Light Upon Light

Five Master Paths to

Awakening the Mindful Self

by

Andrew Vidich

Elite Books
Santa Rosa, CA 95403
www.EliteBooksOnline.com

Library of Congress Cataloging-in-Publication Data

Vidich, Andrew
 Light upon light : five master paths to awakening the mindful self / Andrew
Vidich. — 1st ed.
     p. cm.
 Includes bibliographical references and index.
 ISBN: 978-1-60070-059-0
1. Spiritual life—Science of Spirituality (Organization). 2. Science of Spirituality
(Organization)—Doctrines. I. Title.
 BP605.S19V53 2008
 204'.4—dc22
                        2008011464
             Copyright © 2008, Andrew Vidich

Cover design by Victoria Valentine
Copyediting by Courtney Arnold
Typesetting by Karin A. Kinsey
Image on page192 is from www.exoticindianart.com.

Printed in USA

10 9 8 7 6 5 4 3 2 1

Dedicated to Almighty God working through
all Illuminated Masters
And to my own spiritual Masters, Sant Kirpal Singh Ji Maharaj,
who tore opened my heart to the love of God,
Sant Darshan Singh Ji, who ignited the embers of longing
for the Divine Beloved,
and Sant Rajinder Singh Ji Maharaj, who fanned the flames
with the gift of His Holy joy and service.

Contents

❧

Acknowledgments.. vi
Note to the Reader vii
Introduction ix
   The Challenge of Humanity... x
   How to Use This Book xii
   Overview xiii

CHAPTER 1. Meditation: *The Inner Journey Home* 21

CHAPTER 2. The Seven Core Principles of
   Self-Transformation 49

CHAPTER 3. Kabir: *The Path of Perfect Faith*............................ 73

CHAPTER 4. Rumi: *The Path of Ecstatic Love*............................ 117

CHAPTER 5. Hafiz: *The Path of Joyous Surrender* 161

CHAPTER 6. Guru Nanak: *The Path of Compassionate Service*...... 193

CHAPTER 7. Darshan Singh: *The Path of Self-effacement and
   Positive Mysticism* 229

CHAPTER 8. *The Tale of the Sands* 283

Epilogue..289
Appendix One: *Meditation Instructions* 293
Appendix Two: *Self-Introspection Journal*........................297
Endnotes..299
Bibliography..311
Glossary..315
About Science of Spirituality 335
About the Author...337
Index..349

Acknowledgments

There are so many people who have been instrumental in bringing this book into the light. Each, in small ways and large, appeared at just the right moment to provide feedback, encouragement, and guidance. I would first like to acknowledge my life partner and wife, TAMIR, who not only put in hours of excellent editing but continually encouraged me to improve my English skills, as well. She has been an unfailing friend and true partner in this project in every conceivable way. I owe her a debt of gratitude that can never be adequately repaid. Thank you for your unfailing loyalty and heartfelt love and support.

I would also like to thank my lifetime friend and spiritual brother Eliot Rosen for his excellent editorial work. I believe he deserves much of the credit for the organization and writing style of the book. He constantly helped me hone the message with the right tone and texture, making it accessible to even those who may not quite be ready. Let me not forget my good friend David Middaugh, who was essential in putting together the glossary and in providing ongoing heart-to-heart friendship.

Lastly, I would like to thank my publisher, Dawson Church, whose friendship, editorial advice, and absolutely unconditional support of my work has been an unfailing light in my life. Thank you all for your genuine love and support.

Note to the Reader

This book quotes directly and extensively from the great saints of various religious and spiritual traditions. Enlightened though they were, these saints spoke and wrote in the common parlance of their time, when gender sensitivity was not on the radar. Hence you'll see the word "man" instead of the gender sensitive word "humanity," and the masculine pronoun "He" is used to refer to God.

My deep respect for these great spiritual beings prevents me from altering their quotations in any way in order to make them more gender sensitive. I therefore ask the reader to kindly not take offense at these great teachers' lack of more inclusive gender designations. These great saints knew from direct experience that God was not a "He" or "She," and that males were not inherently superior to females. I hope we can also remember the same despite the limitations of language.

Another sensitive word to some might be the word, "Master," which conjures up the degrading aspects inherent in the master–slave relationship. Yet the word Master, as used in the book, refers to a human being who is, variously, a "master of meditation," "a master of one's own mind," or a "master of the three worlds"— someone whose consciousness has transcended the limitations of the physical, astral, and causal realms. In short, the title is given to one who has become the "Word made flesh," as stated in the New Testament in the Gospel of John, the full embodiment of the Divine Light, the very essence of God, who we may call by various names: Allah, Jehovah, Raheem, Brahma, or the Great Spirit.

It is the author's view that a *true* Master will *always* honor the trust invested in him or her by the student-disciple and has his/her

best interests in mind at all times. The practical solution in searching for spiritual guidance and protection from a Master is to find a
spiritual teacher who is truly genuine and fully enlightened, in every
sense and on every level, and to avoid all those who would abuse the
balance of power intrinsic to the Master–disciple relationship.

Introduction

When he was sixteen years old, the course of Kirpal Singh's life was forever changed when he witnessed a woman's passing into death. She suddenly called her children to her bedside, kissed them, and told them; "I am going." She said goodbye to her husband, then quietly closed her eyes and was gone.

Describing the incident many years later, Sant Kirpal Singh recalled; "I was wonder-struck to witness this amazing sight. Before my eyes, the body was lying there, and yet that which had motivated it was gone. It was still in me but it had left that body; where it had gone I did not know."[1]

According to Sikh custom, the body was cremated. But on the way to the cremation ground, Kirpal Singh saw an inscription on a pillar that read:

> *Beware ye that move!*
> *We too were once like you*
> *Enjoying life to the full.*
> *But alas! Now we are a handful of*
> *dust beneath this stone.*

After reading the inscription, his young heart was pinched with pain. Walking a few yards further, he noticed a young person and an old man with a white beard, both being consumed in the funeral flames. Like the Buddha before him, Kirpal Singh realized that the inevitable end of all life was death.

Reasoning to himself, he asked: "What is it which is in me, but is not in these two bodies?" Three questions took possession of his mind: "Who we are? Whence did we come? Whither shall we go?"[2]

From those fateful moments, the persistent search for the answers to life's deepest mysteries became the ruling passion of his life. Not long afterward, as he read from one of his Bible lessons at the missionary school he attended, his quest was piqued further. While explaining the concept of spiritual rebirth to Nicodemus, Master Jesus stated that, *"Except a man be born again he cannot enter the kingdom of God."*[3]

As Kirpal Singh's search continued he came to understand the need for a spiritual birth, or what Jesus referred to as being "twice born." This second birth was obviously not a physical birth but one of spirit, for as Jesus later said in reply to Nicodemus, "That which is born of the flesh is flesh; that which is born of the spirit is spirit" (John: 3:6).

The concept of spiritual rebirth, second birth, or what in some traditions has been called the birth into the beyond, is nothing new in the annals of spiritual literature. The biographical accounts of all great spiritual masters and saints often begin with the intense desire to solve the mystery of life and death, but sooner or later culminate in a spiritual *rebirth* or *awakening* into the spirit. As in Kirpal Singh's case, this great awakening or inner mystical experience is often ignited by the greatest teacher of all: death.

The Challenge of Humanity

As we enter the third millennium, humanity stands at the edge of a precipice. We as a species have made immense intellectual and physical strides. We now have the ability to travel at super-sonic speeds, heal previously incurable diseases, and communicate almost instantly anywhere in the world. Science has provided us with the means to live longer, compute faster, and live more materially comfortable lives. Paradoxically, the last hundred years of the second millennium have witnessed the unprecedented death of over 100 million people due to war and conflicts, starvation, and epidemics. We have, through the use of these same "technologies," come close to exterminating the entire race and now move perilously close to destroying the very planet that sustains us.

Humanity is faced by a range of seemingly insuperable problems; uncontrolled population growth, diminishing resources, ancient animosities, passion for revenge, racial antagonism, religious prejudice, territorial ambition, and the destructive use of the environment. More importantly, our significant intellectual and scientific gains have failed to bring us any closer to achieving *true civilization* in which the inner human and spiritual needs of humanity have been fulfilled. We have achieved outer material progress at the cost of inner spiritual fulfillment. Indeed, spiritually, humanity as a whole remains in its infancy.

In the view of the great Masters of spirituality all these are secondary or derivative problems — mere symptoms of a great disease. The cause of this disease is the *illusion of separateness*, the notion that we are unconnected, independent beings whose particular welfare can be achieved at the expense of the general good.

The primary challenge now facing humanity is to recognize the unity of all humanity and, in turn, the unity of all life in the universe. It is to realize, not intellectually but spiritually, that despite the superficial differences that divide humanity we are remarkably similar as a species — we have the same inner and outer construction, the same psychological, intellectual, and spiritual characteristics.

Coincidentally, one of the recent discoveries of the genome project was to reassert the ancient truth already proclaimed by the mystics of all traditions: that humanity is indeed one. According to their findings, all humans are 99.9 percent genetically identical. Biologically, we are a single human gene pool with only tiny differences and local variations. Psychologically, we respond to stimulus in the same way with only minor differences. We are all afflicted and affected with the same tendencies, habituated responses, and conditioning no matter our country, race, religion, or ethnicity.

The principle reason for the paradox of our situation is that we have largely failed to investigate the contemplative and meditative experience from a careful, systematic, and scientific way or from a holistic perspective. We have become masters of third-person scientific investigation, but we are mere novices in the arts of critical first-person scientific study. We can use our technology of the outer world to treat previously incurable diseases, but our mastery of the "technology" of the inner world is so rudimentary that we can barely contain the passions that lead us to destroy the very human life we try so hard to preserve. We have studied the machinery of the brain and have vastly increased our knowledge of how the mind works, yet our ability to apply this knowledge to change our own behavior is virtually absent. In short, we know how to *analyze* but not how to *realize*. We can *study* consciousness but not *increase* it. In fact, we do not know *who we are*.

As each of us ponders our collective and individual challenges, we, too, may begin to wonder why we have been placed on this planet and what our ultimate purpose is. It is my hope that this book will help ignite in all of us a passionate desire to understand our higher purpose and, in so doing, answer the most fundamental of all questions: *who are we, why are we here* and *whither do we go at the time of death?* In igniting this search it is my heart-felt prayer that the enlightened words of the Great Masters of the Spirit will help foster and nurture our own critical, first-person investigation into the nature of our own being through the use of the "inner technology" of meditation.

How to Use This Book

Realization versus Intellectual Knowing

There is a vast difference between mere intellectual understanding and experiential realization. Realization occurs only after spiritual principles become *lived truth*. To use an analogy, intellectual understanding is like the word "water," which is only read on a page and cannot be consumed. Realization, on the other hand, is actually drinking the life-sustaining water. We may study the characteristics of water—its volume, various elements, how it changes from liquid to gas—but unless we actually *taste it* we cannot quench our thirst nor have a true understanding of its importance. In a similar manner, knowing about truth is not the same thing as living it. Guru Nanak has said, "Truth is high, but higher still is *true living.*" Fully understanding this simple truth moves us from the byway of the intellect to the highway of divine realization, and from the fast lane of fruitless seeking to the vast lane of profound transformation.

Before the process of spiritual awakening even begins, the prerequisites of an ethical and righteous life and the practice of meditation must be actualized in daily life. My own spiritual teacher, Sant Kirpal Singh, put it simply: "An ounce of practice is worth a ton of theory."[4]

In this sense, it is my hope that you not only "read" this book but "do" this book by living its import. Make it a workbook and not just a good read. To further this aim, I have included "to do" exercises where appropriate, which will help you truly digest the wisdom of the great Masters of the Sant Tradition. The analogy of drinking water teaches us that the acid test of all spirituality is the degree to which we live it and incorporate these truths in our daily lives. Let us not merely read the Masters' words but embrace them in the deepest recesses of our being.

Overview

This book has been written in the hope of inspiring you to put into practice the Seven Core Principles of Spiritual Transformation, as well as the specific Sacred Approaches (technologies) for self- and God-realization given by the great Sant Mat Masters.

Chapter One prepares the way for your receptivity to the Seven Core Principles of Spiritual Transformation by providing an historical, theological, and practical context from which these transformational methods have arisen. The chapter focuses on the importance of meditation as the "inner technology" for the entire process of self-transformation. To my understanding there is no path, religion, or spiritual tradition that has not emphasized the necessity of mastering some form of meditation or contemplative practice—though this meditation may be called by different names in various traditions, such as centering prayer, concentration with attention, contemplation, and so on.

It could rightfully be said that meditation is not only the backbone of our spiritual lives; it is the life-support system for daily spiritual growth. Sadly, for many the absence of a daily meditation practice has resulted in a sense of spiritual disconnection and an often unnecessary day-to-day suffering. To encourage the use of this spiritual-life support system we have provided in Appendix I a simple but highly effective meditation practice given directly by a living saint, his Holiness Sant Rajinder Singh Ji, for use in your daily life. This is a gift to seekers and practitioners and an open invitation to begin the practice of meditation immediately.

As we enter the Third Millennium the final frontier—Inner Space, the realm of the spirit—awaits us. May we all be guided by Light upon Light.

Chapter Two formally introduces the Seven Core Principles of Transformation which spiritual seekers, regardless of their background, will in the course of the progress of the soul's reuniting with its Creator, ultimately integrate and master. The principles are:

1. Deciding Our Aim in Life

2. Priorities (Putting First Things First)

3. Seeing the End in the Beginning

4. Regularity and Habit

5. One-pointed Focus and Quality Effort

6. Patience and Perseverance

7. Flexibility and Adjustment

These Seven Core Principles act both synergistically and holistically. By this I mean that they all act in congruity and in relationship to each other. The successful application of these principles requires that we incorporate them holistically. For practical purposes, however, I recommend that you begin with number one and then work slowly through each successive principle. As you begin to have some success in applying each successive principle, go on to the next. In this way, you may achieve greater mastery in incorporating the principle than trying to apply them all at once. As one progresses, each of the principles become a "habit of mind," which we apply to everything we think, say, or do. With time they become realized or lived truths, which can completely transform our entire lives.

When you begin in all earnestness to live these spiritual principles at home, at work, and at play, you will eventually "embody the teachings" on all levels of your being—physical, emotional, intellectual, and spiritual.

One of the ongoing obstacles to implementing these principles is the highly materialist and often self-centered culture in which we live. For many of us, modern living—with its frenetic pace, competitive drive, and overly materialistic focus—has led to the nearly ubiquitous disease of what I call "general overload." This can include information overload, time overload, financial overload, material overload, and so forth. In today's complex world, we have overwhelming amounts of information at our fingertips but often lack the wherewithal to sift, glean, and prioritize what is timely, useful, and nourishing. This is similar to wanting more food without digesting what has already been eaten; the result is, naturally, indigestion and sickness.

Because most of us find ourselves in this situation, daily spiritual practice is relegated to the "when I have time" list, as if it is but an elective course and not part of the core curriculum of life. It is my hope the light of guidance from the spiritual giants will help you gain a new perspective on the inestimable value of spiritual awakening and its practical application of meditation and contemplative practice in our daily lives.

The Core Principles of Spiritual Transformation have been passed down from spiritual Master to student-disciple in some form since the dawn of self-awakening. No doubt many readers will already be familiar with some or all of these principles, as they have been expressed in a multitude of ways as well as having arisen from diverse sources—not just from spiritual guides and holy texts, but also from the captains of industry, pop psychology pundits, and Western empirical philosophy. If you are already actively working with these principles in your daily life, this book will extend the positive effects in service of self-transformation and developing a meditation practice.

When applied to our spiritual development, each of the Seven Core Principles works synergistically to effect profound and lasting change. While these represent what I believe to be the core principles, there are many others that could be added to these basic seven. What is important here is that the Seven Core Principles provide a practical framework for utilizing the sacred approaches found in the teachings of the great spiritual teachers covered later in the book.

Chapter Three through *Chapter Eight* introduce us to the lives and teachings of five spiritually illuminated Sant Masters: Kabir, Rumi, Nanak, Hafiz, and Darshan. Their ministries span a period of over 900 hundred years, several cultures, and three world religions. Each provides a unique yet truly universal inner and outer road map to spiritual realization. Each of these spiritual paths offer contemporary readers a vibrant and living teaching to meet the pragmatic, day-to-day challenges of contemporary life.

While each of these Sant Masters provides a unique approach, the essential elements of the spiritual path remain eternally the same from age to age. Taken as a whole, they are merely different approaches or varied hues of the same Eternal Light. Just as each stained glass window in a church or synagogue tells a different story or depicts a different theme even as the same light passes through each, in the same way, each spiritual teacher illuminates a different window to the divine—but the Light of Divinity remains the same. Our attraction to one sacred approach or another is primarily a function of the unique individual, the multiplicity of our cultural backgrounds, previous training, and our current life conditions. Each of us responds differently to the same stimuli, and therefore we need different approaches.

It is hoped that the reader will find among these varied offerings the sacred approach that most resonates with him or her. In the end, however, what is important is not what specific approach we most resonate with but whether we have realized those teachings in our hearts. There is not a "Hindu light," "Muslim light," "Christian light," or "Buddhist light"; there is One Eternal Light that has emanated from the same Source, which is Truth. The goal is to realize that *Light of Godhood.* As my spiritual Master, Sant Kirpal Singh, used to say, "To speak of love is one thing; to have that love in your heart is something else."[5]

Appendix One is a verbatim transcript of a meditation instruction given by the contemporary Sant Mat Master of meditation, Sant Rajinder Singh. The reader can easily follow the instructions and immediately begin meditation on the "Inner Light." *Appendix Two* is a self-introspection diary prescribed by Sant Kirpal Singh as a self-awareness aid to one's own thoughts, words, and deeds. This practice allows us to become conscious of our behaviors so that we can bring them into alignment with the spiritual life. Each of these appendices offers a valuable, practical tool from the Masters. Incorporate them into your practice, and you will experience them for the true gifts that they are.

Who are we? Why are we here? And whither do we go at the time of death? In seeking answers to these questions, may we each be twice born, as Jesus exhorts, into the Divine Light that is already within us. For those who are already treading the inner path, may this book offer the leaven of inspiration from the lives and teachings of the greatest of spiritual Masters who have spent lifetimes in this critical, first-person investigation into these divine realities. May their light illuminate the darkness in our hearts and provide *Light Upon Light*.

Sant Kirpal Singh

Chapter One
Meditation:
The Inner Journey Home

All Glory, Beauty, and Joy Lie Within You.[1]
—Sant Kirpal Singh

Meditation is the core practice of almost every great religious and spiritual tradition. Simply defined, it is the key that unlocks the inner doorway to the vast reservoir of spirit within. By learning how to "tap inside," as Emerson put it, each of us can mine the unlimited wealth lying dormant inside us. Meditation has been practiced for thousands of years, and although it has been known by many different names, its core practice remains the foundational practice for spiritual ascension across cultures. For example, what St. Paul called "unceasing prayer" is both in substance and technique the same as what the Hindus call *dhyana,* or concentration. St. Teresa of Avila called it "prayer of the attention," which is remarkably similar to what the Sufis refer to as *mushahada* or *muraqaba,* and what Muslims refer to as *dhikr.* In Tibetan Buddhism meditation is referred to as the practice of Self-liberation through Naked Awareness, or *Dzochen,* It is also referred to as *vipassana* by the Theravadan Buddhist tradition. This same practice of inner attunement has many similarities to *Hitbutdedhut,* or "cleaving to God alone," in the Jewish tradition. From whatever tradition it may arise, meditation in its essence is a technology of self-transcendence leading from illusion to reality, ignorance to insight and darkness to illumination.

Plato told an interesting story about people who were chained to the walls of a cave that had only one opening at the top. Aside from the rock itself, all that they could see when the sun shone through the hole were their own shadows. To them, these things were reality. Then, one day, one of these cave people managed to get outside, where he could see the world of three dimensions. There was so much beauty beyond that which he had seen inside the cave, and he was eager to share it with his friends. When he returned to the cave, however, they all laughed and said that he was crazy. They simply couldn't conceive of anything outside of their own limited experience.[2]

Plato says that this is what happens to each and every one of us: we are so focused on living at the level of our physical senses that we don't comprehend anything more. Meditation can be compared to the experience of the man who discovered the hole at the top of the cave and realized that there was a vast and beautiful world beyond. Although we may hold to the popular notion that "seeing is believing," it is the deeper knowledge born of meditation—that which resides beyond the senses—that is truly real and lasting.

Modes of Knowing

According to the Sant Masters, knowledge can be divided into two kinds: 1) knowledge gained through the agency of the five senses, and 2) knowledge gained directly through the apprehension of the soul.

The Vedic masters also divided knowledge into two main branches, knowledge of this world *(apara Vidya)* and knowledge of the Beyond *(para Vidya)*. The former is the knowledge gained through the five senses and human instrumentation (i.e. microscopes, telescopes, and so on), which is an extension of these senses and proves useful during our life in this physical world. The latter is the knowledge of the soul and God, gained through meditation and the direct apprehension of the higher reality within.

According to many spiritual traditions, the nature of *apara Vidya* is transient or impermanent, and therefore it does not possess intrinsic value. *Para Vidya*, in contrast, is lasting, permanent, and leads directly to spiritual realization. It is this knowledge born of inner realization, which the great sages referred to as *gyan* or *jnana,* that remains for all eternity. Furthermore, the knowledge that this one live principle (called *Paramatma,* or God, by the Hindu sages) is the material and efficient cause of all that exists is known as *Vigyan*. As we seek to re-prioritize our lives, it is of vital importance that we understand the relative importance of both kinds of knowledge.

The Parable of the Ferryman and the Grammarian

There's an instructive parable about a recently graduated college student in India who was filled with ego, especially in regard to his intellectual accomplishments. One day this grammarian needed to take a ferryboat across a large lake. To pass the time, he engaged the ferryman in conversation, inquiring whether the man had ever learned any languages. "No," said the ferryman, "I have not had the chance to study much in my life." To this the graduate replied in a condescending tone, "Well my friend, what a shame, for you have already wasted half your life."

The ferryman was offended, of course, but having good manners he held his tongue. In due course, a storm brewed ominously on the lake and the boat became caught in a vortex of water. Realizing that he could not maneuver the boat out of it, the ferryman turned to the young intellectual and inquired, "By the way, my learned friend, have you ever learned to swim?"

"Certainly not," replied the grammarian. "I have never wasted my time with such silliness."

"Too bad," said the ferryman, savoring the opportunity. "because the boat is about to sink in this tidal wave of a whirlpool. Unless I rescue you, you are about to drown. I think, perhaps, it is you who have wasted all your life."[3]

Although the ferryman in this story lacks formal education, he is nevertheless knowledgeable in the important, real-life matters — in this case, the ability to swim when one really needs to know how! The grammarian, while intellectually astute, is ignorant of the practical, which as we see, can be a matter of life and death.

We, too, may be intellectually well-educated, but if we are ignorant of inner spiritual knowledge then we have "put all our eggs in one basket." In other words, we have lived life based on what is transient and passing, missing the opportunity to connect with the Reality of God within. When the moment of death comes, only the knowledge of the spirit, gained through meditation, will come to our rescue.

Outer and Inner Knowledge

Humans have acquired knowledge of many outer things, both microscopic and macroscopic. We have advanced our knowledge tremendously in the sciences, medicine, and technology; but with all our outer knowledge, have we understood *who we are?* Are we any closer to inner peace, lasting happiness, and realization of the highest purpose in life?

We must ask ourselves of what lasting value is our scientific and worldly knowledge if we still cannot answer three fundamental questions at the basis of our existence: 1) Who are we? 2) Where have we come from? And, 3) Where will we go at the time of death? If we cannot answer these three essential questions, we have built our knowledge — indeed, our lives — on a foundation of shifting sand.

Our situation can be compared to that of a sleepwalker who arises in the middle of the night and walks around aimlessly. If we ask the sleepwalker where she was come from, we will get no reply. Why? Because being asleep, she has no awareness of where she is or what she is doing. Likewise, if we ask her where she is going. She cannot answer, because she does not know. Even if we ask her *who she is* we still get the same non-reply. Although she may appear to be awake, we all know that the sleepwalker is actually sleeping.

In the Sant tradition, the condition of humanity is understood in this same way. We may *appear* to be awake, but in reality we are fast asleep, living in a state of ignorance of our true nature and the nature of Reality. Recognizing that we are in a state of profound ignorance is the first step on the journey to self-understanding and lasting knowledge. It is this knowledge of the True Self that we seek through meditation. As Jesus said, "For what is a man profited if he shall gain the possessions of the whole world but loses his own soul?"[4]

A Case of Mistaken Identity

The overwhelming majority of humanity is suffering from a severe case of *mistaken identity*. We take ourselves to be what our outer labels tell us we are: Catholic, Muslim, or Buddhist; American, Swede, Colombian; midwife, lawyer, artist, and so on. It is necessary, of course, to assume roles while living in the world, but we take them far too seriously, far too often. To blindly identify oneself as *being* one role or another is not only an illusion, but a cause of untold suffering. Throughout history, millions of lives have been lost or destroyed defending these names and forms.

We identify ourselves with these many outer labels because we have lost touch with that divine presence within, our real source, which is God. We are conscious beings, drops in the ocean of all consciousness. This ironic problem of mistaken identity, therefore, is the root cause of our lack of peace, happiness, and inner fulfillment.

The great souls whom the holy scriptures refer to as saints, masters, or prophets have understood who they are and recognized through inner experience the divine presence in every atom of creation. They have realized God completely, and know from moment-to-moment experience that God is the breath of our breath, and the life of our life. He cannot be contained in any image or scripture, nor in any building made of brick and mortar. He is a living presence manifesting in every atom of creation. Therefore, we are actually manifestations of God. In light of this reality, how can one place be more holy than another? How can one race be better than another? The mystic poet saint Sant Darshan Singh Ji reminds us of this truth most beautifully:

> *He is hidden in every instrument,*
> *in every song and melody.*
> *All creation reflects His glory.*
> *There exists not a sparkling wave or fiery star*
> *that does not owe its radiance to His Light.*[5]

Ignorance of Our True Nature

Sadly, instead of feeling the bliss of God's presence, most of us feel despair and emptiness. Instead of experiencing the illumination of the divine countenance, we experience darkness, doubt, and ignorance. Instead of enjoying the certainty and wisdom of God's unlimited power, we are often in a state of confusion and uncertainty. If God's presence is manifest in every atom, then why do we so often feel disconnected from our Divine Source?

While most of us do experience moments of peace and inner fulfillment, these are usually brief and momentary. Too often our lives seem like a series of interruptions, punctuated by fear and insecurity about our future. If it's not financial worries, then it's health concerns. If those areas of life happen to be fine for a while, we then have a problem with a significant other. When our expectations for love and happiness are not met in the way our ego-personality wants them to be, we experience depression and anger.

Are these problems non-negotiable? Are they intrinsic aspects of life that we can do nothing about? Our spiritual technician—the saints—say no. Our suffering is a manifestation of the ego-driven mind, an illusion created in the absence of experiencing our true spiritual nature. Saints say that this ego-driven perception is neither our natural state of being nor the ultimate reality, which, thankfully, it is our destiny to reclaim.

The Parable of the Five Blind Men and the Elephant

Several religious traditions tell similar versions of the following classic parable:

There once was a town in which all the inhabitants were blind. As it so happened, the General of an invading army had his eye on the town, so as a symbolic show of his conquering strength he positioned a massive elephant at the forefront of his troops, dressed from head to toe in awq-inspiring regalia. Very concerned about the menacing threat just outside their gates, the townspeople sent their five wisest men as emissaries to negotiate.

The General instructed his lieutenants to assist the five blind men into the presence of this grand elephant, a rare specimen by any standard. Using the sense of touch, each blind man reached for different parts of the elephant to explore its characteristics. When they conferred with each other to discuss the results of their findings, they were in complete disagreement.

The first blind man, who had grabbed the elephant's tail, said, "The elephant is very thin and wiry." The second blind man, who had grabbed the leg, said, "No, this cannot be, for the elephant felt like a huge pillar, as solid as a tree." The third blind man, who had felt the trunk, said, "No, no, the elephant is flexible and can suck water." The fourth blind man, who had felt the ear, said, "The elephant is like a flapping tent." The fifth blind man, who had inspected the belly said, "All of you are wrong, the elephant is like a huge cauldron." They continued discussing for some time but could not arrive at an agreement as to the true nature of the elephant.[6]

This parable illustrates our condition in this world: The five blind wise men represent the five outer senses, while the elephant represents the nature of reality. Because we rely on outer knowledge gained through the agency of the five outer senses, which are inherently limited and therefore incomplete, we cannot understand the truth.

None of our five senses reflect an accurate picture of the full range of reality. Even our sense of sight, which predominates over other human senses, varies tremendously from person to person. Similarly, we can hear sounds only within a very limited range of frequency, and smell an even smaller range of fragrances. In such a predicament, how can we ever reach consensus on the nature of outer reality, let alone the higher reality within?

We Are Multi-sensory Beings

The good news is we are much more than physical beings with five outer senses. In fact, we are multi-sensory beings. We have five outer senses and five *inner* senses as well. The Sant Masters have said that through these inner senses we can see and hear realities beyond the physical. Unfortunately, few of us have any knowledge of the existence of these inner senses, let alone how they can be accessed. Fortunately, the great spiritual traditions of the world all show us the way through the art and science of meditation.

Early in his discipleship, Swami Vivekananda once asked his revered Master, Paramhansa Ramakrishna, if he could "see God." The great sage Ramakrishna looked at him and without hesitation replied, "My child, I see him as I am seeing you, even more clearly than that."[7] Vivekananda later recorded that it was the absolute certainty of this reply that lead him to fully accept the Master as his spiritual guide. For Ramakrishna, God was a living reality, which he perceived through the inner eye of the spirit. It is through this spiritual eye that we, too, can literally see the true nature of reality.

Entering Higher Realities

The answers to the life's most important existential questions can only be found experientially. As we enter into higher realties through the use of our inner senses, we see that the higher worlds are far more blissful, peaceful, and real than anything we can experience on Earth. It is here that we get a taste of our true identity as soul and understand through direct experience that we are sparks from the ocean of All-light. Once we are reconnected to this inner luminosity, we are able to travel back to these higher worlds at will. We realize that we are not the body, mind, memory, personality self, or ego, but rather an indwelling consciousness that is inherently self-aware, luminous, and loving. Ultimately, who we are is where we are going.

The Inner Journey Home

Spiritually asleep, we are literally prisoners in the cage of the physical body. As we begin to awaken and realize that we are a soul inhabiting this body, then, paradoxically, the former prison of the physical frame becomes holy ground—the temple of the spirit, where the source of all truth resides. Through daily meditation we come to see that *we are spiritual beings having a human experience, not human beings trying to have a spiritual experience*. We come to realize that we have spiritual bodies with which we can traverse higher realms of spirit:

In our astral body we can travel in *Sahasrar*—the astral world. Similarly, in our casual body we can travel through the causal world, or *Trikuti*. As we ascend still higher in the vast inner non-material landscape, we experience the super-casual region known as *Par Brahm* or *Daswan Dwar*. Here the soul moves beyond the region of mind itself.

Beyond the super-casual realm is a region referred to by the Sants as *Bhanwar Gupha,* where the light of consciousness reaches the cumulative luminosity of 100,000 physical suns. Here the soul cries out in ecstasy, *"So Hung"* or "I am that," or, as the Sufis have said, *"Anal al Haq,"* meaning "I am the truth." The soul now knows itself completely and recognizes itself as pure consciousness—no different, in essence, from that of God.

Masters of Our Own House

In order to transcend the physical plane at will in meditation, we must be masters of our own house—in full control of our own body, mind, thoughts, actions, and desires. Then and only then will we be ready to claim our divine destiny and experience the unimaginable beauty and bliss of God. When our time here on Earth is done, we return to the everlasting realms of spirit from which we came to consummate our final merger in God. Yet we need a special passport to make this journey. It is not, of course, an actual credential or qualification, but something far more subtle and precious. The great spiritual teachers tell us that this passport is love. As Sant Kirpal Singh has said, "God is Love. Our soul is Love. And the way back to God is also Love."

As we continue our spiritual practice, our intrinsic inner consciousness begins to reassert itself over our bondage to the ordinary mind. We finally learn that our attention, which is the outer expression of our soul, can be directed and controlled. We realize that we are not at the mercy of every thought and desire that passes through our body/mind. We begin to understand that while we have a mind, we are not the mind; we are conscious beings. To understand our unique predicament, let us explore the metaphor of the charioteer and the wild steeds.

Picture a chariot being pulled by five horses, running wildly in every direction. The driver, who should be in control of the horses, has lost his grip on the reins. Meanwhile, the passenger of the chariot, a wealthy and supposedly powerful man, rides passively in a drunken stupor.

The five horses represent our five senses—sight, hearing, taste, touch, and smell. The reins represent the intellect. The driver is our mind. The passenger in back is our soul or consciousness.

At present our *attention* is dragged at the whim of the five senses, the temptations of the outer sense pleasures; the driver has lost control of the reins; and the owner in back has forgotten his true purpose and identity. In this scenario, we have little or no control over our attention. The moment a desire arises, without reflection or discrimination, we immediately act on fulfilling it. The soul has no control over the mind, and the mind has only limited use of its discriminative intellect. In the absence of true knowledge, desires become like the uncontrolled wild horses and the fulfillment of desires becomes an end in itself. The Masters say that living as a slave to one's unbridled desires makes it impossible to contact the soul.

Different Traditions, Different Metaphors

In the Sufi tradition, slavery to sensual desires has been referred to as the "four birds of prey," namely: the rooster of lust, the peacock of craving fame, the crow of ownership, and the duck of urgency. The rooster of lust sees everything as an object for its own sensual enjoyment. Whatever the circumstances, its attention immediately goes to the level of sense-gratification. The peacock seeks approval for everything it does. Every situation is an opportunity to bring attention to itself. The peacock runs around saying, "Did I mention how much people love me? But enough about me, how do you like my new suit?" It is a junkie for the adulation and praise of others. The crow of ownership seeks to possess everything it sees. This bird believes that by owning more and more it will somehow come closer to happiness. It goes shopping and says, "I've just *got* to have this."

The duck of urgency is always searching through dry and wet alike, like a robber indiscriminately cramming stolen booty in his sack—pearls, pebbles, anything—feverishly fretting, "There's no time. I won't get another chance." Everything has to be done immediately. Every minute another task must be urgently attended to. Surely each of us has been like all four of these birds at some time in our lives.

In Hinduism, these four birds of prey have been called the five thieves: lust, anger, greed, attachment, and ego. Like thieves in the night, they scale the walls of the house and rob the owner of peace, contentment and the riches of spirituality.

The Christian tradition developed similar terms and corresponding representations in the imagery of the seven deadly sins. As articulated by the early Christian father Gregory the Great, these are: pride, envy, anger, covetousness, sloth, lust, and gluttony. From a Christian perspective, these seven deadly sins are a "death of the soul" because, while under their sway, our true nature is obscured. They devour any glimmer of higher consciousness, leaving us empty of all spiritual life and light.

To the spiritually wise, uncontrolled desire is a sort of "misfit love," the counterfeit version of the love of God. When we are lost in desire and identify ourselves completely with our earthly roles, we have no clue to where the source of lasting happiness and real love lies. Attached to that which is impermanent and transitory, we can never experience what is real and lasting within us.

This does not mean that we cannot strive to live meaningful and successful lives in the world. We need to realize, however, that even if we attain worldly success, we will not necessarily be any closer to true happiness, inner peace, or self-realization.

True Wealth is within
Us and the Nature of Desire

Meditation is the means of discovering the source of true wealth within us. It *is* possible to live a balanced, fulfilling life in the world and still be devoted to our spiritual life. As the great Nazarene Jesus Christ said, we can "be in the world but not of it."

If we look carefully at our lives, we see that after satisfying one desire we find we are still not satisfied. Ironically, after fulfillment the residue of desire remains embedded in our consciousness, and instead of feeling more content, fulfilled, and happy, we find no real difference. We may, of course, feel some short-lived satisfaction at having gotten what we desired, but this feeling passes as quickly as night follows day. Then, we find that it brings another round of desires and the cycle of pleasure and pain continues.

Our condition can be compared to that of a man who is hunting birds with a bow and arrow. Instead of shooting the birds in the sky, however, he shoots his arrows at the shadows of the birds on the ground as they fly above. As time passes, he will eventually run out of arrows and fail to catch any birds.

Our attention is those arrows. The birds in the sky are the birds of spiritual happiness. The shadows on the ground are the four birds of desire, which we mistake for true happiness. These four birds drive us headlong into the world of sensual pleasures. When our arrows finally run out—as will our life-breath at the time of death—we will have to leave this Earth whether we are prepared to or not.

By living under the sway of the four birds of desire, the five thieves, or the seven deadly sins, we inadvertently sow the seeds of future discontent each time we satisfy our desires. True happiness lies within, and *those who don't go within, go without*!

Inner Purification and
Increasing Control over Our Thoughts

As we continue the spiritual journey, we are increasingly able to subdue and eventually control our desires. What then arises is an increasing ability to consciously control our thoughts. At present, we have little idea what is going on in the thought processes of our mind. In fact, brain researchers say that we have over 60,000 thoughts per day. Most of these thoughts are largely unconscious, below the level of our awareness. Our minds are like an overgrown jungle with wild animals prowling all around.

On an even subtler level of thought, Buddhists call the uncontrolled mind-stream "the five unskillful states of mind," namely: 1) fear and worry, 2) restlessness and agitation, 3) doubt and uncertainty, 4) depression and disappointment, and 5) anger and resentment. If we examine our lives honestly, we see how familiar these unskilled states of mind are. We have become so habituated to "unthinkingly" thinking these thoughts that, over time, they cannot but spill over to influence our words and actions. In fact, we have become so identified with these thoughts that we think we *are* them. We often fail realize that we have a choice in how we think and feel.

Meditation and the Light of Divinity

Meditation automatically shines the light of awareness into the jungle of our thoughts. When light shines in the darkness, the darkness disappears. All the wild animals run for cover, not wanting to be discovered. The light of awareness dissolves these uncontrolled states. The more we come into contact with the self-luminous presence within, the more awareness we bring into our being. Each meditation sitting, if done with full attention and sincere intention, can potentially open the floodgates of inner luminosity, bringing greater clarity, insight, and peace. Wherever the sun of divinity shines the darkness of desire is dispelled.

In the beginning, the light of awareness is dim, not unlike the light of a single match on a moonless night. Ultimately, enlightened spiritual teachers proclaim that the light of the soul's awareness becomes as powerful as twelve outer suns put together.

As awareness grows, we not only realize how entrapped we have become by our own minds, but we see the door to freedom as well. We recognize our greatness as soul—as a conscious entity, a drop of the ocean of all-consciousness. With steady practice, we begin the journey of inward purification referred to by Saint John of the Cross as the dark night of the soul. Each of us must confront the demons of our own making, our shadow side, and learn the art of controlling the mind.

The Story of the Two Kings

Guru Gobind Singh told a story about a great rishi. This "meditating" king renounced all his possessions and position to live in the jungle, spending his days in meditation and prayer. After some time a new king took the throne, as will happen. This new, war-like ruler, however, was not content with his undisputed reign of the kingdom. In fact, he developed an obsession with conquering the former king, now turned rishi.

So, the king gathered his entire army and prepared for battle. After searching for many months in the jungle, the ruling monarch finally found the former king sitting in the woods, deep in meditation. Arousing him from the depths of his meditation, the monarch challenged the rishi, "Prepare for a fight. I have come to do battle with you."

The meditating former king replied, "Why are you interested in defeating me? There is a far greater rival in this kingdom that no one has yet defeated. That is why I came to hide in these woods." The feuding king demanded to know who this enemy was, fearing the loss of his own kingdom. The rishi replied, "My dear king, this enemy is so great that hundreds and thousands have tried to destroy him but all have failed. My soul shudders in fear when I hear the sound of my enemy's name. Just to think of this enemy causes my heart to quiver."

The King listened carefully as the rishi described his enemy. Finally the king became angry and demanded, "Is your enemy stronger than me?"

The rishi replied, "Even the thought of this enemy destroys my soul. I left everything to escape."

The king demanded once again to know his name, "Who could be greater or stronger than I? *I demand to know his name.*"

The rishi replied, "There is no use in telling you, for you will never be able to conquer him."

"If I can't destroy him, I promise to burn myself alive at this very spot."

The rishi replied, "Alright, but I warned you. The enemy I speak of is none other than the mind."

As the legend goes, the reigning King spent many years trying to control his mind, but in the end succumbed to defeat. Finally, the king had to admit to his failure. True to his word, he burned himself alive at a place called Katasuraj. To this day, it is said one can still find the stone that marks the place of his defeat.[8]

Victory Over the Mind is a Life-long Endeavor

The entire journey of meditation is a process of controlling the mind. Guru Nanak, the first Guru of the Sikh religion, once remarked, "He who conquers his mind conquers the world."[9] No other task remains to be done once this is completed.

The first step in the long journey of spiritual realization is to recognize how difficult this task really is. We must be aware of the immense power of the mind and approach our task with great patience, perseverance, and humility. The process is a slow one, but each step has its unique joys and special blessings. Often, when they begin a meditation practice, aspirants do not realize that the race is not a short sprint, but a long-distance marathon requiring a life-long commitment. This, in fact, is our true work. Many seekers mistakenly expect a quick and sudden enlightenment.

On one occasion, a disciple asked Sant Darshan Singh, "Is it desirable or dangerous to want to have the same experience [that you have had] in meditation?" The Master replied, "It is neither desirable nor dangerous. You have started out on a journey, continue on and never look back."[10] If we study the lives of the great sages and saints we see that they spent years in meditation and prayer. They started on the journey and never looked back. There are no quick fixes and no push-button solutions.

Many years ago, while I was in India with Sant Kirpal Singh, the subject of meditation arose in one of the question and answer sessions. The Master related a story that encapsulated the essence of the meditative journey.

The Parable of the King's Art Contest

There was a town in Greece in which an annual competition was held between the Greek and visiting Chinese painters to see who were the most accomplished artists in the kingdom. The King summoned all his subjects together and proclaimed that each side would have three days to produce the best painting possible. They could use any technique, color, or subject matter, but after three days they would reveal their work before him and the judges. The reward for winning was great wealth and honor.

The King put the Greek and Chinese painters in a great hall and divided the hall in half with a huge curtain. Neither side could see what the others were doing. Each side had a huge wall made of rough marble to paint upon. As soon as the competition began, the Chinese immediately started to paint with great alacrity and speed. On the other side the Greeks took out scrub brushes, soap, and water and began to clean and polish the marble wall of all imperfections.

At the end of the first day the Chinese had already completed an outline of what promised to be an extraordinary painting. On the other wall, the Greeks had not even taken out a single brush, let alone started to paint. At the end of the second day, the Chinese had the beginnings of what looked like a masterpiece of unsurpassed beauty. The Greeks continued their cleaning and polishing.

Word leaked out that the Greeks had not even begun to paint, and rumors flew around the capital city that they were making a mockery of the contest. At the end of the third day, when the judgment time had arrived, the great hall filled to capacity to see which side would win the prestige and wealth that was to be awarded by the King.

When the great moment arrived and the King ordered the curtain to be dropped, most eyes went directly to the Chinese side, as rumors of its beauty had already begun to circulate beforehand. Indeed, on that wall was a painting of great beauty The flowers seemed so real that they appeared alive. Every detail not only mir-rored real life, but surpassed it.

When the King and the audience looked to the Greek painters' wall, they saw to their amazement the Chinese painting reflected on the highly polished marble — but with even more vivid beauty. The Greeks had spent their time polishing the marble wall to such a degree that it had become a perfect mirror of luminosity. The Greeks were declared the winners, for their work was truly flawless and perfect in every way.[11]

In this story, our mind is the marble wall, the painting is our thoughts, and the painters are our inner consciousness. The light reflected back is the luminous essence of our higher Self. Everything in life has its polish, and the polish of the soul is the reflection of the Light of God.

In order to achieve a state of enlightenment we have to polish the mirror of our mind until it perfectly reflects the radiant light of consciousness. This is the essence of the meditative journey. It is a slow, steady process of polishing. Sant Kirpal Singh has said, "The more we come in contact with the Light and Sound of God, the more we become an abode of all virtues."[12] By coming into contact with the primal force of God, we polish ourselves and become reflecting receivers of God's essence. Yet, as deceptively simple as it sounds, achieving purity of this nature is no easy task.

Simran or Inner Remembrance

The great masters of the Sant tradition have revealed that the secret to successful meditation is one-pointed concentration. The secret to concentration, in turn, is perfect remembrance of God. To understand the connection between one-pointed concentration and the inner remembrance (mantra) of God, lets us look at how this inner repetition actually works.

All of us are engaged in some sort of remembrance all the time, constantly shuttling between thinking about the past, present, and future; dwelling on our worries, regrets, and a thousand other things. One moment the mind is thinking about traveling to Hawaii, and the next it is worrying about remodeling the house. The mind moves with such speed that we are not aware of either the nature or extent of our thinking patterns. One definition of the mind might be *that which is never here,* for the minute we try and hold it in one place, it moves to another, thoughts flitting about in perpetual motion. Without knowing it, we're on automatic pilot, recollecting the world in one representational system or another—whether it be visual, auditory, kinesthetic, gustatory, or olfactory, or in the past, present, or future. The result of this automatic recollection is the constant flow of attention outward to the objects of the senses.

Reversing the Spirit Current Flow

In order to succeed in quieting the mind, we need to reverse the flow of attention from going outward and turn it inward. By changing the nature of the content of the mind from worldly to spiritual, we can redirect our attention inward and upward, instead of outward and downward into the world. As the inner remembrance of God increases, the nature and direction of the mind becomes spiritualized. This is the slow polishing process of the Greek artists in the story above. Gradually, as the mind becomes attentive within, stray thoughts begin to subside and decrease in rapidity and down-pulling strength, and the luminous purifying light of our own essence naturally shines through. The final step is the gradual absorption of the mind into the divine Light within. Light becomes greater light.

Inner Absorption and Union

Just as the process of inner purification is slow and gradual, so too is the process of inner absorption. As the attention becomes more fully rooted within, the seeker begins a new phase in his or her journey. The worldly-focused mind is now in retreat, thanks to the effects of constantly remembering God. Inner revelation in meditation becomes continual and permanent. Each day brings greater bliss.

The secret to continued success in this phase of the journey is total surrender and selfless love, which culminates in the ultimate destiny of making ourselves whole once again, which in the Jewish tradition is called *tikkun*—to restore to wholeness our individual spark of divine effulgence. What is the essence of contemplation? To dissolve the illusion of separateness. The secret to successful meditation is love, for what we truly love, we become. When love reaches its zenith, all boundaries of "I" and "Thou" are dissolved. Only perfect love can produce perfect concentration.

Sant Darshan Singh has beautifully summarized the nature and mystery of true love. "Love," he says, "is the golden key that opens the door to the kingdom of heaven. Without it nothing has ever been achieved nor can be achieved on the spiritual path. But, it is difficult to understand the meaning of love, its purpose, and scope. In reality, it is as boundless as God Himself, and to know its full meaning is beyond our limited intellect. In fact, love is the essential theme of all the saints and mystics, for it is indeed the passport to the kingdom of heaven."[13]

If we loved God with the same one-pointed intensity, we would merge with the object of our love and become one with God. The great law of the universe epitomized by Lord Buddha and contained in the Dhammapada states, "All that we are, is a result of our thoughts; it is founded on our thoughts, it is made up of our thoughts."[14] Such love is rare in any sphere, but in the realm of spirituality it is a prerequisite for attaining our final goal. Our love for our Divine Beloved must not only transcend, but dwarf all other loves in comparison.

Bayazid's God Intoxication: "I am the Truth"

Bayazid al Bistami was one of the great early Sufi saints. Once, after a period of deep meditation, he began repeating, "I am God, I am the Truth."[15] over and over again. Being lost in divine ecstasy, he was completely oblivious to what he was saying. Still, such statements are considered heretical in Islam and carry with them the punishment of death. His disciples were shocked. When Bayazid returned from his elevated state, they explained what he had said; but the next time he went into a state of divine intoxication, he once again repeated those words: "I am God, I am the Truth." Now his disciples had no choice but to adhere to Islamic law. With heavy hearts they took up heavy sticks and attempted to punish their Master for his heresy. Miraculously, though, with each blow that they attempted to strike Bayazad, they hit themselves instead.

When Bayazid returned again to normal consciousness, they asked what had happened. He replied, "Whoever strikes a blow upon God will himself be struck down."

The import of the story is that it wasn't Bayazad Al Bistami who uttered the words, "I am God. I am the Truth." God himself had merged with Al Bistami's separate identity when he was in this exalted spiritual state. In dissolution with the divine ocean of all consciousness, we see the same power of God in every atom of creation. This is the Universal Vision of the All in the One and the One in the All.

Sant Darshan Singh echoes these thoughts:

> *What does it matter if I am called a man,*
> *In truth I am the very soul of love.*
> *The entire earth is my home,*
> *and the universe my country.*[16]

This universal vision is attained by love, rooted in love, and sustained by love for all. In order to be successful on this journey, two factors are of immense benefit to seekers: first, guidance from a true Master, and second, a community of spiritual practitioners.

The Value of True Guidance

In the realm of spirituality, the value of a true spiritual master is indispensable. From any physical distance, a true spiritual teacher has the omnipotent power to offer help and guidance to any number of his student-disciples simultaneously by way of thought transference, as well as by appearing to them during meditation on the inner planes of consciousness. With the help of such a true teacher we can transcend our attachments and enter into the realms of divinity within.

We should first understand the value of a guide or teacher. They are not mere advocates of the theory of the spiritual path, but have direct firsthand knowledge of the worlds of the spirit. Authentic teachers of spirituality are few and far between, but the world is never without them.

There are many who can be referred to as the "lecture circuit" variety of spiritual teachers. They can give enlightening discourses, write illuminating books, and have large followings, but have achieved little on the inner spiritual journey. They may look, act, and speak the words of a true teacher, but they are not true denizens of those higher realms. They do not speak from inner authority.

The Attractive Power of a True Saint

Some have compared true teachers to a perfectly ripe peach. If we examine such a peach, we notice that it gives off an enticing fragrance and lusciousness. Its compelling beauty attracts our sense of taste even before we bring it to our lips, and when we do taste the peach we indeed experience a wonderful sweetness. As we digest the peach, our bodies receive the nourishment. Finally, inside the peach there is a kernel or seed. If we plant that seed we can grow numerous other peach trees.

Similarly, true spiritual guides first attract us by the fragrance of their loving, gracious, and spiritually charged presence. Their light-filled countenance has a rare magic and beauty that we find nowhere in this world. After some time we feel irresistibly drawn into their orbit of attraction. When we study their teachings and listen to their words, our lives are immeasurably enriched. Their wisdom and knowledge of the realms of the spirit provide us with a blueprint for the inner journey and a model of how to live our lives.

As we continue to sit in their presence, we enjoy a wonderful sweetness and delicious intoxication that bubbles over into joyous fellowship and innate compassion. To the extent that we feel filled with the love of God, we want to share this love with those around us.

If we are most fortunate, we will seek the secret seed of light that a true spiritual teacher can impart to us. This gift of light, which is the opening of the spiritual faculties by the spiritual teacher, is the greatest of blessings. All great spiritual teachers and saints impart this gift free of any financial charge. These great spiritual beings connect us directly to the power of God within us through the gift of initiation into the mysteries of the Beyond.

Fellowship and Community

One of the often-repeated proverbs that my teacher referred to was that "A man is known by the company he keeps. It is the association which molds our character."[17] That being the case, consciously and intentionally surrounding oneself with spiritually minded people is of inestimable value on the spiritual path. As like attracts like, we draw support, encouragement, and hope from those who are also moving toward the same goal.

While it is perfectly fine to begin a spiritual journey on one's own, in due course the supportive value of the group becomes more and more apparent. Just as in other endeavors we find that we are aided by others' support, so too in the domain of the spirit.

Studies have shown how important our social relationships are in our growth as individuals. We not only learn from others, but also develop friendships that can make a profound difference in our lives. Those who share similar spiritual goals and aspirations are connected in ways that no other connection can equal.

An example that illustrates the importance of the fellowship in a community can be taken from the lives of mountain climbers. The concept is called "roping up." The lead climber ties a rope around himself, and then successive climbers also tie the same rope around themselves. If anyone should fall or lose his or her footing, they are all tied to the other climbers. They therefore have the collective strength of the all the climbers as protection from an individual fall.

Likewise, each of us should "rope up spiritually" with others who are following a similar tradition or path. The power of positive association can never be underestimated; this is particularly so in the arena of spirituality. If we study the lives of those of have achieved success, one of the greatest kept secrets is association. It is said that Mencius, the great Chinese scholar, had many influences during his formative years. But he only took an interest in scholarly pursuits after his mother moved their residence near a school. Soon, it is said, she found Mencius imitating the scholars, researching the subjects and learning about them. In time he grew up to be a great scholar in his own right.

Service Before Self

One of the greatest personal lessons in fellowship and community I have had came in 1973, while I was on tour in India with my master, Sant Kirpal Singh. I was returning from a two-week trip in Kashmir with about a dozen or so disciples in his traveling party. Our Master had been invited to spend the night in a disciple's home in route back to our final destination, Delhi. The hosting family expended great effort preparing for the Master's arrival. For this simple, devoted family, having their Master stay at their home was like having God as their guest. Even though the Master and his party were to spend only a single night, no expense was spared and no detail was overlooked.

Although we had been scheduled to arrive in the late afternoon for dinner, we did not arrive until very late in the evening. Still, when we got out of their vehicles we were showered with great love and affection. The house and grounds had been decorated like a wedding feast with fragrant flowers, multi-colored canopies, and music playing in the background. It felt as if we were not on the earth anymore but had floated up to heaven.

We were ushered to the back of the house, where I was amazed to see an extravagant feast awaiting our arrival. When we got in line to be fed, the *sevadars* (selfless service workers) personally washed each person's hands and face with warm wash clothes. I noticed that the dishes were all warm and fresh, although we were over eight hours late. The sheer variety of flavor, color, and fragrance titillated every sense. It was a banquet fit for a king. We were indeed being treated as the princes and princesses of our divine king, Sant Kirpal Singh. Neither before nor since have I been served with such love and devotion. I doubted that heads of state ever receive such heartfelt treatment.

After finishing our meal at 1:00 AM, we were called upstairs for a final meeting with our Master. As we sat before his awesome presence, one disciple ventured a question: "Master, are we a burden on you?" The Master scanned the room briefly with his piercing blue eyes and then said, "Truly speaking, it has not been easy." Then he paused again, and with a look of immense compassion said, "But love has no burden and knows no burden. Love beautifies everything."[18] I was overcome with emotion, and tears welled up in my eyes. I realized what real selfless service was all about and learned a lesson that I have never forgotten. From that day onward, I have tried to emulate the spirit of devotion and joyous service I saw embodied in those simple, loving people. Such is the value of true fellowship and community on the path.

On another occasion, Sant Kirpal Singh remarked on the value of community on the path. He said, "The highest thing is fellowship, sharing with others what we have. The only thing higher is God realization." These words have become emblazoned in my heart. They have helped me understand that the real worth of a human beings is our ability to live for others, share in each other's sorrows, and give continuously of ourselves. According to the Sufis, it is to reveal "the hidden treasure which is God within us." Sant Darshan Singh Ji sings of this culminating moment on our journey:

> *We are but drops of the same fountain of divine beauty,*
> *We are but waves on the great river of love,*
> *We are diverse blossoms in the garden of the Lord*
> *We have gathered in the same valley of Light,*
> *We who dwell on this earth belong to one humanity,*
> *There is but one God and we are all His Children.*[19]

Chapter Two
The Seven Core
Principles of Self-Transformation

piritual transformation does not usually occur in a sudden moment of transfiguration or enlightenment but, rather, through the slow, steady work of years of spiritual struggle and practice. The final culminating moment is the fruition of applying certain basic transformative principles consistently and accurately over long periods of time. It is these basic or core principles, when applied on a daily basis, that invariably lead to the final moment of spiritual liberation. Unfortunately, when we study the scriptures and writings of the great masters of the spirit we rarely read about how they achieved their spiritual gnosis. It is these often-neglected *core principles*, applied in a critical first-person scientific manner, that are in a sense the how-to manual for spiritual realization.

Principle One: Decide Our Aim in Life

Today, most people can tell you the approximate price of a cell phone, the monetary value of a house, the cost of a college education, even the value of the most ordinary item, like a pair of shoes or the cost of a haircut. But have we understood the value of our own soul? Have we truly grasped the value of our human life?

There is a story of a very poor man who lived in a village. He worked as a farmer but barely earned enough to have a decent house, possessions, or clothes. His neighbors would sometimes make fun of him for his inability to make a living. But, as he was a lover of God, he remained quite content with whatever God had given him. Whatever free time he had he spent in meditation and prayer. Still, some of his so-called friends encouraged him to improve his circumstances instead of wasting his time in meditation. Although the man was quite content, a seed of doubt was planted in his mind: could he be happier if he had more wealth?

One night the farmer had a vision. In this vision, he was told by a divine being to go into the city, where he would find a vast treasure. The poor farmer, influenced by the pressure from others to seek wealth, decided to obey this vision and undertake the journey. He was not used to traveling in the city, however, and was not aware of its laws. He was soon picked up by the police.

"What are you doing, wandering around the streets day and night?" asked the chief of police.

"I am in search of a treasure," the poor farmer answered guilelessly. "I had a vision and was told that I would find a vast treasure here."

"You are a fool," said the police chief. "I have had many such dreams about finding a treasure, but I ignore every one of them. They are useless dreams. For example, once I dreamed that I should go to a poor hut in a village outside the city. The hut had a small stream passing by it. There was a small farm nearby, but the house was a poor one. I was told in the vision that I would find huge treasure there. But I never went there because visions are not real."

As the police chief described the house, the man had a shock. The house the chief was describing sounded exactly like his own.

The chief of police released him and sent him back to his village. But the man was overjoyed at the possibility of this treasure awaiting him in his own front yard.

The man went to the spot described by the police chief and began digging. Sure enough, he uncovered a large treasure chest, filled with enough wealth never to have to work again in his life. He was amazed that all this time there was a hidden treasure right in his own front yard.[1]

In this simple story we see the predicament of our life on earth. At the bidding of society we seek outer wealth and possessions, not realizing that the true wealth lies buried deep in our own soul. True love and happiness can only be found within. In fact, it is *who we are*. Each of us has been given our discriminating intellect for the sole purpose of discovering our divine nature. Unfortunately, we, like the man in this story, have been persuaded to seek happiness elsewhere. How alluring the outside world appears, yet everything in it is impermanent and passing! To fail to realize our true purpose is a tragedy beyond imagination.

My Master has often said that human life is considered the crown of creation because only in the human form can we attain self-consciousness and God-realization. Yet, while I had heard these words many times, their deeper meaning never really sank in. Then one day, while at a satsang in India, he repeated these words once again. Suddenly, as if a bolt of lightening struck my heart, I realized that if what he was saying was literally true, then the only point of my existence was to realize my Self. Every other pursuit was essentially delusory in nature. Even more importantly, my failure to act in accordance with this sole purpose was the source of my continued mental and emotional suffering. In fact, if humans are truly the crown of creation it is because they are next to God. In essence, my master was affirming the greatness of every soul and, in affirming that greatness, consciously bowing to the divinity within each of us. How could he *not* say this again and again? He was affirming the reality of God in each of us.

Every major religion has stressed the importance of human life. According to many traditions the creation of the human form is the highest of all of God's creations. In the Islamic tradition, the creation of the human being is considered even superior to the angels, for the angels cannot know their Maker. Only in the human form can we come to understand our special relationship to God. In the Qur'an, it is written: "So when I have made him complete and breathed unto him of My spirit."[2] Man contains the very essence of the spirit of his maker. In the Bible, we have a remarkably similar passage in which God says, "Let us make human beings in our image, after our likeness."[3] Humans are divine in nature because we share a likeness with our Creator.

In the Hindu tradition, humankind is referred to as the crown of creation. So close is the soul to God that that the Hindus see no real difference. The Highest Self, or Atman, is in fact Brahman, or God. The Kena Upanshad tells us that, "Having given up the false identification of the Self with the senses and the mind, and knowing the Self to be Brahman, the wise, on departing this life, become immortal."[4]

Each soul is divine in origin and in nature. To grasp this is to recognize the priceless value of our own soul and the invaluable gift of human life as a means to return to our Creator.

Principle Two:
Prioritizing — Put First Things First

It has been said that we shouldn't "follow the "soap opera self" of what we *think* we want. In other words, once we have correctly understood the highest purpose in life, we must prioritize our activities around this highest ideal. We don't want to be driven by the 1,001 distractions confronting us on a daily basis, each vying for our attention.

If we are serious about self-transformation, we must put what is truly important on the top of our list. Most of us are aimlessly adrift. We have shifting goals and aspirations, which tend to change or bend with the circumstances. We dig many wells, some five feet deep, some three feet deep, some two feet deep, but nowhere have we found any water because we don't dig deep enough in any one well. The secret to this principle is consistent, deep-seated effort in alignment with our chosen goal.

God First and the World Next

There is a story told of Sant Kirpal Singh that perfectly illustrates how to clarify one's purpose in life. From an early age, Sant Kirpal Singh was a voracious reader of books, to the extent that he had aspirations to accumulate vast libraries in order to feed his hunger for knowledge. He studied hard and excelled in many subjects. After graduating from secondary school, however, he had to make a decision as to what he wanted to do with his life.

Although he was only 16 years of age at the time, Kirpal Singh was an advanced soul ablaze with the love and longing for God. For a full seven days and nights, he engaged in an all-consuming soul-search. At last he realized that he could not successfully fulfill both desires: to realize God and to own big libraries. He came to the realization, in his own simple yet powerful words, that his priorities should be "God first and the world next." From that moment on, Sant Kirpal Singh never wavered from his resolve. Though he raised a family and worked for over 30 years in the Indian government, spirituality always came first.

What stands out from this real-life example is the length of time Sant Kirpal Singh allocated for deciding what he wanted in his life. Most of us never give sufficient time to really deciding our goals. The disappointing result is often half-hearted effort and the wavering of our resolve midstream before our goal is reached. In large part this is due to our not really knowing what is in our heart of hearts to begin with; one day we want this, the next day we want that. Taking the time to really commit ourselves to a goal is required for success. The depth of our commitment is often superficially shallow because we fail to make this commitment.

Many self-help motivational books advocate goal-setting and the prioritizing of goals, yet what these books lack is any mention of the depth of our commitment in the decisional process. It is *intention* that directs *attention*. If the intention is not strong, achieving the decided goal will remain elusive. Deepening our intention, therefore, is the secret of secrets in the realization of our highest ideal. One way to deepen our intention is to reduce the number of goals in our life.

Focusing In, Narrowing Down

Life is short. By reducing the number of goals we wish to work toward, we have more time and energy to devote to that goals most important to us. In this way, we increase our likelihood of achievement. If one studies the biographies of great men and women throughout history, we find with but few exceptions that their greatness and success lies in their single-pointedness of effort. It is not enough to simply prioritize. Too many goals mean that more of these goals will less likely be achieved.

Exercise

Take some time now to create your own list of life goals, then follow the steps outlined below.

- List your goals
- Make room in your schedule to allot a certain number of hours every day for seven days, during which time you will deliberate on the merits of those goals. Are they really what you want?

- Prioritize those goals based on the strength of your commitment. Ask yourself how deeply you want those goals.

- Now reduce the list to a few goals that are most important for you.

Principle Three: Quality, Single-pointed Effort

Regarding the effort necessary to unite the soul with its Creator, it is said that *half-heartedness does not reach up to Majesty*. In other words, there is no place for half-hearted effort on the spiritual path. While each task has its own time frame and its own level of commitment, quality effort is required no matter what we are trying to accomplish.

In the realm of the spirit, the basic law is that we get what we really want. The great spiritual teacher Jesus said it clearly: "For where your treasure is, there will be your heart also."[5] We might fool ourselves, but we can't fool the God within us. Let us, at first, be honest with ourselves. Do we really want what we say we want? If we do, then we will get it!

It is said that if God divided the world into four quadrants and put all the wealth in one corner, all the power in the second corner, all the fame in the third corner, and in the fourth He put Himself, 99.999 percent of all people in the world would be in the first three corners. The question we have to ask ourselves is "Do I really want God?" Success starts with purity of intention.

Let us look at a contemporary example. Cycle-racing champion Lance Armstrong has been hailed as one of the greatest cyclists in the history of the sport. He won seven Tour De France competitions before retiring from the sport in 2006. What is most impressive, however, is the fact that he achieved those victories after recovering from life-threatening cancer. Some of us may wonder about the secret to his success. The answer, in fact, is not mysterious at all: he had supreme purity of intention and unmatched quality of effort. Armstrong endured incredibly body-wracking workouts day-in, day-out, year-in, and year-out. He wanted to win with all his heart and mind. His level of performance mirrored his level of effort and commitment.

In another example, there was once a great Indian wrestler renowned for his strength, physical prowess, and success in competition. In fact, no other wrestler could hold a candle to him. Once, this wrestler was asked how he had reached the top in his field. He replied that he trained not only in the day, but also to keep from freezing during cold winter nights by the Ganges River!

My own Master once told us that, while he was a disciple, he used to meditate all night long. I remember wondering how he had accomplished this feat. "A strong man revels in his strength," he told us, "and a weak man wonders how he got it." Someone then asked whether it was possible that each of us could attain this state as well. The Master replied that "What one man can do another can do—with proper training and guidance, of course."[6]

Success in any field of endeavor is a matter of inner discipline and intention. But Sant Kirpal Singh also cautioned that Rome was not built in a day. In other words, we should not over-stretch our present capabilities, but incrementally develop and improve from day to day.

Changing Our Perspective

Imagine a sprinter who begins a race and, when after running twenty yards he has to jump over a hurdle, thinks, "*Darn it*, what's this thing doing here? It's in my way!" Then, after another twenty yards, another hurdle..."*Darn*"...then another, and another. With this attitude, his frustration grows and he loses focus, risks injury, and gradually loses hope.

Now consider another runner who accepts at the outset that the race is actually a hurdle event and those obstacles are supposed to be there. This puts everything in a completely different perspective! It's the same sporting event with the same number of hurdles and the same distance; the difference is that now the runner sees the hurdles as necessary givens to the race.

We waste an enormous amount of energy and time when we wish things were other than they are. How we see things is all a matter of perspective. The trials and tribulations of life are not annoying obstacles but necessary challenges, a natural part of life. Embracing this positive attitude toward the process of spiritual growth and the obstacles we are bound to face can have a profoundly positive effect on how we meet each difficulty as it arises.

Principle Number Four:
See the End in the Beginning

If you knew you had only one year left to live, how would your priorities change? In what different direction would you steer your life? Recognizing the inevitability of death awakens us to the preciousness of life itself. Each moment is indeed precious precisely because it is irretrievable. When we accept that we have to leave this physical existence one day, we begin to see things with more clarity and foresight.

The Analogy of the Camel and the Donkey

In ancient Arabi, wealth was often measured by the number of camels one possessed. Not only were they valued for their ability to cross long distances with little water, but also for their sure-footedness. One reason can be found in their angle of vision. Unlike many other quadrupeds, camels keep their head high above the road and, therefore, can see far into the distance. With this vantage point, the camel can see the twists and turns in the road and avoid them. They can see where the road is going and how best to get there. Donkeys, on the other hand, have been considered less valuable. One reason for this may be that donkeys normally look downward and, therefore, can only see two or three steps in front of themselves. Their lack of foresight makes them less sure-footed and more likely to stumble and fall.

We, too, would be spared many problems if we developed foresight. If we could always keep the end in mind, we could avoid many pitfalls and needless mistakes. While it is true that we cannot always know how events will turn out, we can at least think carefully about the results of our actions before we start anything. Sant Kirpal Singh put it wisely, "One must first think of the result before doing or even contemplating any deed."[7] Keeping this in mind, many spiritual Masters have encouraged us to see the "end" which awaits us all. Awareness of our own death is not to be confused with morbidity or self-pity, but with a profound understanding that nothing is permanent and everything must pass.

Working through Our Fear of Death

Decades ago I began working in hospitals with the terminally ill, helping them in their last days to come to terms with their lives. Over a period of many years I had the opportunity to see many people struggle for closure at the time of their deaths. This work forced me to face my own fear of death, as well. Over many years, death became an intimate friend and a great teacher.

Until we conquer our fear of death, insecurity, doubt, and lack of courage will plague us. The Greek philosopher Plutonius has said, "Courage is fearlessness in the face of death, which is but the parting of the soul from the body."[8]

People who are approaching death have little patience for empty chatter. They finally understand that life truly is precious, and they seek to maximize their remaining time. This usually means and end to pretense and superficiality. For those who are dying and have a spiritual outlook, the most important thing becomes the giving and receiving of love.

If love is what is important, however, then why should we wait until the end of our lives to express the love in our hearts? If we can recognize now, in this moment, that each of us will have to leave the physical world, then we will be better able to take life in stride and not get caught up in the small stuff. To see the end in the beginning is to see the results of our actions before we do them.

Finding Direction in Life

In order to re-route our energy and focus before it is too late, we must first discern the direction in which our life is currently headed. How can we best accomplish this? By examining the nature of our thoughts before they drag us in the wrong direction. One way to bring this quality of life-changing immediacy to our lives is to imagine that we have only one year to live. With this in mind, we then sit down and prioritize. Even if we have to change course we should relentlessly do what we know in our heart of hearts is in our own highest interests.

Lord Buddha taught that one of the strangest human spectacles is the denial of death: we see people dying all around us, but we do not allow ourselves to realize the inevitability of our own death. Let us not forget the four realities, which Lord Buddha proclaimed after his enlightenment: suffering, sickness, old age, and death. Each of these can be a powerful catalyst for focus and shift.

The Parable of When Death Came to Baghdad

On day, while a certain sultan was sitting in his palace in Damascus, one of his favorite subjects suddenly rushed into the room. Shaken with fear, the youth cried out in distress, "I have to leave at once for Baghdad." He begged the sultan to lend him his swiftest horse. The sultan inquired as to the urgency of his departure, and the young man replied, "Your majesty as I passed through the palace garden a few minutes ago, I saw Death standing there. When he saw me, he threw up his arms as if he were going to threaten me. I must run away from here as fast as possible to avoid Death's clutches."

Taking pity on his subject, the sultan supplied him with his fastest horse. But a short time later, when the sultan entered the garden, he found Death still standing there. Indignantly, the sultan chided, "How dare you threaten one of my favorite subjects." Astonished at his harsh tone, Death replied, "Your majesty, I did not threaten him. I merely threw up my arms in surprise at seeing him here in Damascus, for I have a meeting with him tonight in Baghdad."[9]

Ironically, the harder we try to escape the inevitable the more intently it stares us in the face. Few of us are willing to truly recognize that even the next moment is not guaranteed. Yet to be able to see the end of all things in the beginning changes our perspective. Paradoxically, death makes life precious precisely because life is so fragile and unpredictable. Death brings us irresistibly and gratefully back to moment. Far from being a dreaded nightmare, death becomes a doorway to fully appreciating our own mortality and the infinite sacredness of life itself.

Principle Five: Regularity

Make good habits, it has been aptly said, and the habits will make you. As a beginner on the spiritual path, I struggled for years to appreciate the importance of this priceless piece of wisdom. In creating change, most experts agree that it takes at least 40 days to cement any behavior. Even after 40 days, however, the new habit may not be permanently installed—it may take even longer.

Let's say we want to acquire the habit of meditating for two hours a day: one hour starting at 5 AM, and one hour beginning at 7 PM. The first step is to establish this regular routine in our lives. The grooves of our mind are like machines, which function on pattern. These patterns become etched into the unconscious with repetition. By repeating the habit of sitting for meditation at the appointed times every day without fail for at least 40 days, we create the conditions necessary for this habit to form. Sadly, many people under-utilize the power of positive habit formation and, thereby, fail to create lasting positive change in their lives.

What often happens is that people begin a practice but fail to make it a permanent habit. They do something for a week or two, then somehow get sidetracked and stop. This type of inconsistent action fails to produce lasting change because the habit pattern is never fully set—the activity is not practiced long enough for the behavior to become a part of the person's nature.

Insufficiently reinforced behavior can be compared to a brick that has been shaped but is still wet: it crumbles under any weight. A fully embodied behavior—one that has become one's nature—can be likened to a brick that has been kiln-fired long enough to be solid and weight-bearing. This brick can be used in any place in a building, while the former brick will crumble no matter where you place it.

Regularity, therefore, is a key factor in cementing habit into nature. No one has ever achieved anything on the spiritual path without making his or her spiritual practice "second nature." Spiritual stalwarts become masters of meditation through habitual repetition over time. For those noble, accomplished souls, meditation becomes as natural and effortless as eating and breathing. So, if we truly grasp the import of this principle, we will unceasingly apply ourselves to our spiritual practice until we have formed lasting habits.

The reality is that meditation is *not* what we do for one or two hours a day, but the continual expansion of Self-awareness from moment to moment. It is the abiding awareness of Unity Consciousness. Our first task, then, is to solidify our spiritual practice on a daily basis. British author Samuel Smiles put it this way:

> Sow a thought, and your reap an act;
> Sow an act, and you reap a habit
> Sow a habit, and you reap character
> Sow a character, and you reap a destiny.[10]

The sign of our success in turning habit into nature is when we are irresistibly drawn to our meditation each day, regardless of whether we feel tired or uninspired. When habit becomes nature, if we miss a single day of meditation, we feel a sense of unease or discomfort, as if we've lost something. When habit becomes nature, we are pulled into meditation independent of our personality's passing whims, fleeting moods, or frivolous wishes.

As we solidify our spiritual discipline it enables us to triumph over distracting tangents that threaten to sabotage the achievement of the behavior—in this case, meditation—we have set out to master. Ultimately, our spiritual practice becomes effortless and blissful, a source of daily rejuvenation.

Principle Six: Patience and Perseverance

A fellow spiritual seeker once remarked that another name for enlightenment is infinite patience. Indeed, the cultivation of patience and perseverance is one of the greatest difficulties people face in the process of spiritual awakening. Yet everything in life takes time to develop. We know that seeds germinate at different times. If we sow a bean plant, it sprouts in four to five days. If we plant a carrot seed, it takes two or three weeks. Imagine a nervous gardener who cannot wait for his planted seeds to peek through the earth and, instead, uncovers them every few hours to see how far they have grown. Accepting that there will be a gestation period before we can reap the fruit of our labor is essential to understanding the nature of spiritual growth.

In most worldly tasks we know roughly how long it takes to develop a particular skill or acquire a particular degree. We know, for example, that it takes about four years to complete high school, then another four to five years to complete college. However, it may take much longer if a student only attends part-time, does not put in the required effort, changes majors half way through, or encounters other unforeseeable challenges. In the same way, we cannot know the exact length of gestation in the area of spiritual development. The seed of spirituality is sown in the darkness of our soul, but we do not know precisely when it will begin to sprout and give forth fruit. Impatience kills that growth because it applies an artificial time-line that may be unrealistic given various unknown factors.

Factors in Spiritual Growth

There are three main factors by which we can assess and nurture our spiritual growth—two beyond our control and one within it.

The first factor is our *spiritual background:* what we have accomplished in our past lives in meditation and the ethical shaping of our character, referred to as our *sanchit* karma in the Sant tradition. For example, in a past life we may have reached a certain level of consciousness in meditation. So, for instance, in the present life it will appear that we are making rapid spiritual progress in meditation, while in reality we are just picking up again from where we have left off.

The second factor is our current *spiritual makeup:* the complex constellation of dynamic psychological and spiritual forces that have been released into the present life based on the life-lessons we need to learn. This has been called our *pralabha* karma, or fate karma, in Hinduism and the Sant tradition. These traits can be assumed to have been formed in our various past lives and carried over to the present one. They provide a board framework or blueprint of our general characteristics and propensities. Note that these attributes of "self" are not all of who we are—there is a vast storehouse of unexpressed past impressions lying dormant that may not be meant to seek expression in the present life.

According to the great teachers of spirituality, we have absolutely no control over either our *sanchit* or *pralabdha* karmas. Yet we do have control over a third factor: our *kriyaman* karma, or the intensity of our inner striving. This is connected to the exercise of our free will and the effort we make toward spiritual advancement in this life. The complex matrix of these three interdependent factors gives us an indication of the gestation period of our spiritual awakening and the speed at which we progress. If we can fully grasp this we will realize that patience is the key that unlocks the door to spiritual beatitude.

We All Start Where We Are

Sant Kirpal Singh once remarked that in his entire life he never had a single lustful dream. I was awed by this level of inner purity, which seemed beyond the ken of human possibility. Someone then inquired as to how he had achieved this, to which he replied, "Every saint has a past and every sinner a future." Furthermore, he said, "saints don't drop from heaven, they are made here. What one man can do another can do, with proper guidance and training of course."[11]

Each of us is in the make. Our soul is perfect but, because we are fallible human beings, multiple coverings of mind, matter, and illusion hide our own pristine perfection, which we must work hard to uncover.

In his autobiography, Sant Kirpal Singh mentioned that even as a small child he could see what was happening in far away places, as well as read people's minds at will. Sant Kirpal Singh had this level of inner purity and extrasensory spiritual powers as a result of inner spiritual work done in previous lives. To expect to be able to achieve this level of attainment in a single lifetime, however, would be foolhardy, unrealistic, and contrary to common sense. It might be akin going into a weight room and trying to lift 250 pounds without any previous training. The result would be a hernia! And one would probably never go back in the weight room again.

The secret to success in all things is patience. Only patience removes the limiting veils from over our eyes and opens our heart to the blissful majesty of God's divine secrets. The key to practicing patience is to choose a task that is in proportion to our capacity to act. If we have ninety-nine doubts or irrational fears, we should strive to have ninety-eight doubts and irrational fears. If we are sitting in meditation for 10 minutes a day, we should strive to sit for 15 minutes a day. Each act should be realistically calibrated to be within our reach so that with each success comes a greater capacity to act. Even if we only increase our meditation by one minute a day, then in several months we will have added over two hours to our daily practice.

What is the secret to spiritual change? *Never stop*, say the great sages. Yet I have met many people who complained that they were unsuccessful in their spiritual practices after being on the path for many years. When I ask them how long they have kept up their meditation schedule faithfully, the reply is usually only one or two months, or a year at most.

Once we have embarked on our spiritual journey, we should never look back. Jesus spoke to the essence of perseverance when he said, "knock and it shall be opened to you."[12] Jesus did not say knock for two weeks or two years or two decades, he said just knock and keep knocking. The only way we can fail is by stopping.

Not only is steady effort better than erratic, inconsistent effort but steady effort brings its own special joys. There is no room for the weekend warrior syndrome. Patience teaches us many lessons, most importantly even mindedness and equipoise.

The Story of Two Farmers

Two farmers purchased plots of land adjacent to one other. The first, whose name was Savetime, decided to grow the more traditional crops of wheat and corn, as well as fruits and vegetables. These were quick to sprout and easy to grow, and would certainly fetch good prices at the local marketplace. The second farmer, whose name was Strangeness because nothing ever seemed strange to him after careful consideration, decided to grow something more exotic, which he believed would fetch even higher prices. After studying the possibilities he decided that bamboo would be an ideal crop.

Savetime planted and watered and tended, expecting quick results and an easy time. After the first season's harvest, he sold his crops at good prices at the local marketplace. Meanwhile, Strangeness, who had planted bamboo, watered and fertilized his crop diligently; but by the end of the first season had nothing to show for it. The second season came along and Savetime once again harvested his crops then sold them at the market for descent prices. His farm was prospering, and he was well on his way to becoming a successful and wealthy man. Then the third and even forth seasons came along and, despite the fact that not even a single seedling had arisen, Strangeness was neither alarmed nor concerned but, rather, continued to water and fertilize his bamboo diligently.

Savetime mocked and criticized his friend for his foolhardy choice of crop. "It is evident that nothing has sprouted," he said. "You can barely feed yourself or your family, yet you continue to waste your time. Switch now before it is too late and all your efforts result in ruin."

Strangeness listened attentively and with due respect, but he was not persuaded by his old friend. "In time my bamboo will certainly sprout," he told him, "and when it does I shall be richly rewarded for my efforts."

Finally, after four years of patiently watering and fertilizing his bamboo, Strangeness' seeds sprouted. In fact, no sooner had they sprouted than they began to grow at an alarming rate, nearly doubling its height each day! By the end of that season there was a bumper crop of bamboo that no one could have possibly imagined. Strangeness was the only one who was not surprised. He sold his first crop for exorbitant prices, which more than made up for all his years of patient waiting. And in one year's time he had surpassed his friend and achieved financial success beyond his wildest dreams.[13]

This story illustrates one of the fundamental principles of life. If we can develop patience and perseverance we will not be moved or upset by the seeming setbacks of outer circumstances. Instead, we will do as Strangeness did, tending dutifully and vigilantly to our task despite our seemingly unrequited efforts. Once we start out on the spiritual path we soon realize that life will inevitably present us with countless trials and tribulations, no two of which may be similar. Each of us will face daily challenges and unusual occurrences, which will try our patience and test our inner resolve. If we can pay close attention to the details of each event, however, and accept these daily setbacks as gifts in disguise, then every moment will offer us rich lessons. When we realize that everything is happening for a reason, we see the hand of God guiding us in all our affairs. We now see that nothing is strange and nothing foreign — even the stones have secrets to tell us. The great Masters remind us that there is a place and time and a teaching in everything.

Every horse has its stable,
every beast its pen,
every bird its nest
and God knows best.[14]

Principle Seven: Flexibility and Adjustment

Whenever we set out to accomplish a goal, we must constantly refine and rethink our approach. Many people begin with high hopes and zealous aspirations, only to be thrown off course by the perilous winds of life. Even if we prioritize our goals, practice regularly, and put in a quality effort, life invariably presents us with further challenges. To our dismay, we seldom see even one day going exactly as we had planned.

The secret to success in achieving our goals lies in adjusting to daily circumstances. It is said that even on pre-programmed, computerized flights from New York to London, the computer makes an average of 67 adjustments to its flight-plan per trip. If these adjustments were not made, the flight would never arrive at its destination. In a similar way, many of us fail to reach our goals because we don't make the necessary adjustments to daily challenges as they arise.

This principle was graphically illustrated in my own life early in my disciple-hood. While I was spending time in India with Sant Kirpal Singh, a man came to him and began complaining about several unsatisfactory situations in his life. After giving the man some guidance, Sant Kirpal Singh turned to us and said, "Life is a series of interruptions. Happiness is adjustment to them."[15]

At the moment, I did not think his reply was all that significant. In fact, if I had not written it down in my diary I probably wouldn't have even remembered it. But a few months later, after I had returned to the United States, I came down with a severe case of dysentery, which was so debilitating that I was unable to hold any food in my stomach. As a result I became progressively weaker each day. Within a month or so I was so weak that I could barely stand up or do anything by myself. I began to feel dizzy and light-headed, to the extent that even reading a book became impossible. This went on for about three months.

In the midst of this illness, I recalled the numerous vows I had made before leaving India, including how much meditation time I was going to put in each day when I returned to my home in the United States. At the time they were made I had been fully convinced that I would hold true to my own word. But after succumbing to the illness, these vows seemed nothing but dust in the wind. In fact, due my weakened mental state, I had completely forgotten them altogether. The struggle to just live from day to day was all I could handle. As the days passed on I became despondent, depressed, and though I never mentioned it to anyone, I felt increasingly hopeless.

One morning I got up and remembered the Master's words: "Life is a series of interruptions. Happiness is adjustment to them." At that moment I understood the wisdom from which these words arose, and instantly felt the strength and inspiration to deal with my illness that I had lacked for so long. I finally realized that while much of life is beyond our control, what we can control is the reactions we have. The secret is acceptance and adjustment.

From that time on, I began to see the dysentery as part of my journey. Adjusting to and accepting my situation became the catalyst for my healing. Yes, I needed to persevere in reaching my goals and aspirations; but when life threw me a curve, I had to know when to make the necessary adjustments.

We are always receiving hidden messages from the hand of God, which come in the form of seemingly random outer events. We can view these changes in our plans as obstacles or opportunities, challenges or curses. The choice is ours.

There is a Sufi saying that the true Sufi is who one who feels joy in the heart at the coming of sorrow. If we can adjust to these unexpected happenings with discernment and patience, nothing can disturb our inner equipoise. In the end, they are the secret friends that will make our journey all the richer and more meaningful. In the words of Sant Darshan Singh:

> *Begin to live your life according to your aspirations,*
> *And step toward your chosen goal,*
> *Life is not worth its name unless*
> *We meet the challenges of the times.*
> *Play on the instrument of the heart even if it be broken,*
> *This sleeping world will surely awaken,*
> *But first you must arouse your own slumbering hopes and*
>   *desires....*
> *Why complain of the darkness, Oh Darshan,*
> *Instead illumine the lamp of your own heart.*[16]

Guru Kabir

Chapter Three
Kabir: The Path of Perfect Faith

For Ages past I have been Thy devotee:
How can I now be separated?
The harmony playing at Thy door,
becomes manifest in my forehead.[1]
—Kabir

Kabir is regarded by many as one of the greatest Indian saints to bless the hallowed soil of India. Although his life remains shrouded in myth and legend, this Sant saint and revolutionary figure continues to influence the spirituality of millions of people on the subcontinent and, indeed, around the world. To this day the dates of his birth and death remain unclear and without historical validation. Yet the now legendary story of the manner of his death reveals his vision of transcendent unity and characteristic flaunting of meaningless superstition. According to his biographers, Kabir planned to enter *maha samadhi*—his conscious death—in the town of Magahar, considered by the orthodox Hindus of his era to be an extremely inauspicious place to die. In a poem-song complied in the work *Kabir Bijak*, Kabir refers to the absurdity of such meaningless rituals:

> *You say that he who dies at Magahar will become a donkey,*
> *Have you lost faith in Ram?*
> *If Ram dwells in my heart,*
> *What is Kashi? What is the barren ground of Magahar?*
> *If Kabir leaves this body in Kashi,*
> *What debt is owed to him?*[2]

As the poem narrates, Kabir broke with Hindu tradition and purposely chose to die in Magahar instead of in the "spiritually correct" place, the holy city of Kashi. Immediately after his death, a dispute arose between his Hindu and Muslim followers as to what should be done with his body. According to their respective customs, the Hindus wanted to cremate Kabir; the Muslims wanted to bury him. In the interim, they agreed to lay Kabir's body out on a dais and cover it with a full thirty-two cartloads of flowers. In clear view of all, these flowers were lovingly placed on, over, and beneath the body, covering it so high and thick that it was invisible to his assembled devotees.

Although Kabir's followers were sad at their Master's passing, they were also overjoyed because their teacher was now re-united with *his* beloved, Beloved God. A jubilant celebration continued long into the night as the Master's body lay in state. Finally, however, it was time to uncover the body and decide among themselves whether to burn or bury the body. To the amazement of all, Kabir's body had simply vanished—only the flowers remained.[3]

Throughout Kabir's verses, as well as in the many legends and stories about him, he steadfastly reminds his listeners that the essence of true spirituality and authentic worship is beyond blind performance of outer rites and rituals. Even in his death, Kabir taught that real worship is beyond the limitations of traditions, culture, time, and space. *Real worship is an inner opening of the heart.*

Kabir's simple message is devoid of philosophical encumbrances and artifice. He dispensed with the superfluous mystique of other complex Indian philosophical systems and revealed the inner secret of the path to God, which he called *Sahaja yoga*. He taught that true worship was a matter of direct contact with the inner reality—an experience everyone could have, regardless of caste, tradition, or religion. It is for this reason that he is considered by many to be the father of modern spirituality in India,

At a time when Hinduism was reeling under the oppressive weight of excessive formalism and rigid caste structure, Kabir brought spirituality back to its transcendent core. In addition to reforming Hinduism, he also steered Islam away from zealous fanatics who sought to convert others at the point of the sword. Today, Kabir's verses are sung throughout the Asian subcontinent, found on the lips of both Islamic mullahs and Hindu pundits. Even present-day politicians, educators, and artists dip into the treasure house of Kabir's much-loved verses.

Kabir taught in the language of the commoners, unlike the pundits and mullahs who imparted their teachings in Sanskrit or Arabic, respectively. Yet despite his choice of simple words, he spoke with authority, based on his inner revelation, and he was not averse to using strong, unambiguous language when he confronted bigoted religious authorities of the day. His all-embracing openness of outlook and his simplicity of style endeared him to even illiterate beggars, who even today chant his verses unceasingly on the highways and dusty byways of India.

Perhaps Kabir's most profound offering was his recognition that spirituality is not the monopoly of any one religion, caste, or hierarchy, but a free gift of nature, and that because spirituality is a birthright given by God to all, access to God should also be equal and universal. At the core of his teachings, Kabir stressed the importance of direct contact with a spiritually realized teacher and of the Guru's Word, called *Shabda* or *Divine Word*, which provides the direct link between the soul and the Creator.

Kabir cut through the layers of intellectual verbiage and abstruse doctrine and offered a profoundly simple path that every-one could follow. His unifying vision not only wove together the seemingly divergent threads within Hinduism and Islam, but also helped heal the wounds inflicted by self-seeking religious power brokers. Scholars, commoners, and saints alike attribute India's present spiritual richness to his profound influence in bringing spirituality back to the masses. No method or teachings could be more useful today, as seekers from all traditions and walks of life continue to seek simple, universal methods for achieving lasting inner peace and spiritual progress.

The Universal Path of Shabda Yoga

In the absence of complete historical records, Kabir's modern biographers have found his life difficult to document chronologically. The earliest source available comes from Nabhadas, a devotee who in 1585 wrote a book about saints and holy men entitled *Bhaktamal*, or "Garland of Flowers," which gives an excellent account of Kabir's character.[4]

The few facts we do have about his life can be summarized in a few sentences. Kabir was born in Varanasi around the beginning of the 15th century into a simple family of weavers of Muslim background. He apparently learned the family craft of weaving and later studied devotional practices with a Hindu Guru. From Kabir's poems, it appears he visited a number of places of pilgrimage in search of a true spiritual teacher who could guide him on the path. It is accepted by most biographers that his formal initiation was given by a prominent orthodox Hindu priest named Ramanand.

Now, Ramanand was not considered a realized *Shabda* Saint, but an ardent, well-respected guru who worshipped Lord Vishnu of the Hindu Trinity. Fully aware that no orthodox Hindu would accept him as a disciple because of his Muslim background, Kabir devised an ingenious plan to become initiated. One day, while Ramanand was taking his morning ablution at a river bank, Kabir lay prostrate on the steps of the bathing ghat. In the dim, pre-dawn hour, Ramanand did not see Kabir lying on the stone steps. Ramanand placed his foot directly on Kabir's forehead. Ramanand, startled, cried out "Ram Ram." After this had happened, no verbal interchange occurred between Ramanand and Kabir. Kabir simply picked himself up and silently walked away.

To present-day Western readers, the meaning of this pre-meditated ambush is puzzling at best, but for Kabir, it was a clever plan to sidestep rigid custom and receive initiation from a teacher who otherwise would not grant it to him simply because of his Muslim birth. In India, even to this day, when a Guru touches a disciple on the forehead and at the same imparts a holy mantra—some name of God, in this case, "Ram Ram"—this constitutes the imparting of spiritual initiation.

As the story goes, word got out that Ramanand had initiated a Muslim weaver. Some of Ramanand's disciples asked him why a high caste Brahmin would act in direct defiance of Brahmanic law by initiating a non-Hindu. Ramanand flatly refuted the accusation and asked for them to bring Kabir before him. Kabir was ushered into his presence. Ramanand asked him why he was making this false claim. Kabir respectfully reiterated how Ramanand had touched his forehead with his foot at the ghat (bathing pool) and uttered the words "Ram Ram." Ramanand could not deny the literal truth of his statement and relented by admitting him into his fold of disciples.

The larger irony of the nature of this particular guru-disciple relationship should not be lost to our readers, for although Kabir had sought initiation from Ramanand, it was Ramanand who was less spiritually developed than Kabir. In fact, through Kabir's influence, Ramanand gradually moved away from the outer idol worship and excessive formalism of orthodox Hinduism. Such stories provide us with a glimpse into how Kabir influenced the inner dynamic of Hinduism from within its own walls.

Instead of outer worship, Kabir advocated a *nirgun,* or formless worship of God, based on a path of meditation and the inner repetition of "Ram." Kabir's *"Ram"* was not a mere outer symbol or mantra of the Hindu incarnation of Vishnu, but signified the inner Reality itself, which Kabir referred to as *Shabda* (Word) or *Nama*

(Name). It was the experience of the inner reality of Ram that became the core pillar of his teachings.

Kabir wanted to make it clear this *Shabda* was *videh,* or above the realm of physical existence, and could only be contacted through the soul.

> *All sing of the Shabda without realizing that it is Videh or the*
> *Bodiless,*
> *No tongue can describe it, but the soul may contact it within.*[5]

Kabir distinguishes "religion" from spirituality. If religion is a set of rites, rituals, and prescribed methods of achieving spiritual progress, spirituality is the culmination of those practices, the *experience itself*. Kabir taught that the true purpose behind religion is to unite us to our Creator. Religious approaches may vary, but Truth is One. To further illustrate this truth, the following personal anecdote is instructive:

I am often asked to what religion I belong. My usual response is to say to the questioner, "If you can tell me what religion God belongs to, *that* is my religion." At this point, most people look at me with a bewildered expression on their face, pause again, and ask me what I mean. I then reply, "We all belong to God, not to any religion. Our various religions are merely means to achieve that divine reunion."

God made humans and humans made religion. They are all means to a common end. It was this great distinction that Kabir, in his own time, articulated and brought to the masses. If we are to move beyond the current climate of religious fanaticism and right-wing fundamentalism, it is necessary to understand that God is beyond all labels we may assign to Him.

Experiencing the divine is primary; doctrine is only a secondary footnote to the former. The experience of Divine love alone can take us beyond the prison-house of mind and matter and bring us inner and outer peace. Kabir's essential message can be summarized in the following nine core principles.

1. Recognize our Source— We Have All Emanated from One Eternal Light

In the beginning God created His Light,
And from it were all men made,
Yea, from God's light came the whole universe,
Whom then shall we call good, whom bad?[6]

—Kabir

Kabir's message of divine unity is the preeminent cornerstone of the mansion of true spirituality. To recognize the imminence and all-pervasiveness of the power we call God, Allah, Jehovah, Ram, or our Buddha-nature is the sine qua non through which all spiritual gnosis is born and lasting inner and outer peace is achieved.

Since the beginning of recorded spirituality, saints and mystics have inculcated this highest vision of unity. Though the messengers come and go, their message has remained largely the same. Sadly, humanity continues to forget its essential unity. Out of this forgetfulness arise all wars, hatred, and division. Kabir reminds us of this eternal truth when he tells us that, "In the beginning God created His Light, and from it were all men made."

Prophets, saints, and mystics have testified to the omniscient potency of this great Light, and born witness to its transcendent power, which supports, sustains, and illumines the world. Christians have called it the *Logos*, or Word. In the Gospel according to John we find that "In the beginning was the Word, and the Word was with God and the Word was God. The same was in the beginning with God. All things were made by Him; and without Him was not anything made that was made. In Him was life; and the life was the *light* of men."[7]

Sunni Muslims refer to the same Divine Principle as *Kalma-i-Qadim*, or Ancient Word. Sufis call it the *Nur Allah*, literally the "Light of God." Hindu's call it *Jyoti*, light, and *Sruti*, sound. In the Old Testament, Jews referred to it as The Word and the "Light of Man." Tibetan Buddhists refer to it as the Clear Light. Buddha himself referred to this power as Transcendental Seeing. Through this creative power the entire world was brought forth into being, from the tiniest amoeba to the remotest galaxy in the universe.

The cosmologies of several religions share the belief that God in the absolute state is beyond description, apprehension, or comprehension. That power can neither be fully known nor described. It can, however, be experientially realized by connecting to it through its expression in its non-absolute state—what Kabir refers to as *Shabda* or *Nama*. During his ministry on earth, Kabir tirelessly advocated this direct way of connecting to reality.

A simple metaphor may elucidate the distinction between God Absolute and God-into-Expression: The sun cannot be understood by external observation, inference, or intellectual analysis. Nor can it be approached *directly* by any human-made vehicle, for if such a craft were to approach too close, the intensity of the sun's heat would easily incinerate any protective heat shield.

In the same way, humans cannot know God Absolute directly by using our eyes of flesh or the faculties of mind and emotion. However, Sant Kabir taught that inside human beings is the same light of the Creator, so that if we ourselves can learn how to become a "ray of the sun," then we can ride back on such a ray to the sun itself. By becoming god-like, we can reclaim our inner divinity. Once we connect with this indwelling light we become by degrees more and more "en-lightened."

This Inner Light and Ringing Radiance dwell within every atom of creation and within each and every soul. This indwelling power controls, sustains, and maintains each of us in the human body. Kabir reminds us, as all great luminaries have, that we have a god-like nature within us. If this is so, then there is vast potential in each of us. Indeed, God resides in every soul and each soul has the potential to reach Him.

Kabir tells us that the soul and God are sleeping together in the same bed. God is awake but the soul remains asleep. Through the magic of a saint's touch, the soul awakens. We can better understand this by way of another metaphor. We know, for example, that electricity is present everywhere in the atmosphere. However, to harness its power efficiently, electricity must be channeled through the most effective and appropriate conducting substance. Although electricity can even pass through dried straw, the intensity of the heat given off by the electrical charge will burn the straw instantaneously, making it an extremely inefficient conductor of electricity.

We also know that electricity can pass through water—but again, water is also a poor conductor of electricity. If, however, electricity is passed through the medium of copper wire, it not only passes through easily but moves at high speed, while the medium of copper remains intact for continual use.

Similarly, the divine current of Light is already within us; but in order for us to consciously conduct this current we must become pure in thought, word, and deed, body, mind and soul. Otherwise, we will not be able to withstand the great force and power of God's Divine Current.

Sant Kirpal Singh has said that "We are all micro-Gods. Each soul is divine in nature and therefore God-like." Each of us has the ability to reconnect with this Creative Power within us, but first we must become pure—sun-like, if you will. Once we see divine Light within, we begin to see it in others. Without this experiential unitive experience of Light and the divine, religion devolves into mere rites, rituals, dogma, and doctrine. In time, division and discord between divergent belief systems lead to sectarian strife and hatred.

Instead of seeing the all-pervasive Lord in everything, we see others according to our limited angle of vision. We see mere labels. We see people as male or female, Christian or Jew, black or white, rich or poor, learned or unlearned, good or bad. Perceiving the world in this divisive way is an illusory deception—one of the root-causes of suffering on this planet. From this illusion of separation springs needless conflict: we judge, separate and condemn others. How can there be peace in the world when we have forgotten who we really are?

The Hindus describe our spiritual essence as *Sat-chit-ananda*—truth, consciousness, and bliss, respectively. Until we inwardly realize our true spiritual nature, individuals, families, communities, religions, races, and nations will continue to wage war outwardly. Inner peace leads to outer peace.

The Masters say that there is only one answer to this case of mistaken identity: *realize the One, worship the One, and serve the One in all.* Until and unless we realize this divine unity, there is little hope for lasting outer peace. Until we see that our individual happiness is not separate from the welfare of the whole, we will continue to seek our own happiness at the expense of the greater good. Spiritual communion leads naturally to the universal ground of true spiritual comunity, the only foundation upon which lasting world peace can be built.

2. Find a True Spiritual Teacher and Abide by His Instructions

So hold thy breath in sushmana that thou hearest the unstruck melody
And seek out a Guru that thou seekest not another again.[8]
—Adi Granth

To begin to hear this "unstruck melody," we first have to understand what it is and how we can connect the Divine Sound. Our first step is simple: we need to be humble enough to admit to ourselves that we might not know what this experience is all about.

Plato said, "I am better off than he [a man reputed for wisdom] is, for he knows nothing, and thinks that he knows; I neither know nor think that I know…. The truth is, O men of Athens, that God only is wise."[9] To understand that we do not know, he tells us, is really to acknowledge our ignorance. As long as we continue to believe that we have all the answers, we are not ready to receive the guidance we need.

It is said that only a cup that is not full can receive something new. The cup that is full must first be emptied in order to receive. My spiritual Master would say that the task of guiding learned intellectuals was most difficult. When someone asked why, he replied that, "First they have to *unlearn* what they know already, only then can they begin."[10]

If we think we have all the answers, why bother seeking spiritual guidance to begin with? A precondition of accepting guidance is the recognition of our ignorance of spiritual matters. In this sense, sincere asking is half of knowledge. When our heart truly yearns for guidance, help comes. Then, the second step is to seek the assistance of one who does know—someone who is spiritually competent by virtue of actual realization and not mere book-knowledge or personal charisma.

When I began my search for God almost 40 years ago, there came a point where I had to be honest with myself and admit that I knew virtually nothing about who I was and even less about God. I believed in my heart that God existed, but how could I find Him? I had read dozens of spiritual books, attended numerous lectures, visited mosques, synagogues, churches, and temples—all proclaimed that they had the truth. In the end, I remained confused and unable to decide where to turn. My own efforts were fruitless and I became more and more desperate. I remember thinking one day that there must be a way out. I reasoned that if I could find someone who was in tune with God's will, then by following that divinely attuned person I would be following God's Will. Before such a meeting, how could I really serve God?

At the time, even my concept of God was vague, as it was not founded on any direct experience. Books were helpful to some extent, but were not specific enough to give anything except general guidance. The more I read and studied, the more I realized the necessity of having the guidance of a living spiritual master. Past Masters could be helpful, I realized, but only to a certain point. I knew that I needed a living teacher who could answer my questions directly.

From that day onward I knew what I was seeking, and it wasn't very long before I embarked on a pilgrimage to India to find a spiritual teacher. I dropped out of college and began saving money for my trip. Not long after this decision, I was "guided" by way of multiple, extremely improbable synchronicities to the teachings of His Holiness Sant Kirpal Singh.

On one life-transforming evening, one year before meeting Sant Kirpal Singh physically, I was lifted out of my body and taken to a world of ineffable beauty. There I witnessed universe after universe of inner stars, moons, and suns, each radiating the most exquisite Light. As I watched these wondrous self-illuminating lights sparkle through eternity, every pore of my being exploded with an intoxicating radiance that had no earthly equivalent. This experience shook me to the very core. I had tasted a mere drop of the truth, and I was completely overpowered by its awesome sublimity. I later learned that this experience was entirely the gift of my master. In point of fact, I had not found him, he had found me!

When I finally met Sant Kirpal Singh in the flesh for the first time in October of 1972, I realized that I had been given a direct connection with the very same unstruck melody of which Kabir speaks: the *shabda* or Word. Where is this unstruck melody to be found? Kabir says in the *"sushmana,"* the non-physical, central energetic channel located in and above the eye-focus at the doorway where the two worlds (physical and astral) meet.

Having had this direct experience of the unstruck melody, I began to appreciate the value and indispensability of the guidance of a true spiritual teacher. Kabir and the Masters teach that we need a *living connection* to that Power that is God. For this we need the living touch of a true Master, someone who not only provides the initial connection, but accompanies us throughout the entire journey, providing ongoing inner and outer guidance along the way.

We live in an era in which suspiciousness of gurus is the norm and not the exception—which is not surprising due to sheer number of false gurus, charlatans, and frauds out there. Authentic teachers are extremely rare in this day and age, and in large part due to this prevailing suspiciousness, these true Masters no longer ask for blind obedience but give us a demonstration of their competency at the outset. As Sant Kirpal Singh often reiterated, "seeing is believing." Therefore, if the spiritual teacher is the "real item," they have the power to give a direct experience of the inner Light and Sound, or unstruck melody, which is already within us in latent form, waiting to be awakened by the touch of a true Master.

Such great beings have been known in various traditions by different names, such as Guru, Master, Murshid, Pir, Rebbe, Prophet, and Shaykh. Once we are connected to a true teacher, it is in our best interests to "hold on tight" by abiding by their instructions and aligning ourselves with their core teachings.

3. Align Yourself with the Guru's Word

> *He who knows the import of the Guru's word,*
> *And pays no heed to what another says,*
> *He becomes a man of dispassion and his wanderings cease.*
> *The unsociable Lord he seizes and so seizing,*
> *Abides in the heaven of super consciousness.*[11]
> —*Adi Granth Sahib*

In refreshingly direct words, Kabir reminds us of our task: once we have found a true teacher and received a first-hand experience of the inner light of God and the unstruck melody within, we need to follow their teachings implicitly by abiding in their instructions. The problem many of us face is our reluctance to trust the words of our teachers. We may have read many books, attended many lectures, pondered deeply existential spiritual questions for years, but we find part of ourselves resisting the commitment to crucial aspects of the spiritual path.

Sant Rajinder Singh illuminates this predicament in the story of a man who is being chased by a wild tiger. The man finally comes to the edge of a large cliff and faces a most disturbing predicament: If he does not jump off the cliff, he will most certainly be eaten alive. If he *does* jump off the cliff, he also faces certain death. As he is contemplating his fate, he notices a small branch hanging from the edge of the precipice. He decides to jump onto the branch. He catches the branch and avoids the tiger. However, while he has eluded the tiger, he now realizes he is hanging from the edge of the precipice with no way up. As he looks up he notices that a mouse has begun to nibble away at the very branch he is holding onto. He soon realizes that the branch will soon break and he will fall to a certain death. Facing death once again in a different form, with no apparent way out, he turns to God Almighty for help. Looking heavenward, with an imploring tone, he prays out loud, "O God, *please* save me!" After a pregnant pause, God replies in booming tone, "I will save you, all you have to do is *let go.*"

The man is paralyzed by the import of God's command—let go? He thinks to himself, "What kind of advice is this?" So he looks heavenward and again asks God, "Is there *anyone else* up there I can talk to?"[12]

Let us examine this humorous but meaningful parable closer. The man, like many of us, only turns to God when every other avenue is blocked and all else has failed. Why does it take a catastrophe before we bring God into the equation? Why do we not remember God more often, when times are good? This is a question worth asking ourselves. Most of us entreat God for help at moments of crisis and desperation.

Furthermore, the man receives a reply from God but is not willing to follow it. Why? Because he has little faith and trust in God. Too often we profess our faith in God, but when crisis comes upon us our faith in God similarly falters. Some even question the existence of God. We claim to be religious and revere the saints and their holy books, but if we do not follow their advice and "live the life," it is an empty faith at best.

So if we are able to find a true teacher, it is imperative that we make our best efforts to follow their advice. Today's seekers are sufficiently intelligent to know what we have been asked to do, but we lack the courage and will power to actually do it. One pointed and quality effort is missing. We must ask ourselves why?

In order to follow anyone or anything two things are required: first, we must be convinced of the person authority; and second, we need to have a ruling passion. Without these two prerequisites spiritual progress becomes very difficult. Here Kabir tells us to truly live what the true teacher gives us. Don't go by hearsay. Don't listen to everyone else's opinion. Real faith is born of some direct personal experience of God and not mere blind belief. Without this there can be no true faith. Once we know something of the reality of God, nothing can shake our faith. True faith is always a matter of direct experience. The Master will give us a taste of God. My Master affirmed again and again that "Spirituality cannot be bought; it cannot be taught; it can only be caught."[13]

The true Master gives us a taste of the Guru's Word. This Word is essence of life and light itself. Since life comes from Life, and light comes from Light, a spiritually charged being can transmit his uplifting spiritual power to another being through the law of sympathy. A true spiritual master not only provides us with an initial spiritual experience of inner Light and Sound—the Guru's "Word"—but continues to infuse the disciple/student with ongoing, sustained spiritual support, independent of where each may be living on the earth-plane.

As we have already mentioned, a true master is a rare article, not to be confused with the many so-called "masters" parading the world today. There are many great and wonderful teachers who are *on the way* but a true master *is* the Way. Such Masters embody the Truth and do not merely teach. They awaken others with their spiritual radiation. This is what Kabir means by spontaneous illumination. It is all done through radiation. Words are not necessary. Lectures are not necessary. Even from thousands of miles away this illumination can be transmitted.

To help illustrate this point, take the example of a car's battery. Many of us have had the unpleasant experience of the battery in our car or truck not turning over, especially during the cold winter months. Our first response is to call some emergency automotive service to jump start our vehicle. When the operator arrives, what does he do? He hooks up his fully charged battery to our low-energy battery, connecting the emergency truck's positive charge cable to our positive charge cable and his negative charge cable to our negative charge cable. Once the connections are secure, he starts his engine first and then asks us to start our engine. The charge from his battery flows into our battery and our vehicle (usually) starts right up.

On the level of our senses, when we watch this jump-start procedure occurring, we don't hear, see, or smell anything, yet we know that the electrical current has flowed into our battery from the tow company's charging battery. No one cries out that God's miracle has saved us; we know that nothing miraculous has happened. This is an everyday occurrence and explainable in terms of the basic laws of physics—one charged body conveys its charge to another.

Analogously, a spiritually charged being—call him Master, Shaykh, Pir, or so forth—can also convey energy directly to us through his or her non-physical radiation. This spiritual boost is something like the jump start that opens up our latent spiritual ability to see and hear on the level of consciousness of the soul. When this spiritual transfusion occurs and we have had a palpable experience of a higher order of reality, we know what we have experienced, no matter what others may tell us to discount its validity. Seeing is believing.

Untested spiritual beliefs based on intellect or emotion, rather than direct experience, are the essence of blind faith. Kabir understood the need for the direct spiritual experience of *Shabda* as well as contact with a living teacher.

4. Communion with God— Contemplation and Remembrance

Let contemplation and remembrance be thy two earrings,
Let Gnosis be thy coat.[14]
—Kabir

During Kabir's time it was a common practice for yogis to wear two earrings, one in each ear, and an orange-hued robes signifying their status as a renunciates. These outer symbols were supposed to signify a state of freedom from attachment and desire, but as Kabir points out, outer displays do not necessarily reflect the elevated dispassion of true inner renunciation. The real transformational practice, he says, consists of meditative contemplation and inner remembrance of God.

The same inner criteria for measuring spiritual advancement are just as relevant today. So-called spiritual leaders may wear the distinctive costumes of their particular religious sect and pronounce pompously that their dogmas and doctrine are the "only truth"; they may even become imbalanced by emotional chauvinism and stage mass public rallies aimed at converting others to "the faith." Inwardly, however, these people are still slaves to the dictates of the mind and the senses, to the sway of "I," "me," and "mine." Like the orange-robed yogis of old who wore the outer garbs of spirituality, some contemporary spiritual leaders seek to change others before they have undergone their own inner transformation.

There is also the "almighty dollar" factor, with its acquisitive shopping-mall mentality. Some spiritual groups require would-be students to pay significant amounts of money as a mandatory prerequisite for participation. This is not the way of true teaching. As my Master always said, spirituality is a gift of God and should be as free as the sun and the water.

The initial spiritual boost we get from a true teacher at the time of initiation is like an infusion of capital into our spiritual lives. Based on our spiritual background, our present receptivity, and the grace of the Master, each initiate into Shabda each is given what the Master deems appropriate. Once given, it is up to us to wisely invest this spiritual capital.

In the recently discovered Gospel of Thomas, Jesus is quoted as saying, "He who will drink from my mouth will become like me. I myself shall become he, and the things that are hidden will be revealed to him."[15] To "drink from the mouth" of the Master is to receive his illumination. It is to receive this non-physical Light directly. Once given, it is the sacred responsibility of the receiver to increase this Light with every thought, word, and deed. It is our duty to water the seed of spirituality on a daily basis; otherwise it will wither and die. This is our first task. Out of this remembrance and contemplation comes true *gnosis* — direct knowledge of God. It is worth recounting here the Biblical parable of the sower of seeds, as given by the great teacher from Galilee:

A sower went forth to sow. Some seeds fell by the wayside and birds devoured them. Some seeds fell on stony ground where there was not much earth, and though the plants quickly grew, when the sun came up they were scorched. Having no root, the plants withered away. Some seeds fell among the thorns and the thorns choked the plants and they yielded no fruit. Some seeds fell upon good ground and did yield fruit; some bore thirty-fold, sixty-fold, and some a hundredfold.[16]

In this beautiful parable, Christ explains the predicament many of us face after our first taste of spirituality. The seed sown on the wayside represents those who are given the inner gift but do not practice on a consistent basis. Without consistent practice, the seed of spirituality is not going to flourish.

The seed sown in stony ground grows quickly but, having no root, perishes. This represents those aspirants who fail to prioritize around a guiding purpose. They may practice the meditation, but have no ruling passion in their lives. Such seeds grow quickly at first, but later die.

The third seed is sown in soil, but thorns encroach upon it and choke it from light and water. This represents those of us who are so entangled in the world that we are overwhelmed by the activity of our minds and the environments in which we live. Our lives become so busy and fast-paced that even if we do meditate regularly, we cannot still our minds. It is this last condition that, I believe, afflicts the overwhelming majority of spiritual seekers at one point or another.

Many people perform the outer acts of worship and attend church or synagogue, but how many sit in meditation every day, for one, two, three hours or more? How many attempt to remember God's name internally throughout the day and night, and continuously invoke his presence? In my travels I have found that many people are well read and thoroughly acquainted with the theory of meditation, but very few can honesty say that they meditate regularly.

Although times have changed dramatically since Kabir's day, truly transformational spiritual practice is as rare now as it was then. Meditation and remembrance of God are the true wealth to be accumulated in this life. These should be the prized "earrings" of spiritual wealth. If we were motivated enough to accumulate this kind of wealth with the same ardor and dedication with which we seek the material, we would all be spiritual millionaires!

The hard truth is that time here on Earth is limited, and we cannot pursue and accomplish *all* of our desires and goals. Therefore, we must make what feel like difficult choices, as we cannot *have* everything. We need to set our sights on what is of real, lasting, and of true worth, and then prioritize our time to *seek that!*

Outer wealth is not incompatible with spirituality. Yet unless we are centered in our spiritual practice, an outer-centered, materially oriented lifestyle will be a dangerous distraction often resulting in lack of consistent inner progress. My own Master used to tells us to simplify, simplify, simplify. To be simple is to be strong. To be simple is to accept life.

Kabir taught that the unrelenting pursuit of outer desires produces continuous dissatisfaction, in large part due to the very impermanency of the outer world, which is in constant flux. How do we cure the age-old malady of excessive externality? Kabir's answer is simple: "They who were awake to the Lord's name day and night, became adepts for they were attuned to the Lord." He who remembers God with every breath has nothing to fear in all the three worlds.[17]

During life's trials, we all too often undergo intense suffering as a result of loss of health, wealth, job, loved ones, and so on. When these losses occur—and the Masters assure us that they will—many of us question God's wisdom! "Why do You let bad things happen to good people?" we cry out in our misery. Without right understanding, many people lose their faith in God. They become burdened with the weight of the world and prone to depression and anxiety. It is precisely in trying times that it behooves us to keep our equipoise and recognize our limited human ability to see "the big picture."

The human mind is fallible and subject to error; how can we even begin to fathom the inner workings of the Creator of *all* minds? Yet our opinionated ego-mind assumes that it knows what is right and wrong, good or bad—not only for us, but for everybody else as well! We may whine, pontificate and criticize, but the truth is that we cannot always know what is in our own best interests.

My own Master used to say that the very first step on the spiritual path is to *stop complaining*. Acceptance goes a long way to healing our spiritual malaise. In step five below, Kabir advises that in order to pass through difficult periods of life we must surrender our willful ego at the altar of God's greater Will. This is the basis of true and lasting faith.

5. Accept Both "Good" and "Bad" as Part of God's Divine Will

Learning to gracefully accept whatever comes our way is one of the cornerstones of a true spiritual life. This does not mean we complacently accept those situations in which it is possible to "make lemons into lemonade." Kabir says that acceptance is recognizing that whatever has happened—whether seemingly "good" or "bad"—is part of the divine will, for God has indeed permitted the event to take place.

It is usually easy to accept the good things that happen in our lives, such as a pay raise, honor, or other success. It may take years of inner spiritual work, however, to accept that the seemingly bad, unpleasant things that come our way do, in fact, have a silver lining, even though we may not know what that silver lining is at the time. To complicate matters more, sometimes the so-called "good" may in reality be candy-coated poison, leading to a moral, financial, or spiritual downfall.

In truth, our ability to accurately assess a situation—from an objective, realistic, global, long-term standpoint—is far more limited than most of us would care to admit. This is why we must learn to accept all things and trust in God's greater wisdom. It is to this simple spiritual truth that the saints referred when they said that there are three special blessings that God bestows upon those He loves most: poverty, ill health, and ignominy (bad reputation).

How, one might ask, can poverty, sickness, and ill repute possibly be God's or the Master's special blessings for us? The answer, as saints from various traditions know, is that trial and tribulation have a tendency to turn our attention away from the world and toward the more important eternal realities of the spirit within. Yet, if we can learn to see and remember God in both the easy times as well as the hard—and to accept both as part of God's divine plan—then we will reap a rich harvest of ongoing remembrance, faith, and equanimity.

Sweet is Thy will, say the saints. This level of faith is illustrated beautifully in the following story:

> In the course of conversation, Guru Nanak advocated the supremacy of living by the will of God. The man to whom he was speaking, on the other hand, championed the view that reason and self-will were superior. "Show me one person who truly lived by God's will," the man demanded, challenging the Guru. So, Nanak instructed him to visit Bhai Lalo, a carpenter by profession, who lived in a nearby village. The man was only too happy to comply.

The man traveled to the village and, upon meeting Bhai Lalo, disclosed the reason for his visit. "I will attend to you in fifteen minutes," said the carpenter. As the man waited, Bhai Lalo put the finishing touches on a burial casket, then moved it into his woodworking shop and made an errand to the local bazaar to purchase other burial items. Upon his return, Bhai Lalo was about to address his guest when a messenger came running to the house with terrible news.

"Your son has just had an accident," the messenger told him. "He has fallen down from the roof and died."

Unperturbed, Bhai Lalo muttered reflectively, "God's Will."

When the visiting man asked Bhai Lalo why he was not grieving, the carpenter replied, "Such is the will of God." Then, in a quiet, composed voice, Bhai Lalo told the man that he had to attend to the preparation of his son's body but that he would return soon. An hour or so later, true to his word, Bhai Lalo returned to his shop, greeted the man warmly, and again apologized for his absence.

While he had been waiting, the visiting man had had time to think about the situation. He realized that the casket and burial articles had been prepared *before* Bhai Lalo received word of his son's fatal fall! Caught up in emotion, the man accused him of negligence—for if Lalo somehow knew in advance that his son was going to fall and die, why didn't he try to prevent it from happening?

Bhai Lalo looked intently into the stranger's face and explained with great sincerity. "In meditation," he said, "I was told by the voice of God that it was my son's destiny to die in this way, and that it was in the best interest of all concerned that his earthly connection with me should end at this time. Though I am sad that my son is gone, I am happy in God's Will. Why lament if it is God's will, for it always brings hidden wisdom and blessings? God's Will is always for the best."[18]

Guru Nanak knew that Bhai Lalo had cultivated his receptivity to God's Will through meditation, and that Bhai Lalo was sufficiently tuned into God's "internal guidance system" to know what was to occur in advance. This ability to know God's Will is available to all of us. Compared to this level of gnosis, making decisions and taking actions solely on the basis of reasoning is severely limited. One who fully sees with the inner eye of wisdom is connected to—indeed, knows—God's Will. This spiritual vision is necessary in order to see the true picture on deeper levels of causality. Until such time as we have the inner vision to perceive events correctly, we must have faith that what happens in our lives is for our ultimate benefit. Kabir continues to explore this in step six, below.

6. Rejoice in Whatever Happens

To accept God's will for us is to become worry-free. To joyfully accept God's Will under all circumstances is the most liberating way of being in the world. Yet, this task is a tremendous challenge to our little ego. In a thousand subtle ways, the ego pops up to betray our best intentions, finding fault and casting aspersions on what is unfolding before us. Even when we are able to outwardly accept a trying circumstance by patiently coping with the situation, we are inwardly far from joy. Instead, we question God's Sweet Will in allowing unpleasant things to happen. From a spiritual perspective, even the act of questioning why things happen is a sure indication that ego is alive and well—and a clear expression of our lack of faith.

The Story of Rabia Basra and God's Will

A group of devotees went to pay their respects to Rabia Basra, a woman saint of great renown and spiritual development. In due course, the conversation turned to how a true lover of God should respond to good and bad happenings.

Someone said, "Both good and bad should be borne with patience."

"That is fine," replied Rabia Basra, "but there is pride in this statement."

A second person answered, "One should take delight whether in good times or bad times."

She smiled serenely, "This answer is closer to the truth but still smells of ego."

Another person present then asked Rabia Basra to please tell that what the attitude of a true lover of God should be. She replied, "A truly surrendered soul should be so elevated that such a one feels no difference in good and bad times. In fact, a true lover of God does not distinguish between good or bad and continually rejoices in whatever happens."[19]

Those who fully comprehend the majesty of such a state of equanimity will never doubt God's love and compassion for us. Who can do this? Only one who has rooted out every bit of selfishness and ego from their being. To root out selfishness and ego, we need to move beyond pseudo-worship and enter what can be called "authentic worship."

What is the difference between the two? Pseudo-worship may resemble worship in certain outer aspects, but at its motivational core it is still ego-based—it's all about what we can get *for ourselves*. Instead of performing spiritual practice to experience our essential oneness and to commune with God's love, it turns out the ego is still in the driver's seat. In contrast, authentic worship involves surrendering our individual will in favor of God's Will. When this occurs, we become a conscious co-worker of the Divine.

One of the most soul-stirring true accounts to illustrate the principle is the martyrdom of the great Sikh guru Arjan Dev at the hands of the ruling Mogul dynasty in India. Arjan Dev, the leader of the Sikhs and a fully realized Master, was captured by the enemy and tortured in the public square. Yet even as he was laid out on burning iron plates and red-hot sand was poured over his body, Guru Arjan Dev sang out again and again, "Sweet is thy Will."

Hazrat Mian Mir, one of Arjan's close spiritual friends who was also spiritually advanced and possessed the ability to perform miracles of unimaginable power, was able to exchange some words with him as the torturous spectacle unfolded.

"My dear friend," he said, "for these heinous act your torturers are inflicting on you, permit me to raze the entire Mogul empire to the ground!"

Arjan Dev replied, "Don't you know that I also could do it? But the path of the saints is the path of sweet surrender. Ours is the path of 'sweet is Thy Will.'"[20]

Though this sublime state seems a long way off to us now, it is every soul's divine destiny to experience this lofty pinnacle of surrender. Let us remember that the path of faith is one of trust in the power of God within us. God is not some unimaginable deity in the heavens, but the soul of our soul and breath of our breath.

7. From Pseudo-righteousness to Authentic Worship

Kabir continues to elucidate the path in the following verse:

> *The more efforts the egocentrics make,*
> *The more they fail to swim across the sea of material existence.*
> *For they read the way of works and observe outer discipline*
> *And psuedo-righteousness,*
> *But egotism has burnt their inner core.*[21]

Here the essence of true worship is revealed: it is to love God for the sake of the love of God, and not for any outer reward or fear of punishment. In short, we must seek God, worship God, and love God without egotistical motives. Many of us wonder why our prayers and meditations have become dry and empty, yet in most cases, if we look closely we find that our practice is tainted with cleverly disguised selfish desires. Often, despite our best efforts, we are more concerned with attracting attention to ourselves and accumulating power and recognition than in really loving God and serving his creation. We may outwardly fool the world, but we cannot fool God within, for it is said that God listens to the cry of our soul instead of the rumblings of our mind. Only our sincere intention and aspiration can opens the sluice-gates of grace.

The great Nazarene reminds us that, "Wherever your treasure is, there also will be your heart."[22] We have to delve into our hearts and see what lurks in the darkness. My Master used to say that God gives everyone what they truly want. If we want God we will surely have Him. It is a question of purity of heart—the mechanical performances of outer rituals and disciplines are not enough. Kabir called this pseudo-righteousness. It is not a question of *how much we do* but how *much love* we put into the doing. Confusing the two is a subtle trap to which many succumb on the spiritual path. Remember: it is the purity of our intention that counts.

The Story of Dharam Das

Dharam Das was a wealthy businessman who, despite his religious bent of mind, outwardly took part in the popular practice of idol worship. One day, while Dharam Das was worshiping his stone deities on the banks of the Ganges River, he was approached by Kabir.

"O Dharam Das," said the saint, without introducing himself, "the large stones you have placed before the altar must weigh at least two seers and the smaller ones a quarter."

Dharam Das sneered back at Kabir, who had implied that the idols were merely inanimate stones of a certain weight.

Seeing that he had struck a nerve, Kabir continued. "Have your deities ever spoken to you? Have they ever responded to your prayers?"

Dharam Das looked up again, annoyed, for the stranger had once more maligned his stone-gods. But before he could say anything further, the mysterious stranger miraculously disappeared into thin air.

Some time later Dharam Das was performing a *havan* —a sacred Hindu rite during sacred mantras are chanted while wood, clarified butter, and incense are placed into a fire —when Kabir appeared out of thin air. Once again he challenged the businessman, saying, "O Dharma Das, you think you are a pure Brahmin, but you seem to be a great sinner."

Dharam Das' wife, who was by his side at the time, quickly defended her husband. "Anyone who calls my husband a sinner is himself a sinner!" she exclaimed with derision.

Kabir smiled knowingly and chided, "Don't you know that there are thousands of helpless ants trapped inside the wood you are now burning?" You see, for an orthodox Brahmin, killing in any form is forbidden. Therefore, burning these tiny creatures would by orthodox Hindu standards constitute a most heinous crime.

Dharam Das cried out incredulously, "How dare you accuse me of such a crime! There are no insects in the wood."

Kabir replied, "Well then, why don't you split open the wood and see what's inside."

Dharma Das was momentarily taken aback, but decided to test the veracity of the holy man's contention. Splitting a piece of wood from the sacrificial fire, he found to his horror that hundreds of ants were teeming inside. Although Dharam Das was shocked by what he discovered, he was also in grateful awe of this mysterious holy man, not only for having saved him from a terrible sin, but from appearing out of nowhere to begin with! But when he proceeded to thank his benefactor, Kabir mysteriously vanishes once again.

In the next moment, Dharma Das saw a vision of the resplendent face of Kabir hovering at eye-level. As Dharam Das gazed into the radiant, inspiring eyes of the saint, he became inebriated with spiritual ecstasy. The vision faded,, but in its place was left a burning desire to find out the identity of this holy man. Dharma Das searched throughout the town and across the countryside, but to no avail. He asked everyone he met, but not one other person had seen anyone matching the saint's description.

Then Dharam Das had an idea. He was an extremely wealthy man, was he not? He would sponsor a *yajna, or* spiritual festival, and he would invite all the holy men and women from far and wide. According to Hindu custom, those who sponsor yajnas earn great religious merit, especially when they are offered in loving devotion to the saints and sages. Surely, thought Dharma Das, Kabir would be attracted by such a sincere effort. Even his wife, who wasn't so devout, thought it was a good idea. "Your mysterious holy man is sure to come," she said cynically, "just as flies flock around sugar."

Dharma Das went ahead with his plans and held a series of magnificent yajnas, first in the city of Benares and then in several other locations around India. Each feast attracted hundreds of sadhus, rishis, munis, and fakirs, but to Dharam Das's disappointment, Kabir was never seen among them. Still, Dharma Das threw more celebrations in the fervent hope that his mysterious benefactor would eventually appear. Finally, after footing the expense of so many yajnas, Dharam Das was reduced to pauper-hood. He had spent his entire fortune, but still not accomplished his goal.

Distraught, depressed, and inconsolable, Dharma Das could see no other end but to drown himself. He went down to the river bank and was about to fling himself into the teeming current, when suddenly Kabir appeared before him! Dharam Das was overjoyed to see his resplendent, holy face and kindly smile once again. He fell at Kabir's feet, weeping.

"I have performed dozens of yajnas and have now lost all my wealth," he entreated. "Why have you waited so long to come?"

Kabir smiled knowingly, "Because your wife said that holy men come to yajnas like flies to sugar. If I had come it would have confirmed her belief that all holy men are after money and food. The truly holy have no need of others' wealth or possessions. They do not covet the wealth of others or run after money like dogs after a piece of bread. True spiritual Masters accept no payment for their services and are not takers, but givers."

Finally understanding the truth, Dharam Das bowed in deepest humility and requested initiation into the path of *Shabda yoga*. According to many traditions, he went on to become Kabir's successor in the lineage.[23]

There are several lessons we can learn from Dharam Das's search for God. Two key aspects, however, are particularly relevant: the importance of moving beyond preliminary external practices and the necessity of transcending limited ego consciousness. Like Dharma Das, many of us have become attached to various outer rites and rituals associated with our particular religious tradition. We perform them out of habit and custom, and because they are part of our religious upbringing. But these practices become stumbling blocks instead of aids when they are performed mechanically. Done with little love for God, they only serve to inflate our ego and take us further away from our True Self. In fact, no matter how sincerely they are practiced, outer acts of worship cannot be the be-all and end-all of our spiritual journey; they are stepping-stones to the *inner* worship of God, who is beyond all names and forms.

In this story, Kabir guides Dharma Das beyond idol worship. The holy initiation Dharam Das receives from Kabir represents his entry into *nirgun*, or formless practice—experiencing God without form. Authentic Master's always teach that God is both imminent and transcendent. In other words, God is present in all things, yet not limited to any form. Kabir graciously reminds us of the futility of outer forms of worship when they do not lead to the direct experience of God. Most of us forget that the outer rites and rituals were originally intended to transition us to the real experience of God. So, while there is nothing wrong with these preliminary practices, they lose their meaning and, indeed, become self-defeating when treated as ends in themselves.

In preparing Dharam Das for the inner journey, Kabir had to first remove the seeker's blinding reliance upon outer rites and rituals. Then it was necessary to reduce Dharma Das's ego, which had become inflated with his status as a high caste Brahmin. This was accomplished not by force, but through Dharma Das' own will, as his great wealth diminished with each expensive yajna. As Jesus Christ said, "It is easier for a camel to pass through the eye of a needle than a rich man to enter the kingdom of heaven."[24] This is not because wealth itself is bad, but because such comfort often leads to egotism and complacency. Only when Dharam Das had been brought to a state of destitution, and his heart awakened with sincere longing, did Kabir manifest himself.

Like Dharma Das, we cannot attract God if our hearts are soiled with self-centeredness. So long as our inner motivations are dyed with the color of ego, we will never be able to experience divine oneness. Rather, it is by abandoning our egos that we are able to approach God. Unfortunately, such sincerity is difficult to achieve when we are indoctrinated from birth into the worship of idols for their own sake. Dharma Das learned this lesson the hard way.

Today, more than ever before, we lead ourselves astray through the shallow worship of "sacred" idols. Although it purports to a religious orientation, our culture is largely based on material greed and the excessive consumption of goods. At every turn we find ourselves worshiping at the altars of fame, riches, and power —

the pinnacles of "enlightenment" according to our media and popular culture. Indeed, true spirituality finds itself competing with reality TV!

Not true, many would cry. Certainly such a characterization cannot be applied to the many devout people of faith and committed practice who comprise the moral backbone of our society. Yet I would argue that even many of these follow their religious traditions unthinkingly, out of mechanical habit and custom, and without any real understanding or sincere yearning.

Lacking a direct connection with that Power that is God, we are likely to become caught in the vast net of materiality and the self-serving ego. As Jesus reminds us, "For what is a man profited if he shall gain the possessions of the whole world yet loses his own soul?"[25] We in the West have found material wealth at the cost of spiritual fulfillment, and this state of affairs has lead many of us to experience what might be called a malaise of the spirit—a kind of spiritual bankruptcy characterized by a poverty of love. In many ways, this is worse than material poverty.

Speaking about this very impoverishment, Nobel Peace Prize recipient Mother Theresa said, "When I pick up some starving person off the streets and offer him a bowl of rice or a piece of bread, I can satisfy his hunger. But a person that has been beaten or feels unwanted or unloved or fearful or rejected by society experiences a kind of poverty that is much more painful and deep. The cure is much more difficult to find."[26]

Additionally, those in positions of religious leadership are many times found to preach one set of values and act in accordance with another. Phony gurus have illicit sexual affairs with their disciples, televangelists embezzle millions from their congregations' charitable funds, and people's trust is shattered. In fact, it would not be an overstatement to say that most people today are skeptical of self-professed spiritual teachers—and rightly so. Unfortunately, spiritual authority and influence have all too commonly been used to exploit unsuspecting students and the general public. The sad repercussion of this is that, when these instances come to public attention, our young people equate such hypocritical "leaders" with spirituality itself and quickly begin to lose faith altogether.

As a world traveler, I see an increased interest in spirituality almost everywhere I go. Yet I meet very few people who are able to recognize what authentic spiritual leadership is really about. Like Dharam Das and his suspicious wife, we think all spiritual teachers are after money and fame. Does this mean all spiritual teachers are frauds? Not at all. It just means that we must be able to separate the chaff from the wheat. We must be able to discriminate the real from the false, the authentically spiritual from the material charlatans. We must dig deeper into the great wealth of spirit to nourish our faith.

True spiritual masters are as rare today as they were during past ages, but Kabir reminds us in his teachings and from his example that God does not leave us alone here on Earth. There is always "water for the thirsty and food for the hungry" in the form of saints and messengers to uplift humanity. The law of supply and demand works in the physical sphere, why not in the spiritual as well?

We are living in extraordinary times. Our lives are faster, busier, and more stressful. Advanced technology has afforded us more material comforts than ever before, yet we still find ourselves spiritually impoverished. Although our material environment has changed, our selfish nature has not. Thus, the essentials of the spiritual path remain are no different today than in Kabir's time.

What is the solution to this spiritual crisis? Get out of the *fast lane* of material superficiality and into the *vast lane* of divine consciousness! We must cultivate unselfish love for others and give it freely, completely, and without ostentatiousness. We must offer our lives in the service of God's creation. If we really believe in a life rooted in the spirit, we must be willing to move out of our comfort zone for the sake of love.

8. Practice Loving Adoration

Meeting with the Guru, one drinks the great essence,
And through loving adoration, one is redeemed.[27]
—Kabir

What is the essence of spiritual practice? According to Kabir, it is selfless love for God and all of creation. In the West, the word "adore" seems too intimate and human to refer to our relationship with God. For Kabir, however, to *adore* means to serve one's chosen ideal with self-sacrificing love. But how can we even begin to love our Creator while we are enmeshed in the chains of greed, power, and ego? The following story from Kabir's own life helps us understand this teaching.

Story of Ibraham Ibn Adam

Ibraham Ibn Adam of Balk Bokara was sovereign of a vast kingdom, extending hundreds of miles in every direction. His coffers were filled to the brim with gold and precious stones, and at his command huge armies would venture forth to conquer new lands. With a flick of his hand, life and death decisions were meted out to whomsoever he pleased.

Despite all his riches and power, however, King Ibraham was not happy. You see, beneath the pomp and show of kingship, he was a sincere seeker after truth. He realized that solace could only be found with the help of a teacher who could guide him to spiritual enlightenment. Yet, he did not know where to search or who this teacher might be. Finally, the king could not ignore his soul's longing anymore. He asked many wise people where he might find the greatest teacher, and the name of Kabir was mentioned time and again. After great soul-searching, Ibraham decided to renounce his kingdom and went in search of the saint in the area around the holy city of Benares.

When at long last Ibraham found Kabir living in a humble abode, the former king was welcomed to live the holy man's household as a disciple-in-training. During Kabir's time, the great Masters did not give out the gift of the shabda, or holy initiation, until they saw that the disciple was truly ready. So, for the next six years, Ibraham served Kabir night and day, performing the most menial of tasks without complaint. Not once did Ibraham outwardly express any dissatisfaction or misgivings. He continued in this service with apparent devotion without asking for as much as a crumb from the Master's spiritual storehouse.

Finally, after seven long years, Kabir's wife, Loi, remarked "Dear husband, Ibraham has served you selflessly for the last seven years, is it not time to give him something?"

"He is not yet ready for the inner gift," Kabir replied.

Still his wife protested, "But how is that so? Has he not served you unstintingly, without complaint?"

Kabir saw that she was right. "All right," he said, "let us test him."

Kabir then instructed his wife to have one of the servants' dump a load of garbage from a second story window over Ibraham's head as Ibrahim walked out the front door below. As ordered, the servant dropped the garbage while Loi watched Ibraham's response. When the deed was done, Ibraham looked upward in anger saying, "Had this happened in my kingdom I would have had the culprit's head on a platter!"

Loi was surprised and shocked by Ibraham's response and reported to Kabir what had happened. Kabir nodded knowingly. "Did I not tell you he was not ready for the gift of initiation?" he replied. "In his heart he still thinks he is a king."

Another seven years passed, and each day Ibraham served his Master dutifully. Finally, at the end of the seventh year, Kabir remarked to Loi that Ibraham was now ready. His wife was dumbfounded.

"But I don't see any difference in him," she said. "He seems exactly the same as before."

But Kabir insisted, "No, he's ready. Let us test him again."

This time, instead of household garbage, Kabir ordered the servant to dump the previous evening's "night-soil." As directed, when Ibraham walked out of the house, the servant dropped the human excrement onto his head from the window above. This time, however, Ibraham looked up and said, "Oh God, I deserve even worse than this. I am not worthy of anything. I am filled with sin and filth. Oh merciful God, save me by any means necessary."

Only after fourteen long years, when his service was truly rendered selflessly—without ego or expectation—was Ibraham Ibn Adham finally given the gift of initiation.[28] Nowadays, if these same prerequisites existed, there would be few takers! After all, who has the fortitude, time, and money for such an endeavor? Thankfully, it is no longer necessary to demonstrate one's spiritual worthiness before receiving initiation. What is still necessary, however, is that we seek a competent guide who can give us the inner gift of true spirituality. We must also have some true desire to know God. We may not need to renounce a kingdom or our worldly possessions, but we should have more than a passing fancy to know the Truth. Likewise, while we may not be required to have garbage dumped upon our heads, we must be willing to rid ourselves of our own *inner garbage*. And finally, we must be willing move beyond the mere performance of rites and rituals so that we can begin to worship God *in spirit*, selflessly and without egoistic motives.

9. Become a Spiritual Millionaire—True Wealth Lies In Sovereignty over the Kingdom of Our Heart

Jesus Christ was once given a coin and asked, "To whom does this belong?" "Render unto Caesar what is Caesar's and unto God what is God's," he replied,[29] meaning that the things of this world belong to the rulers of this world, but our soul belongs to God. The key to understanding the import of this quote lies in the word belongs, for the way this word is used relates to the true ruling passion of our heart.

Another story of Ibraham Ibn Adam further illustrates this point: Many years after his spiritual realization, Ibraham returned to his former kingdom and was sitting peacefully on a riverbank sewing one of his tattered, worn-out garments. One of his former viziers recognized him and immediately paid respects by bowing down.

The vizier said to Ibrahim, "My Lord, your ministers have wondered what happened to you after all these years. We beg you to return and take up your royal duties once again. We would be most pleased and the whole kingdom would rejoice."

Thinking to himself the vizier pondered, "There is vast wealth and power at his command, armies to do his bidding and every wish of his ready to be fulfilled instantly. Why would he not want to return?"

Ibraham, like all spiritual masters, was easily able to discern the man's thoughts. At that moment he took his sewing needle and threw it into the river. Turning to his former vizier, he said, "Can you fetch this needle back?"

"But my Lord that is impossible," the minister replied. "It is lost forever in the ever-flowing river."

At that moment Ibraham used his spiritual powers and instantly a hundred fishes appeared, each with a golden needle in its mouth, and presented these needles before Ibraham. Then, Ibraham addressed himself once again to the astonished vizier, "My dear minister, of what use is all this outer wealth and power if it cannot retrieve even one tiny needle? He is a true king who is sovereign over the kingdom of his heart."[30]

True happiness is an *inside* job. For Kabir, the true emperor is the person who has sovereignty over the kingdom of his or her heart. The truly wealthy person is one who is truly contented. Such a one has found the source of all happiness, peace, and joy within.

Many of us today run madly after worldly riches, position, and power. Outwardly, we may *talk* the spiritual talk, but inwardly we are still strongly attached to our material comforts and lifestyle. It is true that, in the West, there are many hundreds of thousands of wealthy people—but how many can claim to be spiritually wealthy? We have traded lasting happiness for worldly rubble.

How does this great delusion occur? It is the ego that has cleverly bartered our inner wealth for an empty bubble. Even those who seek God sincerely are sometimes caught in the meshes of these passing shadows, entangled in countless reoccurring desires. One wonderful way to help diagnose the reason for our lack of spiritual progress is to simply ask ourselves why we forget God. We forget God whenever we are attached outside. What produces attachment? Desire. Each new desire leads further from the center of our own joy. Kabir has said:

> *Let thy mind be seated in the Void of desirelessness*
> *And let the stilling of craving be thy Path.*[31]

The entire spiritual path can be traversed by way of this one simple dictum: *stop craving*. Craving is a form of addiction to what is unreal and illusory. It is a misfit marriage. After all, how can the real mix with the unreal? How can what is permanent be joined with what is transitory? How can the eternal life be joined with that which is dead? We forget that we are conscious beings, created from the great ocean of Light, drops from the ocean of all consciousness. Our essence is self-effulgent and we are limitless beings of love.

If this is the reality, then meditation and remembrance is the true wealth we should all be accumulating. These should be the earrings of spiritual wealth. If we could pursue this inner wealth with the same ardor and dedication with which we seek worldly wealth, we would all reach our destination in no time. Instead, we pursue passing shadows with ever-increasing speed. Even after we get what we want, we want to protect it. We are afraid we will lose it. We don't know what would happen to us if we lost it. This just leads to more fear and anxiety. However, the minute we become open to Truth, we realize that nothing on the outside can ever satiate us. That is when our quest for lasting spiritual wealth begins.

A Spiritual Blueprint: Exercises for Cultivating a Life of Living Faith

As we travel on our inner journey, we can easily forget to actively strengthen and cultivate the quality of faith in our lives. Because it is non-material in nature, it is not surprising that we might fail to recognize its importance. But faith is born of the spirit, nourished by the spirit, and is ultimately the Living Spirit itself. It is the bridge between the physical and spiritual dimensions of our lives. The following practices correspond to the nine core principles outlined in this chapter. Think of them as concrete steps to help you move steadily in the direction of vibrant faith.

1. **Recognize our source.** Let us first recognize the universal nature of true spirituality. We are all one. All religions are expressions of God's love for us. We have all emanated from One Being, regardless of the names we use to address that Universal Being. We belong to One God, not to any particular religious tradition or denomination. All paths lead back to the same destination. Whether we are aware of it or not, we will all return to the same Source. Knowing this allows us to avoid

the pitfall of getting stuck in religious dogmatism or what could be called spiritual *exclusivism:* the belief that we alone have the sole truth.

- Strive for reverence and respect for all religions and saints, regardless of their traditions. They have all come with essentially the same message and from the same source.

- Begin each day by consciously seeing the God in everyone — especially those who seem "different" from you.

2. **Find a competent spiritual teacher.** Why is there such an insistence on the need for a true teacher in the realm of the spirit? It is because true spirituality cannot be taught, or bought. It can only be caught from a person who is a conduit for the divine Source. If we can grasp this simple principle then it is not difficult to see how direct contact with a true spiritual teacher is the shortest route to self-knowledge and God-knowledge. Here is the predicament we face: How can one who is spiritually blind find someone who is spiritually awake? The reality is that we do not find them, they find us. *The Guru appears when the disciple is ready.* All we can do in the meantime is sincerely pray for the guidance of a true spiritual teacher. Below are four criteria that can help guide your search for an authentic teacher.

- In their presence, we experience spiritual upliftment, deep peace, and love.

- They are examples of the teaching they profess and are ethically and morally above reproach.

- They can give us a direct inner contact with the spiritual power within.

- They do not live on the earnings of others.

3. **Attune yourself to the guru's word and abide by his instructions.** Ultimately, our primary task is to make God's will our own. So long as we are disconnected from God's will, we will

experience pain, suffering, and unhappiness. Once we have found a true teacher, the essence of wisdom is obedience to our spiritual teacher's instructions. Let us not forget Christ's exhortation to his disciples: "He that hath my commandments and keepeth them he it is that loveth me."[32] The wisdom and guidance of a true spiritual teacher is a direct affirmation of God's will for us. As John tells us in the Gospel, "And I know that his commandment is life everlasting; whatsoever I speak therefore even as the Father said unto me so I speak."[33]

- Make it a habit to affirm the wisdom and guidance given to you by your spiritual teacher each day, as a part of your everyday life.

- Ask yourself the following questions: Do I regularly doubt or needlessly question my teacher's instructions? When I am around others who are of the world, do I quickly become like them? Am I easily influenced by my outer circumstances, and do I lose faith in my own direction? Do I find it hard to follow even the most simply of instructions?

4. **Commune with God daily through meditation and remembrance.** Every spiritual tradition has emphasized the primacy and vital importance of direct inner contact with God. Once we have received this direct connection, we should make the inner remembrance of God our most important practice. This means at the very least that we should meditate every day. Even if we start with only 15 minutes a day, we should make it a habit. Gradually over time we can increase it to as much as two or three hours or more per day. Saints use the method known in the Sant Mat tradition as *simran,* or the daily repetition of God's names.

- Devote time to meditation everyday.

- Invoke God in your mind and heart, and continually remember Him as much as possible.

5. **Accept both the "good" and the "bad" as part of God's will.** This may seem impossibly difficult at the outset, because we are so used to bargaining and complaining that we can't see clearly anymore. But when we take off our smoky-colored glasses, we begin to see the hidden hand of God in everything. Good and bad, joy and sorrow, poverty and wealth are all part of God's plan for our spiritual evolution. The path of faith is ultimately that of joyfully accepting everything that happens to us.

   - As a vital first step, eliminate the useless and pointless complaining.

   - Try to see God's hidden hand guiding you in all things, whether large or small.

6. **Continually rejoice in whatever happens.** Eventually, a times comes when we no longer distinguish between what seems good and what seems bad. As our faith becomes firm and rooted in our spiritual vision, we see life from a higher perspective. Each day truly becomes a cause for joy and celebration. We not only see the hidden hand of God in everything, but also experience God's loving touch in all that happens.

   - Find something everyday to celebrate and be joyful about.

   - Learn to rejoice in everything that happens to you.

7. **Go beyond pseudo-righteousness to authentic worship.** Most people confuse outer forms of preliminary practice with true inner worship. There is a vast difference between the two. Outer rites and rituals, dogmas, and other such observances are all good in themselves, but are not the be-all and end-all of our spiritual lives. God is spirit and must be worshipped in spirit. Practicing charity, attending one's religious place of worship, and leading an ethical life are stepping-stones to true inner worship. The former are the shell that protects the kernel within. It is for the seed that the shell exists.

- Each day as you practice the daily rituals of your individual tradition, remember that the real goal of all outer practice is the gift of your spirit to God.

8. **Practice loving devotion.** Loving adoration of God is, in its essence, loving and serving God and His creation without selfish motives or egoistic intentions. So long as our worship is tied to personal desires, we still have a long way to go. We may meditate for years and years but make little progress. Why? Because we have made a *business* out of our worship and allowed our egos to rule our hearts. Outwardly, we may impress others with our piety; but inwardly we are spiritually dead. Let us always remember that whatever we truly desire is what we will get.

   - Take some time each day to review your life. Have you really served God and the God in others, or merely our own subtle selfish desires for fame, power, or recognition.

   - A life of true faith demands if nothing else. Seek God for the sake of God alone.

9. **Become a spiritual millionaire.** For the spiritually awakened, true wealth is sovereignty over our desires. Our true purpose should be to accumulate the lasting wealth of divine love and compassion. The simple way to Truth is to stop craving the passing baubles of material life. As we awaken, we come to see that *to possess nothing* is *to possess everything*. It is not necessary to give up all our possessions; rather, we must relinquish our attachment to them. In this way, we open up to God, the ultimate wealth!

   - Make it practice to begin each day by fostering an attitude of inner detachment.

   - Each day, make a vow to eliminate some of your more non-essential desires.

Jalalu'ddin Rumi

Chapter Four
Rumi: The Path of Ecstatic Love

From the Dawn of the first Beginning till the twilight of the last end,
Friendship and love have drawn inspiration from one sole pact,
one single trust.[1]

—Rumi

Thirteenth-century Persian mystic Jalalu'ddin Rumi is considered to have been one of the greatest spiritual Masters of all time. His two major works, a collection of poetry known as the *Divan I Tabriz* and his epic *Mathnawi*, are arguably two of the most well-read books of poetry within the Islamic world. In fact, in 1997 the Christian Science Monitor proclaimed that Rumi had become the best-selling poet living or dead in the United States.[2, 3]

Even before attaining such status—indeed, before he ever wrote a single line of verse—Rumi had already achieved great fame in Muslim society as a brilliant theologian, academic scholar, and full-fledged model of propriety. All this changed, however, one day as he held forth beside a pond with a group of his disciple-students. As the story goes, Rumi was in the midst of erudite discourse when a shabbily dressed vagabond wandered toward the group to listen in on their lesson. After a short while, the man walked directly up to Rumi, pointed to the manuscript from which the great teacher was reading, and asked bluntly, "What is this?"

Judging from the vagabond's outer appearance that he was illiterate, Rumi replied sarcastically, "This, my friend, is the knowledge of which the unlearned can know nothing."

At that, the wanderer, who was actually a fully illuminated dervish (holy man), grabbed the manuscript from his hands and tossed it unceremoniously into the nearby pool. Rumi was aghast, and his disciples threw up their hands in shock.

"Fool," the great teacher scowled, "do you have any idea what you have done? You have destroyed a precious spiritual treasure which can never be replaced."

But before he could go any further, the wandering dervish walked over to the pool, nonchalantly put his hand into the water, and pulled the manuscript out completely dry. To everyone's amazement not a page was damaged. He then handed the manuscript back to Rumi, who exclaimed in amazement at the miracle he had witnessed before his eyes, "What is this?"

"This, my friend," the dervish replied, "is the knowledge born of ecstasy, of which the learned can know nothing."[4]

Thus, the renowned scholar abandoned status and acclaim and was transformed into God-intoxicated mystic. Under the guidance of the enlightened vagabond, Shams i-Tabriz, Rumi attained knowledge of a higher order than that of the mere intellect: the higher knowledge born of direct revelation of God. Rumi's verses and poetry live on to this day and his spiritual stature among saints is acknowledged worldwide.

The Transforming Power of Love

In a much-celebrated passage from the *Mathnawi*, Rumi lays out the miracle of transformation wrought by the all-consuming power of love:

> *Love turns bitter things sweet*
> *By love copper becomes gold,*

By love dregs become clear,
By love pain becomes healing
By love the dead are made living
By love the king is made a slave,
Once more, this love is born of knowledge.
When has a fool ever sat on such a throne?[5]

The reader is invited into his gathering of lovers, where there is neither high nor low and where no formal book learning is required. According to Rumi, love alone has the capacity to totally transform us. His is a path of all-consuming love, where lover and Beloved melt into perfect unity. In this sublime ocean of oneness, separation ceases to exist. Distinctions between Sufi, Hindu, Jew, and Christian pale into insignificance and become meaningless details. Human beings, though different in external appearance, culture, and nationality, are in essence the same on the level of the spirit. We have all been created from one eternal Light, and from that immaculate Light we derive our humanness.

I am neither Christian nor Jew,
Neither Gaber nor Turk,
I am not of East; I am not of the West,
I am not of the land; Not of the sea;
I belong to the soul of the Beloved,
I have seen that the two are One. And One I see, and One I know.
One I see, and One I adore,
He is the first, and He is the last;
He is outward, and He is inward too.[6]

Through Rumi's life and writings he entices us to join the assembly of divinely intoxicated lovers who, from time immemorial to the present day, have basked in a spiritual consciousness that transcends dogma and disbelief, intellectual judgment and opinions. Like all torchbearers of Truth, Rumi invites us to examine what it means to be fully human—and to understand that this very humanity is the key to realizing our inherent divinity. The story of Rumi's journey is, in itself, a perfect map for aspirants seeking such mystical union and spiritual transformation.

The Universal Man

One of the central tenets of Sufi mysticism is the notion of the perfect man, or *insani i kamil*. The perfect saint represents the perfection of the all the qualities embodied in God in the primordial state before creation. The perfect or universal man, then, is the replica of the macrocosm in the microcosm, the connecting link between God and his creation: humankind, in our imperfect state. As such, the perfect man, or *Murshid i Kamil* in Iranian mysticism, is a perfect conduit and manifestation of the light of God.

Who is this perfect Shaykh, or Master? Rumi teaches that "he has shattered the bodily cup, he is the absolute light of God."[7] Having perfected himself and completely merged himself in God, or *fana fil Allah*, he becomes the vehicle for the redemption of all humanity. This process of spiritual perfection and struggle, referred to in Sufi terminology as *jihad al Akbar*, is the real purpose of human life. Unless we can overcome the ego, or *nafs*, and completely submit ourselves in service to God's will, we have not reached the pinnacle of spiritual perfection or fulfilled the purpose of our coming into this world. This process of submission is, in reality, the process of becoming fully human by developing all the noble qualities of compassion, mercy, truthfulness, non-violence, contentment, gratitude, humility, and faith. Without becoming fully human we cannot become divine.

Becoming Truly Human Is Very Difficult

I was once in the holy presence of Sant Kirpal Singh in India when, with his characteristic succinctness, he gave an incredibly insightful overview of the spiritual path in a single sentence: "To become a true human being is very difficult; but once we have become a true human being, God-realization is not difficult."[8] Indeed, a true human being is the fertile soil from which the tree of divinity can eventually mature. It is said that God is perpetually in search of a true human being, but who—or what—might that be? The great Masters would say that he or she is a living embodiment of compassion, selfless love, humility reverence, generosity, and truth. In essence, one *in whom the Love of God is fully manifest.*

It would be an understatement to say that this level of spiritual development isn't easy to achieve. It requires not only dedication and practice, but also an unwavering willingness to move beyond the tyranny of the mind. As Rumi wrote:

> *The intellect will turn my face from you,*
> *Keep your control on it, and I am saved,*
> *Otherwise, I am lost.*[9]

In other words, while the soul is a conscious entity, it has been shackled to the unconscious instincts of both the body and the mind. When we understand that the struggle to be fully human is a battle against what the Sufis call our *nafs,* or animal nature, we are then ready to commence the task of reclaiming our true humanness.

When, as mentioned above, Rumi had his auspicious run-in with the mystic Shams, his conventional world of established order and society was turned upside-down. Almost instantly he broke away from the orthodoxy of his time to embrace a vision of spirituality free from the rigidity of religious norms. Swept into a whirlwind of devotion and spiritual gnosis, Rumi later described Shams in terms almost co-equal with God: "You are the light which told Moses 'I am God, I am God, I am God, I am God.'"[10]

Shams, a true Shaykh, became for him the door to the inner worlds of love. It was said that Shams had been wandering from country to country and community to community in search of a human vessel to be the recipient of his first-hand experience of God. The relationship between Rumi and Shams is one of the greatest spiritual love stories ever told, and although short-lived in terms of physical time, it traversed within a few short years the entire inner landscape of mystical love.

We are blessed that this lover and Beloved, disciple and Master relationship is thoroughly chronicled for posterity in Rumi's writing. From their first dramatic meeting until his final merger with his Master, known in Sufi terminology as *fana-fil-Shaykh*, Rumi eventually realized that he had become the object of his own search: lover had become the Beloved, the drop merged into the ocean. His spiritual journey now accomplished, he had *become* Shams in his true spiritual essence. Thereafter Rumi continued to compose his mystical poems, but his poetic voice became a mouthpiece of Shams himself:

> *He said, since I am he, what need to seek,*
> *I am the same as he, his essence speaks*
> *Indeed I sought my own self—that is sure*
> *Fermenting in the vat, just like the must.*[11]

The mystical union of which Rumi speaks is nothing new in the annals of mysticism. St. Paul echoed the identical theme in a Biblical passage from Galatians when he said, "I am crucified with Christ; nevertheless I live; yet not I but Christ liveth in me."[12] In this exalted spiritual state, the individual ego vanishes and only the soul of the Beloved remains. This is the completion of the first stage of our journey to God: *fana-fil-shaykh*, or merging in the Master, an auspicious precursor to the final stage, *fana-fil-Allah*, merger with God.

In the following seven short verses, referred to as "pillars," this great poet-saint outlines a practical step-by-step approach to becoming fully human through the perfection of love itself.

The First Pillar

> *Anger is the seed of hell-fire: Extinguish this hell of yours*
> *for this is a subtle trap.*[13]

In this quotation, Rumi warns us of the universal human tendency to respond to anger with anger. To be able to control one's temper and be unaffected in the face of abuse is certainly no easy task. Yet Rumi describes the true mystic's response in no uncertain terms: Do not respond in kind. Be as inwardly detached as an inert corpse!

At first, we who live in today's modern world might question the feasibility and wisdom of this advice. After all, most schools of modern psychology tell us that it isn't healthy to hold in pent-up anger. Isn't it unnatural, many might ask, to suppress such a basic human impulse as anger? It is true that, on the surface, Rumi's injunction to remain calm may not appear to be realistic. Yet, Rumi and other great spiritual teachers consider anger to be a form of temporary insanity. From the perspective of someone who is spiritually awakened, anger represents a forgetfulness of our essential oneness with humanity and all creation. This loss of inner integrity or fall from grace carries with it profound consequences not easily perceived by those asleep or half-awake.

We find in the life of the Buddha an instructive story that may help to illuminate Rumi's perspective.

The Parable of the Unaccepted Gift

Once, a man went to Lord Buddha and began to insult him. He continued in this way for perhaps two or three hours, during which time Lord Buddha made no effort to defend himself. Finally, after night had fallen, the man was exhausted and wanted to leave. Still the Buddha remained quietly composed and showed no sign of reaction. Instead, he calmly addressed the man.

"Well, dear friend, just tell me one thing. If one brings a present to somebody and that person does not accept it, with whom does the gift belong?"

The man thought for a moment and then answered, "It belongs to the person who offered it."

Smiling, Lord Buddha then replied, "Well the present that you have brought me today I do not accept."[14]

Like the Buddha, each of us can choose whether to respond to someone's anger. Harsh words spoken by others need not be "taken in" to the degree that they rob us of our equipoise. However cutting and brutal someone's verbal invectives may be, if one doesn't react, the words and feelings are, as they say in the post office, "returned to sender."

To extend the metaphor, consider the fact that each day we receive mail from various sources. Some mail is unsolicited "junk" mail and most of us immediately toss these materials out. Another portion of our daily mail might be regular bills, which some of us do not attend to immediately but place in a drawer or filing cabinet to deal with in a day or two. Mail from a loved one, however, we open enthusiastically and usually read right away. In other words, we respond to different categories of mail as we see fit. In a similar way, it is our choice to respond—or not to respond—in kind to another person's anger. My own spiritual Master once elaborated on this topic by saying, "If anyone says anything to us we should ask ourselves first, is it true? If it is, we should thank the person and act on their advice. If it is not true, we should pray for them."[15]

Anger—An Ineffective Method of Communication

We must ask ourselves whether anger is an effective form of expression. Do people really listen when they are angry? How about when they are addressed out of anger? More often than not, the answer is no. Anger typically arises when desires, expectations, and wishes are not met, fanning the flames of resentment and bad feelings. Unchecked anger fuels the "eye for an eye" mentality—responding to anger with more anger. Within a few short moments all parties are on an uncontrolled emotional roller coaster, the very antithesis of skillful communication!

Scientific studies have shown that frequent or habitual expression of anger is correlated with increased risk of heart failure.[16] According to these findings, anger increases the coagulation of red blood cell platelets, which, in turn, thickens the blood, narrows blood vessels, and contributes to blood clots and heart attacks. Not only is this detrimental to our physical health, but as habit becomes character and character becomes our "nature," the more one allows anger to rule one's life, anger as a pattern of behavior becomes increasingly involuntary and habitual.

How should we respond to someone's anger? Rumi tells us, "Repel thou evil with that which is fairer."[17] Saints repel evil with gratitude and thanks. The ultimate answer to another's fury is *non-retaliation*. By returning evil with evil we only embolden our enemy, showing him that his words have had their intended effect. When we repel evil with an abundance of unconditional, positive regard for the person (not necessarily the behavior or bone of contention), we "put out the fire" instead of feeding it. Rumi tells us that, "The end of this fire is not affected save by the Light. Thy Light alone hath put out this fire."[18]

If we retaliate angrily to anger, we all but encourage those who consciously or unconsciously use anger as a way of escalating the situation. Those who use anger will then feel they've been successful in invoking an angry response. Instead of defusing the situation, such a response only inflames it.

Lessons from an Ancient War

Over 5,000 years ago in ancient India, one family member uttered a few angry words to another; the aftermath, as chronicled in the *Mahabharata,* was the end of an entire civilization. Truly anger for anger, revenge for revenge, and retaliation for retaliation only escalate conflict and, in the end, bring devastation and destruction. On the deepest level of our being, we need to understand how harmful anger really is.

Non-retaliation is for the courageous, not for the timid. The great Masters of spirituality caution us against rash and impulsive actions. Rumi himself tells us that the extinction of anger cannot be affected except through inner contact with the inward Light of the Spirit. "The end of this fire," he says, "is not affected save by the Light: Light alone can put out this fire and we are those who are most grateful."[19] Our ultimate release from the fires of anger comes only through the healing and forgiving power of the Light of God.

Taking revenge represents one's lack of connection to this inner Light. Forgiving the lapses of others, on the other hand, is noble and a sign of one's contact with the inner Light. If people don't give up their bad habits, why should we give up our good ones? If we descend with others into the abyss of anger, we only become like those we preach against. How can that be of any use? Instead, forgiveness has the power to break us free of the vicious cycle of retaliation and revenge.

Exercise in Sublimating Anger:

Perhaps no other character trait is as difficult to eradicate as anger. For many, anger may even seem insurmountable. Yet, once you correctly perceive its inherent destructive nature you can readily remove even its most pernicious manifestations. The first—and hardest—step is to fully and completely recognize that you are the *cause* of your own anger. Contrary to popular wisdom, this is an exhilarating and empowering moment in our journey, for you now know that you have the power to change your own destiny. Once you have accepted your own ability to make this shift, the following practices will help you to move beyond anger when it arises:

1. **Maintain inner vigilance.** This requires that we take notice of the precise moment when we first feel even a slight inclination to become angry. Since anger can arise almost instantaneously, we must act immediately to quell the initial impulse.

- By affirming the destructive power of anger we can begin to loosen its grip on us. These simple words may be of help: I know that anger not only destroys my own inner peace but poisons the entire atmosphere, as well.

2. **Practice remembrance.** Invoking a mantra or chosen name of God is another method that yields terrific results. Of course, we have to remember to invoke the name of God the moment we feel anger rising.

   - The secret to this method lies in shifting our attention away from the object of our anger to the spiritual center within. In essence, the name acts as a method of inverting our attention.

3. **Invoke God's help and assistance.** Once we have turned our attention within, the secret is to invoke the higher power with full attention and true inner need. In the beginning asking for God's help may seem impossible or insincere, but the reality is that our own efforts may not be enough. Ask yourself the following questions:

   - How often do I pray inwardly for God's help?

   - When I get angry, do I rely entirely on my own unaided efforts?

4. **Leave the scene of turmoil.** Many times our attempts to reduce or eradicate our anger fail to work. In these cases we should recognize our need to do something more drastic. One way to help quell the anger within us is too remove ourselves from the immediate vicinity of that which has piqued our anger until we are able to regain inner composure.

   - Go to a quiet room. Sit in complete silence until the anger subsides. Don't be in a hurry. Sometimes an hour or more is needed.

5. **Let go and let be.** Once our anger has subsided we need to release the residual resentment and hurt feelings. The longer

we allow angry thoughts to fester in our minds and hearts, the harder it is to control them later.

- As soon as possible, release these thoughts. Let them go.

- Seek with an open heart to reconnect with this person, first inwardly and then in some more direct way.

- Finally, forgive yourself and move on. Apply the healing balm of forgiveness.

The Second Pillar

He alone is good-tempered who quietly forbears and forgives the bad-tempered and ill-natured.[20]

In this verse, Rumi's reveals the secret of love itself, which is its unlimited capacity to forbear and forgive. So long as we are engaged in the quest for God, Rumi exhorts us to exercise "forbearance with everyone that is unmannerly."[21]

True forbearance is like the ocean: no matter how many thousands of freshwater rivers pour into the ocean, it never loses its salinity—its true nature. Similarly, the majesty of love is that no matter how many people criticize or abuse, us our inner nature does not change.

If we study the lives of great teachers of humanity we see they respond to hatred and evil with kindness and forgiveness. In the Christian tradition, recall when Jesus Christ was asked by one of his disciples how many times one should forgive those who have wronged them. Christ replied that we should forgive others not seven times but seventy times seven times. He implied our forgiveness should be unlimited and unconditional. He adds, "All sins shall be forgiven unto the sons of men and blasphemes wherewith so ever they shall blaspheme."[22]

Most of us find it hard to forgive those we love, let alone those who we do not. When we believe in our heart of hearts that an injustice has been done to us, our mind has a tendency to go on rankling with negative thoughts. We do not greet others with love and openness. We continue to harbor distrust and resentment for years and even decades. Yet to understand the depths of wisdom from which the great masters speak, consider for a moment the inner torment and pain we must live with when we fail to forgive. When we continue to punish ourselves and others, we create in our own mind an internal living hell, allowing those we cannot forgive to "rent space in our brain." In effect, we give up our most precious possession: our own inner peace. Simply stated, one of the great laws of the universe is that without forgiveness there is no healing. Mahatma Gandhi beautifully summarized this truth when he said, "An eye for an eye and the whole world goes blind." Revenge never brings healing. In the absence of forgiveness, anger, jealousy, hatred, and backbiting fester. Our hearts and minds become contaminated with such thoughts.

Sadly, we do not understand the power of forgiveness because we do so little of it. We should ask ourselves, "Unless I am perfect, do I have a right to think others should be?" What, then, is the secret of living in peace and harmony? Acceptance, forbearance, and forgiveness. We may search the four corners of the globe, but in the end this is the sole remedy that can heal the wounds caused by anger and misunderstanding.

On a practical level, forgiveness is *the ability to forget what we want to forget when we want to and remember what we want to remember when we want to remember it.* This does not mean that we should forget the lessons learned in our lives. Rather, it implies that we must become the master of our inner world and not a slave to our lower impulses.

Clara Barton's "Selective" Forgetting

Clara Barton, founder of the American Red Cross, had a particularly effective practice of forgiveness. Once, in the course of conversation, a friend reminded her of an instance a number of years earlier when someone had been cruel to her. When Clara did not respond, the friend asked, "Don't you remember what that person did to you?"

"No" replied Clara, "I distinctly remember forgetting that!"[23]

Cultivating forgiveness is not merely an option on the spiritual path; it is a necessity. This is because when we don't forgive, we add more and more strife to our own lives. The Masters of spirituality, who are attuned to exquisitely subtle levels of reality, tell us that we live in a sort of psychic sea of thought-forms which surround us at all times. When we think evil of another person, those evil thoughts not only travel out from us, but also attract other evil thoughts of a similar nature. It is said that the same evil thought returns with sevenfold strength back to its sender.

How does this work? Through the law of sympathetic vibration. If, for example, a C tuning fork on one side of a room is struck, another C tuning fork on the other side of the room will begin to resonate without being struck. The saints tell us that resonant thoughts work in a similar manner. If someone thinks ill of you or me, or slanders us, what's it to us, really? There's a popular expression in certain circles that what you think of me is none of my business. If we react to other people's negativity, then by being angry and retaliating we become like the resonant tuning fork and magnify the negative energy. If we fully comprehend this truth then we must realize that in holding onto our grievances we only punish ourselves. Therefore when we forgive, we exercise mercy on ourselves. I am of the opinion that we would all go mad—haunted and hunted by our own negative thinking—if we completely repressed "random acts of forgiveness" in relation to the dozens of little slights and insults we may come across throughout a typical day.

To attempt to follow any spiritual path without a daily practice of forgiveness is like trying to row a boat forward while it is still fastened to the dock. Until we release the anger and resentment, our forward progress is halted. Of course, to follow the ideal of love is not easy, for it requires that we constantly open our hearts and embrace others with joy. Unlike people who beg on the streets for money, a true lover begs to give away his or her life. Whatever scripture we choose to study, we find forgiveness a sine qua non for spiritual progress. In a famous Hadith Qudsi, the prophet Mohammed makes clear how far we should go in forgiving others:

> O son of Adam, so long as you call upon me and ask of me,
> I shall forgive you for what you have done, and I shall not mind.
> O son of Adam, were your sins to reach the clouds of the sky
> and were you then to ask forgiveness of Me, I would forgive you.[24]

Forgiveness is certainly necessary to make any spiritual progress, but forgiveness alone is not the end of spirituality; it is only the beginning. If we analyze forgiveness, we see that there is still duality, still a *you* and an *I*. This implies a subtle form of ego, for it is we who think we are forgiving others. In other words, we consider ourselves to be better than others, and the wrong committed against us as forgivable by us.

Yet, who are we to forgive anyone? If we are still committing sins on a daily basis, then what power do we have to forgive others? To forgive others is to release them from the burden of their suffering. It is the Masters, the true saints, who, because of their God-consciousness, have the power to forgive. In this connection, it is an article of faith in Christianity that Jesus "died for the sins of the world." Lord Jesus, dying on the cross in his last moments on earth, prayed for those who persecuted him, saying: "Father, forgive them, for they know not what they do."[25]

Exercises for Developing Forgiveness

I can think of no other quality more necessary for the daily maintenance of our spiritual health than forgiveness. In fact, without it our spiritual life would be in shambles. The first step toward forgiveness, then, is to fully realize how absolutely critical it is to practice on a daily basis. The second step is to fully understand the underlying reasons why it is so essential for our wellbeing. Below are a few things to keep in mind in order to shift your perspective.

1. **Respect everyone.** The first and most difficult task is to recognize, first in mind and later through direct perception on the level of soul, that God resides in everyone. If there is one God-power working in all, then we are all brothers and sisters. Ask yourself the following questions:

    - How often do I inwardly criticize or devalue the worth of another in my mind or actions?

    - Do I tend to make knee-jerk judgments of others people's actions or words, regardless of whether I know enough about the person to do so?

    - Do I expect people to treat me with respect, yet often fail to offer the same to others in equal measure?

2. **Realize that forgiveness washes away inner defilements and restores our peace of mind.** While this task may seem difficult at first, in time we see that we sacrifice more by not forgiving. We give up our own peace of mind. It is our choice whether we go to bed angry and distraught or at peace and inwardly content. Ask yourself:

    - When people offend or criticize me, do I inwardly ruminate for hours or days over their comments?

    - How often do I consider the negative consequences of not forgiving others or myself?

3. **Remember that if we retaliate in kind to anger, then by the law of resonant vibration a negative cycle of accusations and counter-accusations may snowball out of control.** Ask yourself:

    - To what degree do I practice non-retaliation in thought, word, and deed?

4. **Recognize that everyone except the great spiritual masters is imperfect.** This makes it much easier to forgive others. It is important to realize, however, that we do not have the power to forgive on our own. Instead, let us gratefully realize that it is through God and by God that we are able let go of the wrongs others have committed against us. Even more importantly, if we can realize that our own forgiveness is contingent upon the forgiveness we give to others, then we are ready to ask God to be forgiven ourselves. Ask yourself:

   • Do I release and let go of all the wrongs people have committed against me on a daily basis?

   • Do we seek forgiveness every night for the wrongs we have committed against others.

5. **The Essential Practice for Forgiveness:** Consciously and with full concentration visualize those who have wronged you and send them healing, loving, and joyous thoughts. Do this and experience the miracles of love enveloping you on a daily basis. This is, in fact, the litmus test of humanness.

A second similar practice is to sit in silence before retiring, and with deep reverence, offer a heartfelt prayer for the peace and well-being of all sentient life. One of the most beautiful prayers I know, which I often use for this purpose, is the St Francis prayer.[1]

The Third Pillar

When a man speaks well of another,
that good appraisal reverts again to himself....
When a man speaks ill of another,
that person becomes hateful in his eyes.[26]

For many of us who were raised in the West, the idea of hiding others faults seems strange. Criticizing and making fun of people has become a common practice in our media, and is even understood to be socially acceptable in some circles. Almost every-where we go we see people blatantly exposing and criticizing the faults of others. Why does Rumi ask us to refrain from this kind of behavior? The answer is simple. Consider the man who plants thorns and thistles in his backyard: every time he goes out he sees the ugliness before him. When you are the foe of every man, the image of your foes appears before you and it is as if day and night you are among thorns and snakes.

Saints operate by the principle of *Al-Baatin,* an Islamic name for God that means "One who covers or makes hidden." Those who embody the divine qualities of the fully developed human not only refrain from thinking evil of others, but they go a step further and hide others' faults as well. Even though they know of the evil in their hearts, they do not reveal to others this inner condition. Such actions may seem contrary to common sense, as we are so used to exposing others' faults that we rarely ever think of viewing them with compassionate understanding.

Let us ask ourselves why we are so ready to expose the foibles of others. What benefit do we get by broadcasting people's prob-lems and faults? Do we believe that by exposing them that they will change? Or do we think that we will look better to others and ourselves if we make others look worse? If we truly seek to help them, then we must first establish their trust. If there is any doubt in someone's mind as to the integrity of our intentions, will they really confide in us? I think not.

The daily give and take of our human interactions is made up of opportunities God gives to us to help and even protect, not to slander or reveal someone else's weaknesses. Sadly, many of us use a person's weak points to not only expose them to themselves, but also to broadcast their faults to others. To compound the injury, we repeat what we hear about others second-hand, even though it may be no more than unsubstantiated gossip or erroneous hearsay. Some of us may even begin to believe, as my spiritual teacher has said, that we are the unpaid apprentices of the CIA of God. With such practices and motivations, why would anyone be open to seek out our help or protective guidance? The basic law of the universe is love. If we hurt others by betraying their trust and exposing them, we break this law.

Baba Farid, the great Sufi and successor to Muinuddin Chisti, was once asked the characteristics of a true lover of God. He replied most beautifully,

> A lover always shows compassion to others in difficulties, and rather than broadcast any faults they may have, he tries to cover them. He must, furthermore, have these four qualities: First, he makes his ears deaf so as not to hear anything which is not proper; Second, his tongue becomes mute so as to abstain from speaking evil; Third, he renders his eyes blind so as not to observe the weaknesses of others; Fourth, he must be as though lame of foot so as not to visit any place merely to fulfill his lower desires. When hiding others' faults becomes a way of life, we are in fact practicing the highest discipline.[27]

From these instructions we learn that the latent tendencies of our mind are ultimately revealed in our words and deeds. We may think that we can hide, but in one way or another our words and actions betray us. Contrary to popular belief, by concealing others' faults we not only defend their honor but also reveal the generosity of our own nature.

What is the highest love? To act under the law of love which seeks to conceal the faults of others. Such a love goes beyond mere respect, for it actively reveres the inherent Godliness lying dormant within each soul. This requires that we live up to the highest standard of moral conduct, which is non-violence in thought, word, and deed to all living creatures. In the Hindu tradition, this is referred to as *Ahimsa Parma Dharma*, which literally means "non-violence is the highest religion."

When we expose and criticize others, we injure them in thought, word, and deed. We may think that we are correct in exposing the truth to others, but before we do so we should first give them a chance to rectify their behavior. We should remember when a woman was about to be stoned to death for committing adultery they turned to Jesus for advice. He replied that whoever had not sinned should cast the first stone. Who has the right to condemn others? Only he who is without sin. Yet truly spiritual people not only refrain from injuring others in thought, word, or deed, they extend their help and compassion to all. The spiritual path begins with non-injury, but should lead to a state of active compassion and universal mercy.

Exercises in Non-violence and Concealment of Faults

We are all guilty at one level or another of finding fault and criticizing others. The seemingly innocuous little criticisms we all indulge in from time to time may appear harmless, but are they? From a spiritual perspective, indulging in these habits is worse than the eating the rotting meat of a dead relative. This may sound gruesome, but in fact from a spiritual perspective it is entirely true. Practicing non-violence and refraining from criticism of others is the bedrock of our spiritual sanity. It is not an option but a necessity. Here are a few helpful aids in working with this practice:

1. **Recognize that by criticizing and thinking evil of others we hurt them, whereas by protecting the dignity, safety, and well-being of others, we gain their trust and love.** Ask yourself:

   - When I criticize others, does it really make the situation any better?

   - How do I feel after publicly exposing or finding fault with others?

2. **Remember that no one has appointed us as the moral police of humankind.** Whenever we think ill of others, judge them, label them, or put ourselves above them in our mind, it eventually comes back to us by way of the law of cause and effect, for as we have judged, so shall we be judged. Ask yourself:

   - When I judge, label, or think ill of others do I feel that I am better than they are?

   - Am I aware that each time I criticize or find fault with others I invite the same back onto myself?

3. **Reciprocity is the Law.** Remember that whatever we do to others we are actually doing to ourselves. By exposing the faults of others, we expose our own faults in the end. As yourself:

   - Would I like my own faults exposed in front of others?

   - When I criticize or find fault with others do I have that person's best interests in mind?

   - What are my motivations for finding fault with others or exposing their faults?

4. **Respond with love,** regardless of the emotional responses that another person's actions may initially trigger in us. If someone has erred in some way, as we all do, approach them in private and lovingly bring up the issue in a non-judgmental but instructive way. If they do not listen, or if they react, then know that you have done your best in good faith, and thereafter pray for their welfare. Ask yourself:

   - How often do I respond lovingly to others by offering to help them correct their error or fault?

   - How often do I approach others non-judgmentally and in private to instruct them compassionately in a better way of doing something?

The Fourth Pillar

God out of the perfection of His mercy and waves of his compassion bestows the rain of mercy and moisture on every barren soil.[28]

For Rumi, true compassion arises out of the source of all love, which is God. The entire universe is a manifestation of the Creator's mercy and compassion. The eternal Light of God sustains the heavens and earth and all sentient beings. Like the sun, which continues to shower its light and warmth on everyone regardless of age, sex, religion, or nationality, a true human being is a conduit for the unlimited compassion of God. The light of compassion issuing forth from God should pour through us, showering its blessings on whomever we meet. This, in fact, is the true definition of unconditional love. To recognize compassion as the very ground of our own being is the first step in expressing compassion to all.

Sant Darshan Singh echoes this spirit when he says:

> *Embrace every man as your very own*
> *And shower your love freely wherever you go.*[29]

True love is selfless. Antoine de St. Exupery, author of the classic book *The Little Prince,* tells us that "true love begins where there is no recompense."[30] Our compassion should extend to all creation, even to those who have wronged us. Jesus it is very clear in the Gospel of Mathew about the condition of one who follows the way of love: "Love your enemies, bless them that curse you, do good to those who hate you, and pray for those who despitefully use you and persecute you."[31] Not only did Jesus not preach revenge, but he advocated unmitigated forgiveness and compassion. His gospel was a living testament to the power of love. He told those who would be his disciples, "Ye have heard that it hath been said, 'An eye for an eye, and a tooth for a tooth': But I say unto you that ye resist not evil; but whosoever shall smite thee on thy right cheek turn to him the other also."[32] His path was the path of perfect compassion, forgiveness, and grace.

When Mother Teresa was asked about forgiveness she replied, "Every human being comes from God, and we all know something of God's love for us. Whatever our religion, we know that if we really want to love we must first learn to forgive before anything else."[33] On another occasion she remarked, "Holiness is not a luxury for the few; it is not just for some people. It is meant for you and for me and for all of us. It is a simple duty"[34] Although many of us feel that these kinds of actions are reserved for a select few who have attained cosmic awareness, in actuality they are a part of a normal state to be attained by everyone. From the viewpoint of the spiritually awake, to live in any other way is to deny one's full humanity and block the ultimate source of joy from blessing us. Indeed, the secret to a joy-filled life is a life of compassion and service.

When a television interviewer visited Mother Teresa he told her, "The thing I notice about you and the hundreds of sisters who now form your team is that you all look so happy. Is it a put on?" She replied, "Oh no. Not at all. Nothing makes you happier than when you really reach out in mercy to someone who is badly hurt." "I swear," wrote the interviewer afterward, "I have never experienced so sharp a sense of joy."[35] When we live only for ourselves, we trap ourselves in our own ego.

Love with conditions is not love at all, but a subtle form of selfishness. To love others in the hope of some gain, whether short-term or long, whether here or in the hereafter, is only another form of lending with interest. In fact, we can never attain true and lasting happiness until we give up attaching conditions to loving others. Hazur Baba Sawan Singh, in a letter to his most devoted disciple, once wrote, "If others do not give up their wicked ways, why should we leave our noble ways."[36] To act in the spirit of compassion is to act in accordance with our true nature.

Each of us has a precious jewel within us. When the prophet Mohammad was asked, "What actions are most excellent?" he replied, "to gladden the heart of a human being, to feed the hungry, to help the afflicted, to lighten the sorrow of the sorrowful, and to remove the wrongs of the injured."[37] In truth, this was not just philosophy, but was modeled in the prophet's own life. For instance, when he returned a victor over his former enemies who had plotted and nearly killed him on numerous occasions, he sought neither revenge nor justice. Instead, he freed them from their captivity and forgave them their wrongs.

This deeply held moral code is noteworthy in the wake of the current misunderstanding of the core values of non-jihadist Islam:

> *O Prophet, say to the prisoners in your hands:*
> *If God knows of any good in your hearts*
> *He will give you better than what has been taken*
> *From you, and He will forgive you;*
> *Surely God is all forgiving, all compassionate.*[38]

But for a true Muslim or one who has fully surrendered to God's will, even this is not enough. In one of the more famous Hadith, the Prophet was asked how one could recognize those who are of the faithful. His reply was that, "You will recognize the faithful, for they show mercy to one another, love one another, and are kind to one another as if they all were of the same body. When one member of the body ails, the entire body ails.[39]

The Story of Bhai Kanehiya

Compassion of such magnitude is the hallmark of the saints, prophets, and true disciples. During the time of Guru Gobind Singh, the Sikhs were in a desperate fight for survival against their Mogul rulers. It was the duty of a devoted follower by the name of Bhai Kanehya to distribute water to his wounded fellow soldiers on the battlefield. He carried out his task with absolute conviction, yet in addition to giving water to his fallen Sikh comrades, he offered refreshment to injured enemy forces as well. His fellow soldiers objected, thinking he was a traitor, and brought the matter to Guru Gobind Singh. When his case was brought before the Guru's court, a complaining soldier testified against Bhai Kanehiya by saying: "whenever a enemy soldier has fallen in battle, Bhai Kanehiya gives water to them with the result that they revive and begin to fight again."

The Great Guru was fully aware of his beloved disciple's compassionate intentions, but in a firm tone of voice demanded from Bhai Kanehiya an explanation to defend his actions.

Bhai Kanehiya replied, "Master, I give water neither to the Sikhs nor to the Muslims. I give water to You alone. Wherever I see the Light of God shining, I give water to that person."

The Guru then spoke to the assembly, saying, "Bhai Kanehiya alone has understood the true meaning of my teachings." He then gave Bhai Kanehiya a box of medical supplies and instructed him to not only give water to wounded enemy soldiers but to also to apply balm and bandages as well."[40]

Such compassion arises out of a vision of unity and not intellectual effort. When we see the Light of God shining in every atom of creation, who then is high or low, who is good or bad, who is enemy or friend? Saints and true lovers of God see all mankind from a level of universal oneness. They draw no distinctions between believer and non-believer. It may sometimes be difficult for us to understand this level of compassion, in part because we have not rooted out the inner violence within us. When *ahimsa,* or non-violence, becomes the ruling passion of our life, inner and outer conflict disappears. Brute force is transformed through compassion and humility.

During the partition of India, when the new state Pakistan was created to make a new home for Muslims, millions were forced into exile: Hindus left their homes to relocate in India, which Muslims left India for Pakistan. During the two-way mass exodus, atrocities were committed on both sides. Radical mobs of Hindus and Sikhs killed innocent Muslims. Muslim mobs killed innocent Hindus. Thousands of men, women, and children were slaughtered by marauding groups on both sides.

Knowing the horror of this situation, Hazur Baba Sawan Singh deputed Sant Kirpal Singh to provide safe passage to a large group of Muslim refugees who had been dislodged from their homes and had arrived in Beas. They were dispatched in lorries, but on the way the vehicles were stopped by a mob who threatened to kill them. The lorries were brought back to Beas, and he was told that the attackers were in pursuit with the intention of killing them. Kirpal Singh went alone to speak to the rioters, and found them ready for murder. He explained to them that it would be against the tenets of Sikhism to take the lives of those who had sought refuge with them, and that the Muslims were like their brothers. At that, two old men from the murderous throng stepped forward and thanked the saint for saving them from committing sacrilege against their own religion.

When the Muslims were about to board the lorries, Sant Kirpal Singh spoke to them, "For a long time we lived together like brothers. Now we are passing through a very disturbed time and their lives are in danger. Will it not be better if we parted in friendship after embracing each other?" The Sikhs, who had been ready to cut the Muslims' throats only moments before, now hugged them, and they all wept together.[41]

One may well ask how it is possible for one man, armed only with the power love and compassion, to disarm an entire battalion of vengeful killers. How is it possible to transform raised swords into loving embraces? What power can alter the imminent slaughter of innocent humans into a caravan of security and safety? The answer: unconditional love and compassion. Indeed, the power of compassion is the basis of the life of the spirit. It can transform the most hateful and horrible humans into loving and kind beings. How is this accomplished? First we must enter into the sanctuary of our own being and experience this divine quality for ourselves. Only then can we invoke the power of compassion in others. Ultimately, compassion arises out of the experience of divine unity, when we realize that whatever we do to others, we ultimately do to ourselves.

To experience compassion is to recognize that any wrong or evil a person has done is the result of their mind, not their soul. All of us are redeemable. Saints do not drop from heaven; they evolve over the course of time. Enlightened beings, having suffered greatly themselves, are able to have compassion for others who have suffered. They have seen the "little Hitler" inside themselves, but have known it to be false.

If we see a diamond in a toilet bowl, will we flush it down the drain? Those who know the diamond's value would never do so, no matter how soiled it may appear. A connoisseur of jewels knows that no amount of concealing dirt will alter the diamond's value. The soul, like a diamond, has an inner nature that can never be altered. As we begin to progress spiritually, we begin to see the ever-pristine Light of God within us. When we see the divine presence in each human being, we honor and revere them. We know the unlimited potential in each soul and never doubt—even for a nano-second—the power of love to transform others.

Exercise in Developing Compassion for Others

The practice of compassion is something everyone can readily appreciate as a significant part of spiritual development. The problems arise when we realize how little we actually do it. The following steps will help us to incorporate compassion into our own everyday nature.

1. **Recognize that the very essence of our being is compassion,** a by-product of love. It is who we are.

   - Affirm this reality in your conscious thoughts in some way everyday.

2. **Experience the Light of God in oneself.** To fully practice compassion, we must experience the divine presence in ourselves first, only then can we see it in others.

   - Each day make it a conscious habit to work toward seeing God's light in all life forms.

3. **Hate the sin not the sinner.** To act contrary to this principle is to deny our inherent humanity.

   - As often as possible, reach out to help someone who is experiencing difficulty. If nothing else, at least lend a compassionate ear.

4. **Honor the pristine beauty and greatness of every soul** by recognizing that everyone is perfectible and redeemable. There is hope for everyone no matter his or her past.

   - Starting today, do at least one act of kindness for someone you do not know well.

   - Greet others as if they are your long-lost friends.

The Fifth Pillar

It is through humility that water avails against fire; for fire stands up whereas water lays prostrate.[42]

What is the real meaning of glorifying God? It is to see ourselves humbly in relation to the greatness of God. So long as we do not see God's greatness, we cling to our limited ego. The real cause of our spiritual ruin is the idea of "me and mine," which creates the *illusion* of our separate existence. To know God's Unity, then, is to be consumed in the presence of the One. As Rumi says, "If you wish to shine like day, burn up your night of self-existence."[43]

Have you ever asked yourself why we are not attracted to arrogance but rather to humility? People who speak only of themselves and their achievements are concerned with themselves and have little interest in others. Rumi tells us that on the spiritual path, we should assume the qualities of the earth and become humble in spirit:

> Let us examine the qualities of the earth. First, it is always beneath our feet. It never assumes a position of prominence. Second, no matter what weight is put upon it, the earth never complains. And finally, it supports all life on the planet. Without the earth, life as we know it would not exist. Like the earth, a truly humble person avoids the limelight, is continually grateful, and never complains about circumstances. A great teacher once told a parable in which someone asked the earth what troubled it the most. The earth's reply? "I can bear all burdens, but I cannot bear the burden of an ungrateful heart."

The way to true blessedness is the way of humility. The words of the shepherd boy singing in John Bunyan's *Pilgrims Progress* are worthy of note:

> *He that is down need fear no fall,*
> *He that is low, no pride;*
> *He that is humble ever shall*
> *Have God to be his guide.*
> *I am content with what I have,*
> *Little be it or much,*
> *And Lord, contentment still I crave,*
> *Because thou savest such.*[44]

In nature, too, we see this principle exemplified. The willow tree survives the storm because it easily bends, whereas rigidly stiff trees break at the first winds. In a similar way, the fruit-laden tree bends down of its own accord, offering its fruit to everyone. So, too, does one who has found God. He or she offers their gifts to all, for they see God in everyone. This is true humility. Rumi tells us:

> *The affair of spiritual poverty is beyond our cunning intellect;*
> *Do not look at poverty with contempt*
> *Because dervishes are beyond both property and wealth*
> *They are the sovereigns of the heart,*
> *Giving away their "life" with open hands.*[45]

When we clear our hearts of everything that is not God, we invite God into our hearts.

The Parable of the Gates of Heaven

Once a seeker of God found himself at the gate of heaven. The gatekeeper asked him, "Who are you?" to which the seeker replied, "A teacher." The gatekeeper then asked the man to wait at the gate and went in to confer with his superiors. After a while he returned and said that he could not let the man in, as there was no place for teachers in heaven. He was told to go back and "wash the dust of dead words clinging to him in the waters of silence."

The seeker left and decided to go into retreat. Every day he sat in the silence and imbibed the message of the saints. He prayed to be the servant of all God's creation and, gradually, his spiritual consciousness became sufficiently elevated that he was truly humble in spirit. When he returned to the gates of heaven, he was again asked who was there. This time he replied, "I am the servant of all." The gates of heaven immediately opened and he beheld the Divine Beloved's face, pure and beyond compare.

It is ego that prevents us from seeing the divine in others and in ourselves. The great Sufi Saint Ansari of Heart summarized the reality of the seeker's life when he declared:

> *If thou wouldst become a pilgrim on the path of love,*
> *The first condition is that thou become as humble as dust*
> *and ashes.*[46]

The ego derives its strength from the assumption that it is, in fact, the *doer*. So long as we assume *doer-ship*, we must reap the results of our own actions, whether good or bad. Those under the sway of ego all operate under this fiction. We assume power where there is none. So long as we continue to take credit for our own actions, we must bear the consequences for them.

The secret of the great ones is that they know God is the real doer. They pass all credit on to God and their own spiritual teachers, who are at one with God. There were two qualities that deeply impressed me about my spiritual Master: the first was his compassion, and the second was his humility. I remember one incident that to this day continues to bring tears to my eyes.

It was during the scorching month of July and Master had been spending hour after hour attending to the various needs of his large spiritual congregation, many members of which had traveled long distances to attend. As the birthday celebration of his Master approached, the oppressive intensity of the summer heat took its toll on most people. The only relief was an occasional rain that cooled things off briefly. Every minute of the Master's waking day was filled with his non-stop giving—in fact, it was almost embarrassing to witness such a manifestation of his seemingly unlimited compassionate love.

Everyone knew that the Master was giving twenty to twenty-two hours every day to serving humanity in this way. One day, someone who was moved by his compassion-in-action praised the Master for his superhuman efforts. Upon hearing this praise he remarked, "But I have done nothing. It is all the grace of my Hazur [his Master] and God working overhead."

We had heard this reply many times, but somehow it was different at this moment. One of his disciples was unable to understand how he could say this and asked, "Why is it that you never take credit for anything you do? Surely, you can't expect us to believe this? We daily witness your superhuman acts of kindness and love for all us. How can this be?"

My teacher answered in the spirit of all illuminated beings, "You people think I am lying. I tell you what I see. God is doing everything. I do nothing. It is all God's grace and compassion." In the face of such humility, all one can do is bow down in complete self-sacrifice. To say that we were taken aback would hardly describe the impact of this profound disclosure. In that moment, I realized that his humility was an absolute affirmation of God's greatness: Master Kirpal Singh had become so completely empty of self that what flowed through him was an inexhaustible river of the purest, sweetest water of compassion and generosity.

As I learned, becoming humble is not about abasing oneself, but about glorifying God. The truly humble person is oblivious to his own humility. Ironically, the more concerned we are with developing humility the harder it becomes to do so. Conversely, the more absorbed we become in the grace, beauty, and majesty of our Beloved, the more oblivious we are to our own self. To give up the ego is to renounce our separate existence once and forever. It is to assert our companionship with Love itself. There are no shortcuts in this difficult task except the constant and ecstatic experience of the Beloved's love, grace, and beauty.

What is the ultimate measure of our progress on the spiritual path? It is to recognize that whatever separates us from others also separates us from God. Only when our consciousness is in tune with our essential oneness will we be a truly humble person, gifted with a wondrous feeling of peace. Once we have recognized the ego and its deceitful ways, we will no longer allow it to steal away our happiness.

Exercises in Developing Humility

1. **Be grateful for all things and content in all circumstances.** This is the first step to living in the will of our Beloved. Ask yourself:

   - Do I begin each day with an act of gratitude?

   - Do I find at least one thing to be grateful for everyday?

2. **Avoid feeling superior to or better than others.**

   - Try for an entire week to see everyone as your teacher.

3. **Regard position, wealth, and fame as you would dung or filth.** They have no value in God's eyes.

   - Each day make it a habit to glorify and praise God, the source of all gifts.

4. **Be the servant of all.** Do not try to dictate in a superior way to others. Instead, seek to serve others quietly and without attracting any undue attention to yourself.

5. **Realize that there is a divine purpose behind all life.** If this is true, then we have something to learn from everyone.

6. **Remember that God is the only doer.** Pass on all credit or success to God or one's own spiritual teacher.

   - Make it a practice to take responsibility for errors that go wrong in your day-to-day affairs, but pass on any and all praise to God and your spiritual Masters.

The Sixth Pillar

> *The one who gives without expectation of any gain,*
> *that one is God, is God, is God.*[47]

Generosity is the foundation of our being. With every breath the saints give without thought of any return, here or in the hereafter. This is because, when we are connected to our divine source, we see every act of giving proceeding from God's unlimited bounty.

The prophet Mohammad has said, "Whoever knows for sure his recompense on the day of Judgment, that his reward will be ten for one, at every moment a different act of generosity will issue from him."[48] How could such a being refrain from giving, for they see every act of kindness and generosity returned tenfold?

For Rumi, generosity proceeds from experiential *seeing*, not from reasoning. "All generosity arises from seeing compensation from God: those who see God's unlimited bounty never fear of giving nor withhold their acts of generosity."[49] Viewed from this angle, true generosity is a product of spiritual perception. When our inward eye sees the recompense of every act of generosity, what then is there to withhold? The root of the matter is our connection to the Divine, which is the unlimited source of all goodness and all gifts. We are not the giver. All gifts proceed from God, and yet we are its beneficiaries.

Sant Kirpal Singh once spoke about the meaning of being truly human. He said, "The highest thing there is...is fellowship. Sharing with others what we have. There is nothing greater. The only thing higher is God Realization."[50] At that moment, I understood that there was really nothing to strive for on a personal level. What I needed was to learn how to live selflessly. To live for others and share with them selflessly is all that is needed.

True spirituality is the recognition of the greatness latent in each soul. We bow our heads because we see each soul as a divine gift to humanity. It is from this wellspring of humility that true fellowship arises. How can we seek to usurp the rights of others if we see divinity in each soul? Greed, envy, and jealously arise from a lack of faith in the bounty of our Creator. This means that fear is merely the absence of love.

Lord Jesus, being in full unity-consciousness, knew that everything happening to him — even His crucifixion — was in reality a gift of God's love for him. Compelled by faith, he willingly underwent tremendous torment and trial for the benefit of others.

It is often our fear of the future that causes us to withhold. We act from greed because we believe that there will not be enough for ourselves and our own. Yet, true generosity is rooted in an attitude of abundance. The more we can give, the more we are gifted. God, the source from which all gifts flow, is unlimited. Our capacity for giving expands to the extent that we open up to the Divine, for we see that we never lose anything when we give.

An instructive story from the life of my own teacher helps shine light upon the nature of true generosity. When his uncle fell ill and was taken to the hospital, Sant Kirpal visited him in the hospital often. One day, he noticed that the patient in the bed next to his uncle was not being attended to properly, so he offered his assistance to this man as well. His uncle, however, voiced an objection. He could understand Sant Kirpal Singh's selfless service to him, as he was duty-bound by familial obligations; but what right did this complete stranger have over his nephew's services? Sant Kirpal Singh replied simply and beautifully, "Not only does he have a right over me, but all creation has a right to my service."[51]

Such is the magnanimity of true saints and Masters. They recognize all humanity as their true family. When we see the light of divinity in each and every soul, we too will offer ourselves in service to that Light. True men and women of God do not come for any segment of society, race, or religion. They come for all humanity. They come only to give.

Contrary to conventional wisdom, embarking on the journey of love is not a burden, but rather a release from the prison house of the petty self. Total and complete giving is really another name for complete and flawless love of the Beloved. The path to the abode of divine love begins with little acts of kindness, but ends with the total and complete giving of oneself. If we are serious about embracing the path of ecstatic love then we must give everything over to God. As we embark upon this journey, we find to our surprise that each act of giving fills us with greater passion for God and an even greater capacity to give. Here are a few practical steps we can take to inculcate a spirit of generosity into our daily life.

Exercises in Developing Generosity

1. **Realize that one of the highest principles in life is fellowship, or sharing with others what we have.** Then we begin to experience the true joy that arises out of sharing our gifts. Ask yourself:

   - What responsibility do I have to make the world a better place for my children and future generations?

   - To what extent do I feel I am contributing to increasing peace and joy in the world?

2. **Remember that true generosity arises out of inner contentment and fearlessness.** Only then can we begin to shift our sense of lack to one of abundance. Ask yourself:

   - How often do I consciously act to make others' lives better?

   - How often do I feel a sense of lack or fear that I won't have enough?

3. **Recognize that all humanity is our family and that each of us has a duty to serve everyone equally.** This is the first pillar on the path of service and generosity. Ask yourself:

   - How often do I think of others outside my immediate family?

   - How often do I actually give of myself to others outside my immediate family?

4. **Reconsider our definition of spirituality.** Instead of thinking in terms of what we can attain through spiritual practice, we must think of our spiritual life as a continuous act of giving. If this is true then the more we can give, the more we open ourselves to the unlimited gifts of the spirit. Ask yourself:

- How often I make it a point to hide my acts of goodness or giving?

- How often do I give to others without pre-calculation or desire for recompense?

- Most of all, how often to I give joyously and from a sense of abundance to whomever I meet?

The Seventh Pillar

Do not assume a virtue which you do not possess...like Pharaoh:
If you are a jackal, don't act like a peacock.[52]

The theme of hypocrisy finds expression in a variety of places in Rumi's work. He continually reminds us of the dangers of all forms of self-deceit, but especially of portraying ourselves as other than who we are. We should, he exhorts, be as transparent as an empty glass. Oftentimes, however, we prepare one face to meet the public and another in dealing with our friends and family. Such deception is born of ego.

Living in the Light of Truth

To portray ourselves as we are, without self-deception, is the essence of integrity. My own master set a powerful example of this in his everyday life. For instance, while he dressed in the simplest of white cotton clothes—which were often frayed or missing but-tons—his bearing and presence were the essence of majesty. He would often tell us that we must be true to our own selves and without self-deception. In this way, too, he was a living example. On one occasion a disciple asked to speak with him in private about some personal matters. But his reply astonished me. "There is noth-ing private with me," he said. "Everything here is above boards, all clear."[53] From that day onward each of us was made aware that we live in a transparent universe where nothing can be hidden or concealed.

Each morning the Master blessed us with special "darshan sessions" in which he would ask each of us how much time we had put in for meditation and what we had seen. At first I felt fear and trepidation, as I was revealing everything about who I was to people I did not even know. Yet I quickly got over my fear when I realized that there was nothing we could hide from the master. He knew everything that was going on not only in our thoughts but in our daily meditations, as well. Ironically, the sessions that had, at first, seemed very scary became a place of great refuge. No subject was taboo, and people gradually opened up to him about everything. In this atmosphere of total honesty I felt a peace and tranquility that cannot be imagined. One example that helped me understand this teaching will forever remain engraved in my heart.

During the month of July an attractive young woman arrived from the United States. Master had showered her with much love and attention for the first two weeks of her stay, even addressing her on occasion by her first name. Each day she would come to the morning darshan session wearing a new, colorful, attention-grabbing outfit. While no one paid much attention to her, this was certainly out of the ordinary, as it was accepted custom that everyone avoided drawing attention to or herself unnecessarily.

One morning, Sant Kirpal Singh looked her straight in the face and asked her what her name was. Everyone was taken by complete surprise because he had been addressing her by her name for the last two weeks. He then turned to someone sitting next to her and asked that person who she was. The person said, "Oh Master this is such and such, she has been here for the last two weeks." Master nodded knowingly and then shook his head back and forth. Looking directly at her he said, "Acting and posing will get you nowhere. One day dressed like this, the next like that. Be true to your own self."

It was a lesson for all of us. I realized in my own way that I too was "posing" in order to impress others. Indeed, upon deeper reflection, I could see how we all act and pose to gain attention and bolster our image of ourselves. Sant Kirpal summarized the essence of true discipleship when he said that a disciple "never boasts of his valor or intelligence, but seeks to help others surreptitiously. He dislikes the limelight. He shuns publicity and feels shy in large crowds. He does not like acting and posing, but is always unassuming and natural in his behavior."[54]

One of the most treacherous pits many seekers fall into is the desire to be recognized. We want other people to notice us. We may publish many books, give stimulating lectures, and receive prestigious awards, but if these acts are done primarily to gain outer recognition, we reap an empty harvest of self-deception. With each step in the direction of self-seeking outward approval, we move further away from the truth within us.

Rumi's own life is a perfect illustration of a transformation from external recognition in the eyes of the world, to inner spiritual realization. Before he met his master, Shams, Rumi was a well-respected and recognized expert in Hanifi law, Quranic studies, Hadith, and theology. He had been groomed by Borhan al din to succeed his father as the spiritual preceptor in Konya. It is said that as many as ten thousand disciples would come to hear Rumi's Juma prayer on Friday. However, when Rumi met Shams, he renounced every act of pretense and abandoned the adulation of his many disciples. This complete and total renunciation was made possible by his overpowering love for his spiritual teacher.

Living the Message

Someone asked Mahatma Gandhi, "What is the message of your life?" He replied, "My life is my message," meaning that our lives should be an embodiment of the change we seek. Our words will then have impact on others. Why do people so often ignore the advice others? Why is it so rare to find anyone we can truly trust? It is because most people do not practice what they preach. True spirituality only begins when our thoughts, words and deeds are in alignment. Only then can we be considered "honest" in the true sense of the word. Sant Rajinder Singh tells us, "Honesty begins where ego ends."[55] When we are finally brought before God's court, we will be judged by our actions, not by our pious pretensions.

Those who seek nearness to God never portray themselves as other than who they are, because they know that nothing can be truly hidden. In contrast, the ego is ready at any moment to try to claim for itself what, in fact, only God can claim. In many of Rumi's poetic verses and stories, he reminds us that the truly spiritual person does not make grandiose claims or speak proudly about his own spiritual attainments, for to do so violates the sacred tradition that one's inner spiritual experience should remain a secret between lover and Beloved. Furthermore, to reveal this secret decreases one's spiritual wealth and increases the ego. It may also have the consequence of making others jealous. Paradoxically, for those sufficiently sensitive to spiritual vibrations, one's true inner condition cannot be hidden, for it radiates out of every pore of one's body.

Chaitanya Mahaprabhu was an Indian Master who lived in the early part of the sixteenth century. This God-intoxicated saint's favorite way of remembering God was the continuous repetition of the phrase "Hari Bol," which literally meant *Glorify God*. It so happened that one day he met a group of men washing clothes, and while standing beside them he said, "Hari Bol." Every person sees others from his own level, and because the washer men thought he was a beggar, they ignored him. Chaitanya Mahaprabhu repeated it once, then again, and finally a number of times. Finally, one washer man replied sharply, "I am not going to say it," but Chaitanya Mahaprabhu put all his attention on him and told him that he must. It has been said that even one glance from a Master is enough to uplift a person, because it reaches the very depths of the soul. The washer man thought, "Oh well, he is very insistent, I will say it." So, he repeated the words "Hari Bol." Immediately upon repeating the words he became so intoxicated that he started dancing around ecstatically repeating "Hari Bol, Hari Bol." The other men wondered what had happened and drew around him asking, "What is the matter with you?" He said, "Hari Bol!" The minute they heard him say the words they, too, became intoxicated. Whoever said Hari Bol began dancing with intoxication. In the end the contagion spread and soon the entire place was full of people dancing with joy, all repeating "Hari Bol, Hari Bol, Hari Bol."[56]

Sant Kirpal Singh called this story an example of *changing others through radiation.* This is the true spiritual revolution that can change the world. All other revolutions, whether political, economic, or social, cannot change a person's heart as deeply as spiritual transformation—for unless a person's heart is changed, no real change has occurred.

When our thoughts, words, and deeds are in harmony then we can change others without out even speaking. Every step we take toward the goal of honesty is a step away from ego. Spirituality begins where hypocrisy ends. The divinely realized beings who live in this way are the real treasures of this world, guiding humanity toward real peace and lasting change.

The path of ecstatic love requires us to be true revolutionaries of the spirit. We must have the boldness of heart to renounce all except love itself. Let us not forget that the word ecstasy literally means *to stand outside of oneself.* Therefore, personal interest and selfish gain are foreigners in the land of true love. To portray ourselves in a manner that is inconsistent with our inner nature is to dishonor the face of love. The lover should seek only the glory of the beloved. Here are a few steps we can all take to develop greater sincerity and root out hypocrisy.

Exercises in Developing Honesty and Sincerity

1. **Always portray yourself with scrupulous honesty.**

- Take note of how you feel when someone says something flattering but not true about you. How do you react inwardly?

- Pay attention to your relationship to your own faults. Do you subtly seek to hide them, even at the expense of others?

2. **Pay attention to pretenses.** Pretentiousness usually arises out of a subtle feeling of arrogance, either born of ego or arising from disdain for others. Knowing this, consider the following:

- Do you seek attention or subtly separate yourself from others by your dress, behavior, or speech?

- How often do you become defensive when others do find out about your mistakes?

3. **Recognize that outer accolades, honors, and awards will all be forgotten.** This is a great first step in becoming more inwardly attuned.

- Ask yourself whether you seek recognition for your acts of goodness. If you do any kind deed, do you seek to disclose it surreptitiously to others?

- Ponder whether your meditation and prayer stem from truly seeking God's unlimited bounty, or if they are sometimes used as attention-getting acts.

4. **Seek to be honest with yourself.** It is a common truth to say that we can deceive others but we cannot deceive the God within. Nevertheless, the reality is that most of us do not recognize where we deceive ourselves. Here are a few tasks to consider doing daily:

- Note your actions and continually ask yourself to what extent they are serving only your own self-interest.

- Ask yourself how often you openly or secretly try to justify your actions, regardless of circumstances.

Hafiz

Chapter Five
Hafiz: The Path of Joyous Surrender

From the Dawn of the first Beginning till the twilight of the last end,
Friendship and love have drawn inspiration from one sole pact,
one single trust.[1]

—Hafiz

afiz has long been honored by spiritual seekers, mystics, and saints as one of the greatest spiritual masters and lyric poets of all time. While he is still relatively unknown in the West, throughout the Persian-speaking world one hears his verses sung and recited in the bazaar, on the radio, and at spiritual gatherings. In the Middle East his collected works, or *Diwan,* is held in such high esteem that his words have been cited and quoted by spiritual masters and religious authorities as well as politicians, educators, and literary giants up to the present era; and the tale of how Hafiz came to be a Sufi is a legendary throughout the East.

Hafiz's Conversion

When he was a young man of twenty-one, Hafiz worked as a baker's assistant. One day, while delivering some bread to a mansion, he happened to catch a fleeting glimpse of a beautiful girl on the terrace. With that single glimpse he fell madly in love with the girl, yet she did not even notice him. To make matters worse, the girl—who was from a wealthy, noble family—was so beautiful that many referred to her as *Shaik i Nabat,* or "branch of candy." Not only was Hafiz a poor baker's assistant, but he was short and physically unattractive. The situation was hopeless.

As the months went by, Hafiz made up poems and love songs to celebrate his longing for the beautiful young girl. Day and night he sang his poems, and people began to repeat them. In fact, his poetry was so touching that it became popular all over Shiraz. Hafiz, however, was oblivious to his new fame as a poet—he thought only of his beloved.

It was said in those days that anyone who kept vigil at the shrine of Baba Kuhi for forty full nights in a row would be granted his heart's desire. Desperate to win the affections of his beloved, Hafiz undertook this near-impossible spiritual discipline: Each day he went to work at the bakery. Then, every night he went to the saint's tomb and willed himself to stay awake. Remarkably, his love was so strong that he succeeded in completing the vigil.

As day broke on the fortieth day, the archangel Gabriel appeared before Hafiz and told him to ask for whatever he wished. Hafiz had never before seen such a glorious, radiant being. "If God's messenger is so beautiful," he thought, "how much more beautiful must God be?" Gazing on the unimaginable splendor of God's angel, Hafiz forgot all about the girl, his wish, everything. There was only one thing he desired. Without a second thought he told the angel, "I want God."

Gabriel then directed Hafiz to a spiritual teacher who lived in Shiraz. The angel told Hafiz to serve this teacher in every way and his wish would be fulfilled. Hafiz hurried to meet his teacher, and they began their work together that very day. That teacher was the venerable mystic Mohammad Attar.[2]

In this remarkable story we see the broad outline of a path of joyous surrender to the overpowering force of divine love. This vision touches the farthest horizon and yet it is grounded in daily contemplative practice. Hafiz's spiritual thirst (*gham*, or profound sorrow), ignited by the love of a beautiful girl, propelled him to the holy precincts of God's presence.

Humans need a human connection to understand the divine. We cannot approach God intellectually. The shaykh, or living master, connects us to the divine. Through the intimate, loving association with a perfect teacher whose presence is an embodiment of divine beauty and love, we are able to taste a tiny drop of the ocean of God's grandeur. Once we have tasted even a single drop of this vintage our hearts are irresistibly drawn to the source. Hafiz illuminated a path of surrender to this love (*zaat*), acquired through the perfection of noble qualities (*sifat*). This is the path of the actual experience. To a starving, thirsty man, mere intellectual knowledge of bread and water has little value. We need to become drunk with God's love. The way to our innermost home is through surrender to the blissful embrace of God's love.

The Life of Hafiz

Despite the recent interest in Hafez we still know very little about his life and work. What we do know comes mostly from anecdotes and biographical sketches, references by other writers, legends, and the poems themselves. Most biographers now agree that Hafiz was born in Isfahan, in what is now central Iran, somewhere between 1317 and 1325. His father, Baha ud-Din, was said to be a merchant who moved to the city of Shiraz while Hafiz was still a young boy. Not long after their arrival, his father died, leaving the family in difficult circumstances. Nevertheless, despite these hardships he managed to acquire a rigorous classical education and was considered to have an encyclopedic knowledge of the Qur'an, its jurisprudence (*fiqh*), interpretation (*ijtihad*), and sayings of the Prophet (*Hadith*). He was fluent in both Persian and Arabic, and it is said at a very young age had memorized the entire Qur 'an—an accomplishment which won for him his name, Hafiz, or literally, "one who recites."[5] This alone may give us some indication of his prodigious literary and spiritual genius.

The Divine Trust and Treasure of Love

The vast bulk of Hafiz's work deals directly with the themes of mystical love, surrender, longing, and guidance on the spiritual path. His mastery of the spiritual path, its twists and turns, highways and byways earned him the most distinguished honor accorded in the Islamic tradition: the titles *lisan-al-ghayb*, or "tongue of the invisible," and *tarjuman al asrar*, or "interpreter of the mysteries." Considered by most to be the unrivalled master of the classical Persian *ghazal*, a brief and strict lyric mode, Hafiz expressed some of the most elevated spiritual insights couched in lyric verse. His consummate poetic art paints a multi-faceted panorama of the vast inner landscape of the mystical journey as it is portrayed in the relationship between the *murid*, or disciple, and the spiritual teacher, or *Murshid*.

The three essential symbols of Hafiz's mystical poetry of love—and, indeed, the work of many Persian mystical poets—are those of the *cupbearer* or dispenser of the treasure of love, the *wine* or love itself, and the *ravaged heart* or lover who is the receptacle for this divine love. This great treasure of love, the poet tells us, is also a profound sorrow (*gham*), a "continuous restlessness of the heart," as Muhammad Iqbal once described it.

The entire mystical journey is a path of return through the ever-increasing longing for love. This longing is, in fact, a treasure bestowed upon man by God. This profound longing—which began at the moment of creation but continues throughout the spiritual journey—is, indeed, without end. Persian mystics referred to it as a treasure of sorrow (*ganj i gham ishiq*) for it is a gift of infinite worth that is only fully realized through the death (*fana*) of the little self or animal ego (*nafs*). Hafiz begins his exposition of this mysterious journey by explaining the soul's unique predicament:

The Lord of pre-eternity (sultan-i-azal) *offers the Treasure*
   of Sorrow (ganj i gham i ishq)
That we may descend into this ravaged dwelling (manzil-i-
   wiraneh).[4]

In these lines, Hafiz takes us back to the primordial beginning of creation, when God is said to have stated in a famous sacred saying (*Hadith Qudsi*):

I was a hidden Treasure; I loved to be known,
So, I created creation, in order that I should be known.

Though perfect in everyway. God had a latent wish to know Himself through Himself. This latent wish manifested when He decided to become many from one. At that instant, God said, *"Kun fia Kun,"* or "be and it became," and all creation sprang into being. At that command billion of souls were created, each a part and parcel of his own essence. Ever since that primordial moment, each soul has been on a quest to return to its source. This journey is only consummated when each soul becomes a unique expression of the divine essence, like a tiny mirror reflecting back to God his perfect and ineffable love for himself. In this way God's secret treasure becomes known and the experience of his infinite love is realized in every part of his manifold creation.

The simultaneous pouring of God's being into all creation, and the love of these creatures aspiring to be reunited to the source of their being, form the two arcs of Iranian mysticism: descent (*qaws-i-nuzuli*) and ascent (*qaws-i-uruji*). These twin movements, one originating from pre-eternity (*azal*) and the other starting from man and flowing back to God in post-eternity (*abad*), is the cosmic topography from which Hafiz articulates his vision of self-surrender.

The Predicament of Man

Hafiz takes us back to the moment before recorded time and reveals the unique predicament in which man finds himself. It is man alone who has been given this unfathomable gift: It is said that when God created man he asked the angels to bow down to his new creation for God had created man *in his own image.*

The great spiritual master and Sufi poet Sant Darshan Singh tells us, "What is that image? God is love. Since man is created in his image, he too is love. Man is born out of love it is his very nature."[5] Why were the angels asked to bow down to the creation of man—because they lack that special quality which is born out of love and compassion? Sant Darshan Singh continues, "They cannot become one with God. To do this they must assume the human form. Only then can they achieve salvation.... It is only through the path of love and compassion that they can gain communion with God."[6]

Angels, though perfect in devotion, lack compassion—for they never err. The soul is the epitome of God's creation, the very "image of God Himself"; therefore, the human form is a part of God. The special and unique capacity of humanity is our ability to share in the suffering of others. If it were only a question of devotion, the angels would already be perfect in this capacity. But the angels have not experienced the difficult trials and tribulations of human life. They have not been able to "share the afflictions, the restlessness, and anguish, nor the pain of separation which has fallen to man's share."[7] Man is superior because he contains in him both *zaat,* which is pure essence, and *sifat,* which is noble qualities and special attributes, acquired through intense trial and suffering. It is man's unique ability, through his experience of love, to grasp the absolute essence of God. Such a designation raises man above all creation to the level of a micro-God.

In the next verse, Hafiz not only alludes to this visionary journey between *azal* and *abad,* but also to the special pact and divine trust (*sifat*) given to man at the moment of his creation:

> *From the Dawn of the first Beginning till the twilight of the
> last end,*

Hafiz: The Path of Joyous Surrender

Friendship and love have drawn inspiration from one sole pact,
one single trust.[8]

Reference is made to a passage in the Qur'an describing the gathering of all souls together at the beginning of time, when God reminded them of the sacred trust bestowed upon them. On that day of promises, he asked, "'Am I not your Lord?' They said, 'Yes.'"[9] From that moment, each soul agreed to accept the obligation to follow God's divine commands and acquire the noble virtues of love and compassion *(sifat)*. At that singular moment, each of us set out on a journey to return to God by becoming perfect yet unique embodiments of his unfathomable light and love.

In the second line, Hafiz reminds us that our very existence proceeds from God's unfathomable mercy and grace. Therefore, all love and friendship should be directed to God, as he is the sole source of our very existence. Though seductive and alluring, this world ultimately proves empty and illusory. Everything in this world is temporary—even our bodies are like rented houses, which each of us must one day vacate. Sadly, we have forgotten who we are and whence we have come. We pass our days here searching aimlessly, but in the end nothing satisfies the deep longing of the soul to know itself.

But the soul is dragged by the mind to the outer sensual pleasures. For most of us it seems all but impossible to make any steps toward our goal even when we are inclined to do so. Even the most ordinary habit seems impossible to overcome, let alone the deeply ingrained habits of mind and intractable emotional loops. How ironic that God has asked us to lead pure and unsullied lives, yet we find that every step is beset with countless temptations and difficulties. Instead of turning our attention inward, where we could find lasting joy, we find it impossible even to turn our eyes away from a passing illusory pleasure. Hafiz aptly describes our condition when he says:

*Man has been tied to a raft and left in the midst of the high
seas with the warning, "Beware, lest your clothes get wet."*[10]

The lasting fulfillment we all seek eludes us because we are
unable to extricate ourselves from the quagmire of physical temptations. The slow process of realizing that nothing in this world can
ever satisfy may take one year or a hundred lifetimes; but ultimately, as Hafiz beautifully tells us, through countless births and deaths
and often great trial and tribulation, each soul finally recognizes the
source of all felicity and love lies solely with our Creator.

The Awakening of Human Consciousness

The moment the first flickering of self-consciousness awakes
within the soul, it remembers its divine origin; and as soon as it
recollects the sacred trust bestowed upon it, the soul is overtaken
by a powerful nostalgia to return to its source. This journey, which
began the moment we were separated from God, will only end the
moment we reenter the eternal divine consciousness. This is the
journey from pre-eternity to post-eternity, from *azal to abad*, from
form to formlessness. As we commence this inner journey, we realize that we are more than a body; we are conscious spirit. In fact, as
Jalalu'ddin Rumi tells us, we have inhabited many bodies and jour-
neyed through many kinds of forms to reach the station of human.
In a rare passage, Rumi reveals the evolution of the human spirit:

*I died as a mineral and became a plant,
I died as a plant and rose to animal,
I died as animal and I became a man.
Why should I fear? When was I less by dying?
Yet, once more, I shall die as man, to soar —
With angels blessed, but even from angelhood
I must pass on; all except God doth perish.
When I have sacrificed my angel soul,
I shall became what no mind e'er conceived,*

Oh let me not exist, for non-existence
Proclaims in organ-tones, "To Him we shall return."[11]

The Path of Infinite Longing

When we begin to see our human life in these terms we can appreciate the exalted wisdom with which Hafiz and other great Sant masters speak. With each step in our journey the soul moves closer to understanding its essence as love. This is the path of infinite longing—a journey fully explored and mapped out by a long line of great spiritual giants, including such ascending stars as Farid ud din Attar, Jalalu'ddin Rumi, Baba Farid, Nanak, Kabir, Swami Shiv Dayal Singh Ji Maharaj, Sant Kirpal Singh, and Sant Darshan Singh.

In the opening ghazal of Hafiz's *Diwan*, he masterfully maps out the essential elements of the path of joyous surrender, through valleys of doubt and self-importance to wisdom and selfless compassion. He skillfully summarizes the soul's treacherous journey from illusion to reality, selfishness to selflessness, and from death to immortality.

Oh Saki, bring around the cup of wine and then offer it to me,
For love seemed easy at first, but then grew difficult.[12]

In this opening couplet the aspiring lover invokes the Beloved beseechingly, for he now realizes that the journey of love is an arduous and difficult affair. The novice on the path may at first be fooled to think that his or her progress will be rapid and without difficulty. But, it is not long before he realizes his mistake. The lover implores the *Saki*, or Spiritual Master, to fill his cup with the wine of love. He has recognized that the Spiritual Master, or Cupbearer, is the mediator between himself and God. Since the Master has merged his soul with that of God, he now becomes the conduit for the grace and power of the Almighty. The lover recognizes that there is no access without the aid of the guide. This realization is an important

turning point on the path toward God, for the seeker who understands that his efforts alone will never secure the precious gift of
love has already been graced with right understanding. The very
act of asking is itself a form of submission and a step in the direction of grace.

In my travels all over the Unites States I have found hundreds,
indeed thousands of seekers—but few who are actively seeking
help from a spiritual teacher. When asked why so few people in
the West seek a Spiritual Master, Sant Rajinder, the Master of the
Sant lineage, replied, "In the West most people feel they can do
it themselves and therefore are not willing to seek out a spiritual
Master."[13] Yet, reflecting on my own feeble efforts, I have come to
realize that I not only can't I do it myself, but I need all the help I
can get. When we learn to put aside our pride and ask for God's
help we are in a position to receive. Such a seeker understands that
divine love is the sole remedy for his suffering, and the Cupbearer
his sole hope of deliverance.

> *Flooded with their heart's blood are those who wait for the scent*
> *That the dawn wind may spill from her dark musky curls.*[14]

Anyone who has tasted even an atom's weight of divine love
becomes overwhelmed with desire to meet the Beloved. Even a little
taste of that exquisite bliss floods their hearts with yearning. These
lovers awake each morning propelled by an ineffable urge to see the
divine friend. Hafiz compares the scent of the Beloved to the *nafeh*,
or musk bag of the graceful gazelle. In traditional Arabic poetry,
the scent of the Beloved is said to arrive on the wings of the dawn
wind. The lover arises every morning in hopes that the dawn wind
will carry the scent of his Beloved. From that scent, he can trace his
way back through the wilderness of the heart to the abode of God.
Ironically, like the musk deer, the scent *nafeh* of the Beloved is not
outside, but inside the lover. It is generated and sustained through
intense yearning and continuous longing. This quality, in turn, is

the result of both our own efforts and the gift of the spiritual friend. Here the friend is not God Absolute but the Cupbearer or guide on the path—one who has reached the destination and can take others there as well.

Stain your prayer mat with wine if the Magus tells you so,
For such a traveler knows the road, and the customs of its
stations.[15]

In this second verse, the entire path of self-submission is explained and justified. In Iranian poetic traditions, the *Pir-i-mughan* (literally Master of the Magi) referred to the Zoroastrians and unbelievers who were unconstrained by the Islamic law and its prohibition against drinking. The *Magus* was the dispenser of wine at the tavern. Here however, the word Magus refers to the *Pir, Shaykh,* or spiritual master, who guides his disciples through the various stations and states on the spiritual path and is the dispenser of the spiritual wine of love.

Hafiz may also be alluding to the fact that the cupbearer or dispenser of the wine is often scorned by the orthodoxy, which neither understands true spirituality nor is willing to accept the authority of the God-intoxicated saints. The truth of this statement is born out when we study the lives of the great saints throughout history. Buddha was scorned and ridiculed; Prophet Mohammad suffered numerous assassination attempts and ultimately had to flee for his life; Al Hallaj was executed; Guru Arjan Dev was made to sit on burning hot plates; and Christ was crucified. Hafiz was well aware of the fanatical elements within Islam and often disguised his verses in order not to raise the eyebrows of the orthodoxy. This verse, however, appears to be an exception to this rule.

In the mystical traditions of Islam, the masters of the path speak of two kinds of stations: *hal* and *maqam*. The former is relatively temporary and the latter a more stationary or permanent state. These states and stations come to the disciple's heart as a result of his own efforts and strivings, and the grace and guidance of the spiritual master. In the second part of the couplet, Hafiz tells us that only the spiritual master truly knows all the hidden difficulties and pitfalls of the path. In this seemingly simple verse a whole world of mysticism is revealed.

To fully comprehend the depth of meaning contained in this verse we must first understand that, for a devout Muslim, the prayer carpet is considered to be the most sacred possession one owns. Secondly, equally *haram* or forbidden for any self-respecting Muslim is drinking wine or alcoholic beverages. For one's spiritual guide to ask one to dye one's prayer carpet in wine would be tantamount to heresy and punishable by death. How could any Muslim possibly follow such an injunction? To do so would imply an outright abnegation of his religion and faith. Here it is important to know a few facts of Hafiz's life in order to fully understand the extreme nature of his poetic admonition.

We know that, in the early stages of his career, Hafiz worked as a baker for some time; but by his late teens or early twenties he began to write for a wealthy patron who was a vizer for the Shah Abu Ishaq of the Il Khanid Empire. It was under the reign of Shah Abu Ishaq that his literary career was first established. It is said that Abu Ishaq was a tolerant and easygoing ruler who was also artistically inclined. While we do not know exactly when this poem was written, it is quite likely that it could have been written at the end of peaceful Abu Ishaq reign, or perhaps during the more violent period of Shah Shuja', which was characterized by some of the most inhuman acts of ruthless aggression recorded in the annals of the Persian Empire. During that time, the Il Khanid Empire was under constant attack and, while Islam was the primary religion of the period, it was enforced through violence and bloodshed.[16] To have uttered such advice in such times would have been not only a revolt against Islam, but against its despotic rulers as well.

Whenever the verse was created, it is certain that by the time it was spoken Hafiz already held an important university post, and that his poetry was held in great respect throughout the region.[17] His seemingly blasphemous edict, in this case, could not have gone unnoticed. In fact, by some accounts it is said that when he wrote this hemistich, or half verse, it resulted in an outcry throughout the country. As word got out, Shah Abu Ishaq was duly informed of Hafiz's heretical statement and asked his Caliph to look into the situation. During those times the Caliphs were masters of Islamic law and were responsible for all matters of religious jurisprudence. Therefore, Shah Abu Ishaq requested that his Caliph investigate the matter and render a judgment.

As the story goes, all sorts of pressure was put on the Caliph to take serious action against Hafiz. But because he was a wise man and had personally met the great mystic, he knew he could not reach a decision without at least investigating the matter personally. The Caliph proceeded to visit Hafiz, in hopes of returning with a suitable explanation. When he arrived, he asked Hafiz, "You have written a verse which declares that one should dye one's prayer mat in wine if the master tells one to. Surely, a man of your status must understand that such a verse can cause uproar in the hearts of your listeners. However, I am sure that in writing the second half of the hemistich you will certainly explain yourself to everyone's satisfaction. Naturally, on my own I would not have bothered but I have been commanded by the Shah to investigate this."

Hafiz replied, "My dear Caliph I have a mystic friend who lives some distance off, first go to him and do whatever he says then, when you return to me, I will explain the meaning of the verse." The Caliph began to have some doubts. "I have come to him in good faith and acted in accordance with the command entrusted upon me," he thought. "Why is it that Hafiz has not answered me? Surely, he could have given me some sort of reply." Almost instantly, the Caliph began to have doubts about Hafiz's status as a great mystic. He began to think to himself, "Not only has he not replied, but he has sent me off on an errand, which seems to have no connection with my inquiry." He continued to question in his mind why Hafiz was acting in such a strange manner. He thought perhaps Hafiz was trying to buy time until he could come up with a suitable answer and justify the verse.[18]

The Caliph is not unlike any of us who come to meet a great teacher and evaluate that teacher according to our own level of understanding. Whatever advice they offer us is run through the litmus test of our own intellect. We seldom give much credence to their words, nor do we understand the depths of their wisdom. In fact, most of us know very little of the true value of a spiritual teacher. Not only was the Caliph having doubts about Hafiz, but he was also somewhat offended that a man of his status should be sent off on an ordinary errand. His ego was pricked.

Upon reaching the mystic, the Caliph explained the entire story and then said, "My dear friend Hafiz sent me here and told me to follow your instructions and then he would explain the meaning of his verse." The mystic listened to him and then, in a nonchalant manner, replied, "All right, we will talk about it later. For now I want you to go to the house of a certain prostitute on a certain street in a nearby town."

The Caliph could not believe what he was hearing. How could he, the esteemed doctor of the law, be asked to go to the house of a prostitute? What an outrage. He had never heard such nonsense in his entire life. One mystic tells one to dye one's prayer mat in wine and the next to go to the house of a prostitute. To even think of such an action would be the downfall of any man of God. But for the Caliph of the Shah such an order was sheer madness.

We have to understand this story in our own terms today. Even the notion of a perfect guide is today very much open to debate. For many seekers, the need for a guide is still very much in question. In today's world, most of us have little faith in spiritual teachers and still less interest in following them. We have seen so many false gurus come and go, each one embroiled in one scandal or another. To entertain the notion that a perfect teacher or master exists is already a leap of faith for many of us. But to follow such a teacher when it goes against the grain of our culture, education, and religious training requires a level of faith and surrender rarely seen in today's cynical world. Let us not forget that when Jesus began his preaching only 12 disciples had the courage to follow him. Most ridiculed him, others had little faith, and still others betrayed him.

Yet, this was exactly what Hafiz had in mind when he sent the Caliph out to visit his mystic friend. He wanted to test the Caliph's faith. My master used to say, "Wonderful are the ways in which a true saint tests those who come to them." A true spiritual master has no interest in money, power, or fame and is beyond the confines of ego. The entire spiritual path is, in reality, a path of controlling the ego or little self. The essence of the spiritual journey is summarized in the saying, "Put one foot on your ego and the next step will be in God's lap." However, to control the ego is no easy task. Almost all traditions agree on this point: unless the ego is controlled spiritual attainment is impossible.

What could the Caliph do? Because he had been sent on a mission to investigate the meaning of the verse, the truth was that he had little choice. If he came back without a verdict, his own life would be in jeopardy. So he did as the mystic said. But while traveling to house of the prostitute he began having grave doubts and concerns about the sanity of Hafiz and the second mystic. His mind was filled with terrible thoughts.

This is how most of us act on the spiritual path. We may be given an instruction, but when we find that we are incapable of obeying the instruction we come up with a hundred reasons why we should not do so. Most of us are not following any faith except the dictates of our own mind. If we look carefully at our inner lives we see that even if we want to apply ourselves spiritually, our mind stands in the way and we do the opposite. Submission to God's will or surrender to a higher authority is out of the question when we have no control of our own mind. To understand our own fundamental helplessness in the face of the mind is the first great spiritual lesson we all must face. And to follow even the simplest act of spiritual instruction requires us to have some self-discipline and self-control.

What is the essence of surrender? It is to be able to submit to the will of God in all things. But this is obviously easier said than done. The Caliph was being given a lesson in how far he had been able to control his own mind. When he reached the house of the prostitute, he seated himself in the reception room. While he waited an attendant of the house came by and served him some food. Once again, his mind acted up and he began having doubts about his actions and concerns for his reputation. He wondered what would happen to him if anyone saw him here.

After a short while a young lady entered his room. He noticed that the young lady was dressed in fine clothing and was perspiring from head to foot, trembling and shaking. The Caliph rightly observed that this is hardly the behavior one would expect from a prostitute. As he observed her more closely, he noticed she was halting at every step and trembling more and more. Having become aware of her trepidation he put her at ease and said, "Don't worry I am not going to touch you. But kindly tell me, how is it that you are in such a plight?" The girl replied, "I am the daughter of a respectable man. When I was very young robbers came and plundered our street and carried me along with them. They sold me to the owner of this house, and because the prostitute you have come to see is away today to be with a nobleman, I have been pushed in to take her place. I was raised in a righteous fashion and have led a chaste life by the grace of God and from my own conscience; I know that this is not the right path. I would rather die than engage in this sort of activity."

As the Caliph continued to listen attentively, he was filled with compassion as he remembered that many years back he had also lost a daughter when robbers had plundered his house. As they continued to talk he asked, "Can you tell me about the town in which you were living?" The young girl replied, "I cannot remember exactly but it was something like...."

The Caliph was greatly surprised, for it sounded very similar to his own town. He further inquired, "Do you remember the name of the street on which you lived?" Once again relying on her memory she replied, "I am not entirely clear but it was something like..." The Caliph became even more animated, as it sounded very similar to his own street. Finally, the Caliph asked, "Can you tell me the name of your father?" The young girl replied, "Sir, I do not recollect exactly, but I believe it was...."

At that the Caliph burst into tears as he realized this was his own daughter standing before him. In that moment he fell to his knees and offered a prayer to God Almighty for having reunited him with his long-lost daughter. In that instant he not only realized his own folly for having doubted the wisdom of Hafiz, but a wave of gratitude overwhelmed his heart.

He immediately contacted the owner of the house and paid the requisite price to redeem his daughter from the bonds of slavery. He then set off to Hafiz's friend's house. With tears in his eyes, he remonstrated himself for having doubted the intentions of these mystics: How could he have ever passed judgment on these great saints; how could he have wondered about their noble acts? How childish he was to have trusted his own mind. How ignoble to have uttered such callous words when, in reality, these saints were acting solely in his noblest interests. Why had he been cursing these great saints when, in reality, they were performing the greatest act of kindness? He then fell at the feet the second mystic and begged for forgiveness. "I have misjudged you, but you acted only to save my daughter's honor. I am an ignorant fool who has no grasp of the depth of vision from which you speak. I now see the extent to which I am shackled by my own limited intellectual understanding, which is blind and biased. You saints see with a panoramic view and are unconcerned with the worldly praise or blame. You give us love and we recompense you with evil, we disrespect you and you bless us and guide us."

After the Caliph shed may tears, the mystic replied, "It is all right; do not trouble yourself so much." The Caliph pleaded, "How can God ever forgive me for my terrible curses and doubts?" Once again the kind-hearted mystic reassured him, "My dear friend, whatever you have done you have done without malice, but only because of your lack of spiritual vision and understanding. Please don't bother yourself with this anymore. You continue to have my blessings. Now forget about all this."

Suddenly remembering his original purpose he asked, "What about the hemistich? I have been instructed by the Shah to return with an explanation of the verse. I still have no answer." The mystic replied, "Go back to Hafiz and he will complete for you the remaining second hemistich, which will provide you with an explanation."

The Caliph returned with his daughter to Hafiz where he prostrated himself in all humility at his feet. He then burst out in tears and related the entire story to Hafiz. He cried out, "We are mere mortals, incapable of understanding the depths of your wisdom. We have no inkling of your peerless wisdom and guidance. Since we have seen many charlatans, we assume all teachers are frauds. We see you as wolves in sheep clothing and have even lost faith in spirituality itself. Since I have no inner experience, I think everyone is spiritually blind like myself. I have been so filled with ignorance and arrogance that when a saint tries to help me I blame and curse them. How can God forgive my behavior? I am at your mercy. Please forgive me though I am in no way deserving." Hafiz said nothing but blessed his visitors. The Caliph then remembered the instructions given by the other mystic and said, "Your mystic friend has requested you to complete the second hemistich which will explain the full meaning of your verse to us sinners and mortals." Hafiz then completed the verse:

> *For such a traveler knows the road and the customs of its*
> *stations.*[19]

The Caliph then took the verse back to the Shah who could see plainly the meaning, which, Hafiz intended. The verse was then published for all the kingdom's inhabitants to see and the furor died down in the empire.

Truly speaking, surrender or submission to God's will is an exalted station on the spiritual path. The concept already implies that we have completed the course in controlling our mind. How many of us are like the Caliph, unable to control our mind for even a few minutes of the day? To do so is a gift of God, which, comes when we have recognized in the depths of our unworthiness and helplessness. To receive help, we must first recognize our inability. Asking, it is said, is the half of knowledge. Whoever believes they can achieve everything solely through their own efforts will always be filled with ego. Such a person puts a wall between himself and God. It is the veil of ego tha prevents us from recognizing that, along with our own effort, guidance and grace is required.

In this story, the Caliph, like many of us today, has to pass through the fires of purification. As our ignorance and vanity are exposed, we begin to develop the noble qualities of humility and compassion, which are prerequisites for true submission and selfless love. Love not tempered in the fires of humility can never touch the purity of God's throne.

Hafiz continues his ghazal with the following verse:

> *What security is there for us here in this caravanserai?*
> *When every moment camel bells cry, "Pack up the Loads."*

Hafiz here employs the traditional image of the caravanserai, which is a caravan of merchants and travelers, en route to other cities for trading purposes. In Hafiz's times, people rarely traveled alone because of the risk of bandits and thieves. There was safety in numbers. By traveling in large caravans, merchants were assured at least some safety and security. However, despite the caravans' seeming security, the wayfarer was still at the mercy of the shifting sands and the exigencies of travel. At any moment, the caravan might have to move on to avoid danger or possible plunder.

Hafiz compares the caravanserai to this fleeting world, which bewitches us with the effervescent pleasures of the senses. While we may get some immediate satisfaction from these sense pleasures, we fail to get any real security or lasting happiness. Hafiz warns the spiritual aspirant that life is not what it appears to be. There are no guarantees; in this world all is fleeting and impermanent. Hafiz joins the great chorus of all spiritual luminaries who teach that life is like a momentary bubble on a great sea. Let us not forget the supreme doctrine of impermanence (*anuka*), the cardinal teaching given by the Prince of Peace, Buddha: Nothing is lasting, nothing is permanent, and *everything* is transitory. For many of us, this sounds like just another spiritual truism. But the reality is that the kaleidoscope of colors, sounds, and sensory impressions has mesmerized us all. As we look around, we see everyone falling into the seductive but illusory traps of petty power, transient fame, and temporary wealth.

The Story of Ebrahim Ibn Adham

There is a wonderful story from the life of Ebrahim Ibn Adham, who, before becoming a great sheikh and spiritual teacher, was the ruler of a vast kingdom. It is said that once, a man came to see the king. This man was so horrible to look at that none of the royal party could bear to set eyes on him, and even the servants dared not to ask his name. Yet the man came solemnly and stood before the throne.

"What do you want?" demanded Ebrahim.

"I have just joined this caravanserai," said the man.

"This is not a caravanserai, you madman. This is my palace!" shouted Ebrahim.

But the man would not be dissuaded. "Who owned this palace before you?" he asked the king.

And the king replied, "My father."

"And before him?" asked the man.

To which the king replied, "My grandfather."

Still the man was not satisfied. "And who owned this palace before him?" he asked.

"So-and-so," Ebrahim told him, growing impatient with the impertinence of this lunatic.

But still the man questioned. "And before him?"

"The father of so and so."

"Where have they all departed?" asked the man.

To which Ebrahim retorted, "They have gone. They are dead."

At that the man simply nodded and said, "Then is this not a caravanserai which one man enters and another leaves?"[20]

Life here is a caravanserai. Some of us are companions for a day, some a week, others a few years. Our homes and possessions come and go with such speed that we cannot keep up with the frenzy of buying and selling. We have sought security in a world of impermanence. If we look at our life, we see that most of it is spent trying to make ends meet. From dawn to dusk our day is spent earning money, which is spent quicker than we can make it. These bodies and homes will not last.

Hafiz reminds us that what is permanent is love acquired through spiritual practice. But how much time do we spend in our spiritual practices? How much time do we spend in meditation and prayer? The real journey is that of the soul from the world of empty shadows to the world of light. How many of us have consciously embraced our spiritual work as our preeminent goal? This is real submission and real surrender. It is also the highest security.

To surrender is to fully embrace the reality of love. When we fully understand this, we achieve the state of equipoise. We are not bothered by change; we know change is inevitable. We do not place any hopes in this world, for everything here is transitory. To understand this is to understand the nature of the ravaged heart (*manzil-i-wiraneh*). This heart is the place where we embrace the lessons of change in order to become fully conscious human beings.

Hafiz continues:

> *In the end, my life has drawn me from self-concern to ill repute.*
> *How long can the secret of our assemblies stay hidden?*[21]

In this hemistich Hafiz outlines the paradoxical nature of the spiritual path. As beginners on the spiritual path, most of our concerns revolve around our narrow self-interest. We see everything through the smoke-colored glasses of our limited egos. As we mature we begin to realize that praise and blame, name and fame, poverty and riches, and health and sickness are all the same. They ultimately have no bearing on the spiritual journey. Why? Because they are all transitory, impermanent phenomena. Only the Saints' gift of selfless love is of lasting value.

Hafiz reminds us that everyone one of us will one day be tested. We will each have to ask ourselves what we really want. If we want riches, we will get them; if we want power, we will get that; and if we want honor, we will get that. Those who want only God, they, too, will get what they desire. We have to ask ourselves what we really want. Jesus reminded us this of point when he said, "What is a man profited if he gains the possession of the whole world but loses his own soul."[22]

In the second half of the hemistich, Hafiz reveals the secret of the mystic's heart: it is the joy of union with God. And how is this achieved? Amazingly, it is attained simply through the continuous and ever-flowing remembrance and invocation of God. It is said in the Qur'an, "Remember me and I will Remember You,"[23] and again, "Remember your Lord much and glorify Him in the evening and in the early morning."[24] The way to approach God is through the power of remembrance.

Kabir tells us, "Comforting is God's Name. All ills it cures. Remembrance of God's Name leads to Him besides."[25] Just as water gets poured through cloth to free it of all impurities, so, too, is remembrance like a hidden sieve through which we need to pass many times. Through this constant remembrance of God, we are purified of all that is not God. If we want to boil everything down to one essential practice, it is the remembrance of God. In fact, one saint has said that the only sin is forgetfulness. Through the forgetfulness of God we commit all kinds of horrible acts.

Once Tukaram, a great Indian saint, gave a lecture on mantra. "Mantra is great," he said. "Mantra takes you back to God." Someone shouted from the back of the room. "How can you say that a mantra takes us back to God? If I say 'bread, bread, bread,' will that get me bread?"

"Sit down, you filthy scoundrel," Tukaram shouted. When the man heard this, he became furious. He began to shake, and his hair stood on end. Even his necktie began to vibrate. He shouted, "You call yourself a saint, and yet you use such a filthy word against me?"

"I am sorry, sir." Tukaram replied, "Please be calm and tell me what happened."

"You have the audacity to ask me what happened. Don't you realize how you have insulted me?"

"I used just one abusive word, and it has had such a powerful effect on you." The saint said, "When this is the case with an abusive word, what makes you think that the Name of God, which is the supreme Truth, does not have it's own power and will not also affect You?" If an abusive word can make our blood boil, why shouldn't the Name of God have the power to change us.[26]

Tukaram has said, "When the name of Ram [God] is on the mind, Liberation is in your hand." The divine secret to which Hafiz alludes is the ever-flowing and ceaseless remembrance of God. It is the connecting link between God and us. Why should the joy of union be experienced by only a few hearts and members of the assembly? It is high time that this truth be shouted from the house-tops and broadcast on our iPods.

In the final stanza, Hafiz gives us the peerless council of a seasoned traveler:

> *Hafiz, if you desire her presence, pay attention,*
> *When you find the one you seek, abandon the world and let it go.*[27]

The literal translation of this first hemistich is, "If you desire his/her presence/attention, Never be absent/or fall into oblivion." Here Hafiz offers the remedy for securing the gift of divine union: in order to be with the Beloved, we must be absent from the world.

In Sufi mysticism, *gha'ib* and *hudar*, absence and presence, are paired opposites. If our attention is in the world, it is not on God; and if it is on God, it cannot be in the world. My master, Sant Kirpal Singh, used to say the same thing, "The true lover is awake inside and asleep to the world."[28] Yet, at present, we are all awake to the world and asleep to the divine presence.

This does not imply that the seeker should abandon his responsibilities and retreat from the world. Not in the least. Rather, one should detach one's heart from the love of the world and anchor the love in God. Even if one were to retire to the mountaintops or jungles, one could not escape one's own mind. It is inner detachment that is required. Hafiz tells us that if we seek the divine presence, we must "abandon the world, let it go." Jesus Christ reminded his disciples to live in the world but be not of it. Our lives should be like the lotus flower, which, though it floats on the mud and filth of the pond, is never sullied by it.

Cultivating this inner detachment, however, is one of the most difficult of all tasks. Detachment does not mean indifference or lack of concern for others. Quite the contrary, it is an act of the greatest compassion. For it is only when we are free of our own attachments and limitations that we can direct our love selflessly and fearlessly for the betterment of others. True love of God implies the love of His creation.

The Story of Abou Ben Adhem

One night, while Abou Ben Adhem was sitting alone in his house, an angel suddenly appeared before him. In his hands this angel held a book containing the names of all the people who loved God. Now, Abou Ben Adhem was a very saintly man. When he looked at the angel's book, however, he saw that his name was missing from its pages. This saddened him greatly, yet when he addressed the angel he prayed only that if one day a list were drawn up of those who loved their fellow human beings, his name might be included there. A few days later, the angel appeared once again, bearing the same book. This time, however, it had been revised. The angel explained that when he had related the man's request to the Lord, God said, "Make a new list of those who love the Lord, and put the name of Abou Ben Adhem at the top!"[29]

True love of God requires us to act in the service of His creation. We must not only raise our hands in prayer, but offer them in service to our brothers and sisters. Jesus exhorted his disciples to "love one another as I have loved you."[30] In order to comprehend the full meaning of divine love we must extend our love not only to all humans, but to all sentient life. Our universalized vision of life embraces all creation. Such a love seeks nothing for itself but, rather, offers itself in perpetual sacrifice to others. It is a love that continually expands and grows in compassion for others.

Our life itself is but an insignificant offering at the altar of God's love. This, in the end, is the treasure of sorrow (*ganj i-gham*) and the reason for our descent into this world. Since love, like God, is beyond measurement or calculation, it continues on throughout eternity. Ultimately, Christ tells us, "As the Father hath loved me so have I loved you. Continue ye in my love."[31] The Sufi poet and saint Sant Darshan Singh Ji encapsulates the great paradox of this supreme gift in writing, "Love has only a beginning, it has no end."[32]

In the end, Hafiz's message is clear: we must continually give thanks to God for whatever He gives us, whether it be pleasure or pain. In time we come to learn that pain is the cleanser and also the healer. The great saint Baba Farid summed up the essence of the path of joyous surrender when he said: "If anyone suffers trouble or pain he should consider that he is being cleansed of his sins. He should know that all happiness and pain come out of the love of God has for us. If anyone as much as worries about his condition, he commits a sin against his faith in God."[33]

A truly centered person will have faith in the love and mercy of God no matter what the circumstances may be. Such like faith is as rare in the East as it is in the West; but it is, nevertheless, the secret to a life of inner bliss and peace.

The path of joyous surrender is certainly not the easiest path to the divine, for it requires a rare sense of acceptance of life along with a powerful faith in God's plan for us. However, once we decide to fully surrender, no path is more joyous. Although we may initially feel a loss of individual will, it is quickly replaced by an attunement to a more perfect, all-embracing divine will. There can be nothing more joyous and more life affirming that to become *a conscious co-worker of the divine plan,* as Sant Kirpal Singh used to put it. Let us review some of the essential steps that will empower us on this journey and open us up to a life of divine beatitude and spontaneous joy.

1. **Realize that each of is here to fully realize God's infinite gift of love.** Sometimes the hardest thing in the world is to realize is that each of us has come to fulfill a unique, sacred calling. There is indeed a divine purpose behind the life of everyone who comes into this world. No one has been created for nothing. In fact, there has never been nor will there ever be another person exactly like you. Our unique life has been created to express the special gift of love already within us. Only by fully embracing this purpose can we come to know who we are and why we have been sent here. Here are a few things you can do daily to begin this journey:

   • Accept your *divine uniqueness*. This means no longer seeking to compete with anyone for God's love. Accept that you are special and irreplaceable in God's eyes.

   • Learn to *love yourself unconditionally* for the unique soul that you are.

   • Begin each day with an affirmation of the gift of this divine love within us all.

2. **We humans have been given pure essence (*zaat*) and the opportunity to acquire noble qualities (*sifat*) through intense suffering.** The special noble quality acquired only through human suffering is the quality of compassion. Once we understand that compassion only arises through the experience of suffering, we come to accept suffering as a necessary part of life's journey. This special quality of compassion and mercy completes our essence (zaat) and makes each of us a unique and perfect expression of God's love. Ironically, it is in embracing our faults, mistakes, and failures that we discover our true humanity and perfection. Although this may sound difficult at

first, by beginning to accept suffering as a necessary ingredient on our journey we can more easily learn to surrender the really difficult things in our life. Here are a few simple practices to assist you:

- Each day, make a point of *readily and spontaneously accepting* whatever may come to you. Keep it very simple. Just accept it.

- When you experience physical or mental suffering of any kind, do not immediately push it away; instead, *accept it unconditionally* as your teacher.

- Begin to see your own suffering as your *long-lost friend* helping you to develop more compassion and empathy for others.

3. **Recognize that all love—from the most selfish to the most is selfless—is a reflection of the primordial gift bestowed upon each soul at the moment of its creation.** What this means in simple terms is that every expression of love, however base or sublime, comes from God. On a practical level it means that we need to see God as the *source* of all love in our lives. Normally most of us seek love and friendship from various expressions of human love, whether it be spousal love, parental love, or platonic. In this new vision, we come to see all our relationships supported and sustained directly by God Himself. This is something radically new for most of us. We do not seek in this new vision to sustain our love through anything other than God. In time, we do not seek to acquire love at all. We come to realize that it is already in us. Instead we seek *to express it.*

Ask yourself the following questions:

- Do you experience pain when your friends do not pay you as much attention as you would like?

- Do you feel that people do not sufficiently acknowledge your presence when you greet them?

- Do you feel hurt when your children no longer see you as their primary relationship?

- When a loved one forgets to call, write, or stay in touch, do you feel abandoned?

- How much time do you spend thinking about how people should treat you?

- Do you become depressed when people forget your birthday, anniversary, or other special day?

- How much time do you spend thinking about what you can do for others instead of what they can do for you?

- How much time a day/week/month do you spend actually *expressing* simple acts of love to others?

4. **Realize that the Path of Love is arduous and difficult.** For most of us this realization itself seems a contradiction in terms. After all, isn't love supposed to be joyous and fulfilling? In the beginning, many seekers do find the spiritual path filled with seemingly endless vistas of bliss and peace. But within a year or two distractions and diversions set in and many find the initial joy and happiness to have been lost or at least diminished. Here are a few questions to consider:

- Do you have preconceived ideas about what the spiritual journey should be?

- When the initial phase of excitement wears off, how do you respond to the daily challenges given to you?

- What are you currently doing to help yourself through these difficult times?

- As the journey seems to become more difficult, do you lose faith and zeal? And if so, why?

- To what extent are you willing to accelerate your efforts in the face of continued difficulties?

- How often to you realize that each difficulty is a gift to increase your faith and ability to surrender?

- How often to you surrender with love and joy in your heart to the new challenges presented to you?

5. **Follow the Spiritual Guide's advice even if it goes against traditional wisdom.** Here many in the West will wonder at Hafiz's admonition, for it seems to imply the abandonment of rationality and common sense. But, in fact, Hafiz asks us to trust a higher wisdom, born of a higher knowledge and more elevated perspective. If you don't have a spiritual teacher, consider the following:

  - Until such a time as you have found an authentic master, follow the injunctions of your chosen scripture.

  - If you have found a true spiritual master and are convinced of his or her authenticity, make every effort to follow the farsighted vision of your guide.

6. **Realize that everything in this world is transitory.** There is no true "security" here whatsoever. If each day we could fully realize this truth, we would save ourselves endless worry and headaches. Most of our fears arise from attachment to the allurements and temptations of the sensual and material life. But when changing circumstances cause these comforts and enjoyments suddenly disappear we suffer. The good news is we can change that.

  - Make it a *practice* to not place too much emphasis on your material needs and comforts. This way, when the day comes that they disappear, you will feel little attachment or suffering.

  - Start today by making a list of everything you really don't need and either pass it on to others or dispose of it.

  - Seek to be simple, for simplicity is strength.

Here is a list of questions that can help you assess how much emphasis you place on the outer life versus the inner life:

  - When you lose a cherished heirloom, how do you feel?

- How do you feel when valuable personal property is stolen?

- If you had to downsize to a much smaller apartment or house, how would you react?

- Do you find yourself frequently wanting to shop for no particular reason?

- How often do you experience a sense of peace, joy, and happiness regardless of whether your outer needs are met?

Can you be completely happy without any material comforts?

Guru Nanak with his companions Mardana and Bala.

Chapter Six
Guru Nanak: The Path of Compassionate Service

To live for others is the highest norm
He alone liveth who liveth for others.[1]

—Nanak

Though little-known in the West, the fifteenth-century North Indian poet-Saint and founder of the Sikh religion, Guru Nanak, helped ignite and lead one of the most significant spiritual resurgences in the history of the Indian sub-continent. Journeying thousands of miles on foot across three continents, Nanak ushered in a new age of spirituality based upon total equality, compassion, and service to all creation. Of course, his timeless message of spiritual community based on universal brotherly love is not the sole monopoly of the Sikhs. Nanak belonged to all humanity and all humanity belonged to him.

The stories of his early spiritual transformation and miraculous enlightenment are well known throughout the Indian Sub-continent. His father was not a mystic, but a businessman by trade. Fearing Nanak's continued retreat from the world and social responsibilities, he sent his son to Sultanpur to be employed in the service of the local Nawab. Once there, Nanak was successfully engaged as an accountant in the service of the commissariat, and for about two years led a seemingly normal life. His father had hoped that this newfound employment would fix his son's attention on his worldly duties and away from his spiritual pursuits. But, like all great luminaries, Nanak could not ignore his spiritual longings and aspirations for long.

Fate caught up to him early one morning, when he and a friend went to the nearby river Bain for their daily bath. As the *Janam Sakis* tell us, after plunging into the river that morning Nanak did not reappear. His companion and friend, Mardana, waited patiently for him to resurface but he was not to be found. Fearing the worst, Mardana quickly sought the assistance of the local Nawab, who had great affection for Nanak. At his instructions, the river was dredged thoroughly by divers, but without success.

Three days later, and much to everyone's amazement, Nanak miraculously reappeared in the town as if from nowhere. Nanak, however, was no longer his old self. The splendor of his face was dazzling to look upon and his eyes bore the stamp of otherworldly light. The inspired youth had been wholly transfigured. Whatever had happened in those three days remains a mystery, but Nanak now radiated a profound spiritual power and his words carried the weight of inner realization born of communion with God. Not until several days later did Nanak break his silence with the enigmatic utterances that "there is no Hindu and no Mussulman," and, "one must labor to earn one's living and share one's earning with others."

Baffled by these messages, the local Nawab asked Nanak to explain what he meant. He replied:

> Let compassion by thy mosque, faith thy prayer mat,
> And honest living thy Qur'an.
> And modesty thy circumcision, contentment thy fast,
> Then verily, thou art a true Muslim.
> [Let] good deeds be thy Kaaba, and truth thy Prophet,
> And thy prayer be for God's Grace.
> And thy rosary be of His Will then
> God will keep thy honor.[2, 3]

For Nanak, compassion and faith in God were the cornerstones of spiritual practice. The outer accouterments of one's religion mean little if one does not possess the inner qualities that they symbolize. Modesty, contentment, and good deeds were the essence of true spirituality, which could not be trapped within the confines of sectarianism or narrow religious dogma. My own Master summarized Nanak's universal vision of peace by saying that "he bore witness to the glory of one God, one brotherhood, one law, the law of human fellowship and love."[4]

Over five hundred years later, this message continues to touch millions upon millions of seekers who daily sing Nanak's praises and recite his luminous verses. True to the essence of his vision, Nanak transcended religion—today he is venerated by Muslims, Sikhs, and Hindus. A popular Punjabi saying illustrates the extent of this veneration: "Baba Nanak the great man of God, the guru to the Hindus and the pir of the Mussalman."[5] During his own time, this vision of a universal spirituality based on quiet, gentle, and unostentatious service of the poor and needy, reverence for all saints and religions, and a true fellowship of the spirit helped to heal bitter wounds of religious fanaticism and corruption inflicted by inter-religious hatred.

A Call to Service

Nanak was born on April 15, 1469 in a small village called Talwandi, located about fifty kilometers to the southwest of Lahore. He was the son of two poor parents at the lowest rung of Hindu society, yet while growing up he exhibited many spiritual qualities and attributes. It became clear to both his immediate family and friends that Nanak was a specially gifted child. At a very young age his proficiency in both reading and writing caused his teachers to remark they had little to add to his knowledge. So, after completing his basic studies, he was sent to the local *madrassa* to study both Arabic and Persian according to the religious customs of his day. There he quickly mastered both languages, as well as the study of the Qur'an.

Perhaps one of the more revealing incidents of his early childhood involves the investiture of the sacred thread among caste Hindus. Like baptism among Christians or bar mitzvah among Jews, this ritual defined the moment of spiritual birth in the Hindu tradition of his time. When the presiding priest approached Nanak to bestow upon him the sacred thread, Nanak would have nothing to do with any ordinary thread, however symbolic. After several attempts to convince him failed, Nanak went into a spiritual reverie and sang to his priest:

> *Let mercy be the cotton, contentment the thread*
> *Continence the knot and truth the twist*
> *O Priest if you have such a thread*
> *Do give it to me.*
> *It will not wear out, nor get soiled, nor be burnt nor lost,*
> *Says Nanak, blessed are those who go about wearing such a*
> *thread.*[6]

Inspired utterances like these made it increasingly clear to the immediate family that Nanak was no ordinary youth. As he grew into early adulthood his moments of spiritual transcendence continued to appear with increasing regularity. His keen spiritual discrimination already recognized the futility of ceremonial rites and rituals that were devoid of inner meaning or significance. True baptism, he understood, was not merely an outer symbolic rite but an inner awakening of the spirit and a direct contact with the Truth within oneself. It was a birth into the beyond, and a true unveiling of the transcendent light within oneself.

Let us remember that Nanak's message came at time when religion had become lost in excessive formalism, ceremony, rites, and empty ritual. The Muslim *Qazis* had become corrupt and more interested in amassing wealth and power than in devotion to God.

The Hindu Priests had forgotten God altogether and were worshipping idols. Castism had become the rule of the day and true brotherhood and sisterhood were frowned upon.

By the time Nanak was born there had been as many as sixty foreign invasions of India between the eleventh and fifteenth centuries. Timurlenk—known in the West as Timurlane—had attached the Punjab not once but many times, leaving the countryside pillaged and plundered. A succession of Muslim invaders followed, including Jasrat Khokhar, Faulad Khan Turkbacha, Sheikha Ali, and finally Barbur. The Lodi Kings continued the oppression and converted thousands by point of sword. Those who resisted were massacred. The marauders even believed that there was religious sanction for their wanton looting and destruction. As Hasan Nizami Nishapuri noted in *Taj-ul-Maasir*, when Qutbuddin Aibak took Meerut he massacred about a hundred thousand Hindu males.[7] Each successive wave of oppression brought greater and greater lawlessness, poverty, and devastation.

As we look back at Nanak's times we quickly realize that the misuse of religion for fanatical ends has a long history and is not new to contemporary times. For this reason, Nanak's message has special importance for us today. We, too, live a world where the ideals of equality, compassion, and the dignity of man have been forgotten in the midst of misguided, fanatical rhetoric. In many places of the world women remain second-class citizens, children are abducted to fight as soldiers, and over a billion people do not enjoy the freedom to worship as they please. Today, as in Nanak's time, religion has become a mere shell without its inner kernel. Instead of being a force of unity, social order, and brotherhood it has become a force of destruction. In reality it is not the *faith* that is the problem, but the *faithful*. No religion has ever preached hatred or the destruction of innocent life. Nanak could well have been describing the situation today when he railed against the inhumanity of man.

Kings are butchers, they treat their subjects with gruesome cruelty.
The sense of duty has taken wings and vanished.
Falsehood is rampant over the land
As a thick veil of darkness, darkness darker than the darkest night,
Hiding the face of the moon of Truth.[8]

This was the world Nanak inherited, and to which he addressed himself.

The Path of Compassionate Action

Nanak's message was not just a revamping of the age-old truths, but a brilliant re-envisioning of spiritual equality and compassion. It was a redirection to the inner reality, which alone has the power to dispel the dark clouds of hate and fanaticism. A popular legend tells of how he traveled to Kailash, where he spent time with the sadhus who sat immersed in deep meditation high in the Himalayas.

Nanak greeted the sadhus and inquired as to their well-being. They spoke of their blissful state while meditating in the solitary caves high above the tumult of the world. Nanak chided them for escaping from the suffering of the world. What good was all their piety if it only benefited them? He then guided them to leave the snow-clad Himalayas and engage their spirituality to help suffering humanity. Our spirituality, he insisted, was not for us alone, but for the benefit of all. It is not enough to bow our heads in prayer; we need to also raise our hands in service as well. The first lesson we have to learn in this world is brotherhood and sisterhood; and the last lesson, after learning all philosophy and mysticism and after all our efforts, is brotherhood and sisterhood. If we have practiced meditation for thirty years but have not awakened in us the spirit of brotherhood, then no progress has been made. It is a living brotherhood and sisterhood of the spirit that he called for. That means that talking about brotherhood is not enough; we must do something concrete about it. We must realize the one source of all, which pervades everything. From that vision of unity, each of us is called to do whatever little we can in the service of this brotherhood.

Once, while taking a bath at the Ravi River, the voice of God guided Nanak:

> *Repeat my Name — Sat Naam.*
> *Mingle with men uncontaminated by the world.*
> *Worship my spirit and power.*
> *Meditate on my glory.*
> *And serve the poor and the needy as thyself.*[9]

Nanak was thirty years old when he sent forth from Sultanpur to spread his message. From that moment leaving family and comforts behind he exhorted others to connect directly to the power of God, which he called *Sat Naam,* the eternal light of God. Once we see the reality of God within ourselves we can begin to see it in others. It is only through direct experience of this Divine Light that we could serve the poor and needy as our own self. Inspired and literally guided by the light of unity, he began to address the ever-increasing wounds inflicted by religious fanatics, misguided priests, and mullahs. Bearing witness to the unconscionable suffering of his countrymen, Nanak's heart opened in prayer for the grace of God:

> *O Lord, the whole world is being consumed in the invisible*
> *   flames of fire,*
> *O save the world in this hour of darkness.*
> *Raise all unto Thee.*
> *Raise them in whatever and however a way Thou mayest.*[10]

Perhaps one of the greatest treasures of spirituality ever written is the opening treatise to the *Guru Granth Shahib,* the sacred scripture of the Sikhs known as the *Jap Ji.* Nanak lays out in this short but highly condensed introduction the essence of a compassion-centered spirituality. It is a work of unparalleled beauty, universal in scope, pragmatic in its methodology, and unmatched in its revelatory power. In one of the concluding stanzas of the *Jap Ji*, Nanak provides a simple, insightful, yet pragmatic blueprint for spiritual transformation. The great Master offers six essential principles for traversing the inner mystical journey. These steps are the prerequisites for a total inner transformation and ultimate enlightenment experience. Like a condensed code of inner technology, each verse reveals more and more every time it is reflected upon and practiced. These verses bear no religious stamp or narrow dogmatic position but, rather, facilitate a paradigm shift from the unreal to the Real born out by Nanak's own personal experience.

> *Make chastity your furnace, and patience your smithy,*
> *The Master's word your anvil, and true knowledge your hammer.*
> *Make awe of God your bellows and with it kindle the fire of*
> *   austerity,*
> *And in the crucible of love melt the nectar divine.*
> *Only in such a mint can man be cast into the Word.*
> *But they, alone, who are favored by Him can take unto this Path.*
> *O Nanak, on whom He looks with Grace,*
> *He fills with ever lasting peace.*[11]

Make Chastity Your Furnace and Patience Your Smithy

In the first verse Nanak lays out the prerequisite for the dawn of the higher life. Here chastity refers not merely to the outer physical body, but to inner spiritual purity as well. Spirituality begins and ends with inner purity. Once asked to summarize in a few words the essence of his teachings, Sant Kirpal Singh replied, "Be good, do good, and be one."[12] Explaining further, he noted that in order to do good we must first be good, and that the best definition of inner goodness was righteous thoughts, words, and deeds. From the wellspring of pure thoughts, words, and deeds, purity and holiness would follow. What does it mean to be holy if not to be who we really are? We are beings of light made in the image of that Light of All Lights. When the greater light enkindles our lesser light it is Light upon Light.

How is this purity attained? Through purity of thought, which consists of the continuous remembrance of God that effaces our entire seemingly separate being. Such a lover never forgets God even for a nanosecond. Nanak tells us of his own experience, "If I forget you Oh God, even for a fraction of a minute, this amounts to me more than fifty years."[13] From this overflowing remembrance the vision of God's radical oneness and unity is revealed.

All religious and spiritual traditions have emphasized the need for inner purity. Did not Jesus tell his disciples, "Blessed are the pure in heart for they shall see God"?[14] Purity is the inner key that unlocks the treasures of divinity within us. A wonderful story told by Sheikh al Akbar Ibn al Arabi demonstrates this point. Once, in his travels, he met a highly evolved Sufi sheikh whose inner remembrance consisted solely of the word *Allah*. Sheikh al Akbar asked why he did not use the traditional liturgy given out by most Sufi orders, consisting of the phrase *La illah ilallah* —which literally meant "There is no God but God," or more generally, "There is no reality other than the reality of God."[15] He replied, "If I were to die while half-way through the recitation 'There is no God,' then I would die denying God's reality and be sent to hell. I cannot afford to take such chance." To forget God even for a second is actually the cause of all our problems, for in this way we remove ourselves from the love of our creator. In this, all awakened teachers agree: we must begin our inner journey through the constant invocation of God's remembrance. The heart should be like a pure tablet on which the Name of God is emblazoned in light.

In the second part of the first verse, Nanak continues his metaphor and points to the necessity of patience and perseverance on the spiritual journey. We have already discussed why patience is of such importance in any endeavor we embark upon. But it has even greater relevance in the field of spirituality. Many of us in our Western culture have become accustomed to pushing a button and achieving our desires. Seldom do we pause to consider that for every task there is a time period. Oddly enough, we know that it takes years and years to become a doctor or to earn a PhD; but when it comes to spirituality we expect sudden transformations and instant enlightenment.

There is in one of Aesop's fables a story about an old crow. This parable serves as an excellent analogy for the spiritual path in general, and meditation in particular:

> [The old crow] was wandering one day in the wilderness and became thirsty. He had not had anything to drink for days. Finally, he found a jug that had a little bit of water in the bottom. The bird reached its beak into the jug to try to drink, but his beak could not touch the bottom. At first he did not know what to do. It seemed there was no way he was going to be able to drink the water. He then had an idea. He started to drop one pebble at a time into the jug. As each pebble was dropped in the water the level gradually rose up. One by one he added more and more pebbles to the jug. For a while he thought it seemed useless because he still could not reach the water. But after a while enough pebbles were put in, the water rose and the crow could drink it and satisfy his thirst.[16]

The seed of spirituality is planted in the darkness of the mind and only gradually, at its own unique pace, sprouts forth into the light. If we look at nature we see that everything has its own gestation period. When I was in India with my master someone once asked him how we can progress more quickly in meditation. He replied, "More practice." The questioner was not satisfied and asked again, "Please tell me what is the real short cut." Again our master said, "Still more practice." He then added, "Still more practice and spend time in the company of a true Master."[17]

Many years ago, when I first was initiated, I fell into a common trap and believed I would be able to make rapid inner advancement in a short period of time. Raised in a Western society, my little ego expected quick results and wanted them *now*. Only many years later did I come to understand how deeply rooted my impatience and ego really were. I had returned to India for my tenth or eleventh trip with high aspirations. The weather in Delhi was beautiful and there was an intensity of light in the surroundings that uplifted my spirits. I fell into the required daily routine of meditating eight to ten hours a day, and within a week or so I felt the strength to continue into the night. Not surprisingly, however, despite being physically able to sit I felt blocked and internally frustrated with my progress. I began to expect greater progress and became inwardly agitated and subtly ungrateful when nothing happened.

As I continued to sit, my impatience only increased. Intellectually I knew that I should be grateful for whatever I was receiving, but the subtle desire to have more needled me internally. Despite my best attempts to stop clutching I realized that I had been cleverly and subtly sucked into the *expectation game.* This is an all too common error which occurs as a practitioner begins to put more time in for meditation and then comes to expect better results as a result of his or her greater efforts. Nothing could be further from the truth in reality. The expectation of greater progress is born of our ego and selfish desire. The essence of meditation is to reduce the ego. If our meditations begin to increase our ego in any way something is drastically wrong...as I soon learned.

The following evening a small group of Westerners were invited to have dinner with Sant Darshan Singh. The Master was unusually animated and jovial. As he gleefully entertained us with his playful humor he made a remark in passing which summed up my inner dilemma. After casually remarking about one thing or another he turned to me and half-jokingly said, "And here is one of our great stalwarts on the path." I realized instantly the noose I had drawn around my own neck. While no one in room but me knew what he was referring to his point hit home like a nail in rib. My ego had led me to expect that I actually deserved something for my efforts. In that moment I suddenly realized that no matter what I did, I deserved nothing. I could not earn anything. I was far from a stalwart. Indeed, if all my actions were totaled they would only demonstrate my unworthiness. Whatever I had been given was still *all grace*. I could claim nothing. With a pang of deep remorse I realized that no one could ever earn the gift of love. My duty was simply to sit: to sit with a simple love; to sit without expectations and with a heart filled with gratitude for what I had already been given. It is not our efforts alone but gratitude, thanksgiving, and, most of all, surrender that open the door to further grace.

Seek the Highest Knowledge

Nanak continues:

> *[Make] the Master's word your anvil and true knowledge your hammer.*

Here the great teacher reminds us of the necessity of right understanding. We must develop true discrimination, or *vivek*, as it is called in Hinduism. The words of our teacher should be the guiding light of our life. All great teachers of spirituality have pointed out the difference between knowledge of this world, *paravidya*, and knowledge of the beyond, or *aparavidya*. The former is the knowledge of the sciences of this world, which are always changing and impermanent. They are useful in our careers and our maintenance of our physical body, but cannot be of much use to us spiritually. The latter is the knowledge of the beyond and is born of direct experience of God. It is only this revelatory knowledge, born from the transcendent Light of God, that is called true gnosis by the awakened ones.

What, then, is true wisdom? It is to understand the real value of these two kinds of knowledge. Sadly, most of us spend 99 percent of our time accumulating knowledge of this world, which cannot help us spiritually. In fact, it can often become a distraction and an end in itself. We may accumulate many degrees and read hundreds of volumes yet still be spiritually bankrupt. By the time we reach our sixties, or even earlier, we may begin to forget what we have learned and gradually remember less and less. Such knowledge is ephemeral and illusory. Even the information we do have becomes outdated and useless. New discoveries in science, technology, and medicine are constantly revamping and invalidating older theories. For example, in the field of medicine doctors need to recertify every so many years just to keep their license.

We have become the masters of third–person scientific investigation, but we are mere novices in the arts of critical first-person scientific investigation. One of the principle reasons for this paradoxical situation is that we have largely ignored the careful, systematic, and scientific investigation of contemplative experience from a combined third-person and first-person perspective. We can use our technology of the outer world to treat previously incurable diseases, but our mastery of the "technology" of the inner world is so rudimentary that we can barely contain the passions that lead us to destroy the very human life we try so hard to preserve. We have studied the machinery of the brain and have vastly increased our knowledge of how the mind works; yet our ability to apply this knowledge to our own experience remains at a near standstill.

The mystics point to another supersensory knowledge based on direct intuitive illumination that is beyond physical perception. True knowledge, they assert, is based on first-person experience and acquired without the agency of the five senses. Such knowledge is transformational and permanent. It does not change, alter, or decay. In a sense, it is the mother of all sciences and is trans-cultural, trans-sense, trans-temporal, and pre-existent. This is what

Plato referred to as the knowledge of divine ideas, or what in Islam is called knowledge of God's Names.

This does not mean that we should abandon the empirical sciences or scholarly investigations in the various academic fields, for they have important practical uses in advancing our cultural and world civilizations. However, we must understand the relative merits of each and apply them both if our civilization and culture are to advance beyond their current state.

Nanak reminds us that that this first-person scientific knowledge is the knowledge of our own soul, which is the gift of a saint. Nanak called it the *Naam,* or name, and *Sat Naam,* or truth eternal. This is none other than what his contemporary Kabir referred to as *Shabda.* The early Christians referred to it as Word, or *Logos,* and Jesus Christ referred to it as the Holy Spirit. The Upanishadic sages spoke of it as *Jyoti* and *Sruti.* It is, in fact, what many scientists have called the unified field theory that explains everything. Regardless of what we call it, though, this inner Word cannot be written or apprehended by our physical senses. Nor can it be taught or intellectually assimilated. It is the primal Divine Power responsible for all existence and for the creative expression of the universe. This Divine effulgence is lying dormant within, us but can be awakened by the revelatory touch of a realized being.

Kindle the Fire of Holy Awe

Nanak continues:

> *Make awe of God your bellows and with it kindle the fire of austerity.*

Here the great sage encourages us to live in holy awe of the divine presence, which stimulates us to be untiring in our efforts to realize God. What is awe? It is the recognition of the all-pervasiveness and majesty of God's power. This is the secret of accelerating our inner progress. We may give to charity, attend church, assist the needy, and have a spotless reputation in our community but still be far away from God. For example, I may be a model citizen, perform my duties with integrity, and be considered honorable and righteous by my peers. But if I am cut off from my spirit—from the source of my own existence—then I am still far from God. Ethical life is a stepping-stone to spirituality, but not the be all and end all. Unless we are conscious of God on a moment-to-moment basis and have a direct experience of His presence, we are still very far from a spiritual life. It is interesting to note that the word *sin* literally means to miss the mark. From the perspective of a true knower of God, to forget God is truly to miss the mark; and to remember Him is the beginning of all holiness.

To progress inwardly we must cultivate an awareness of that power in every moment. Our remembrance must be suffused with the deepest reverence. As someone growing up in a Western society the concept of awe was almost meaningless for me. It was not until I met my own teacher that I had any idea of what it truly meant. I remember sitting in my master's presence for the first time and literally feeling awe-struck with holy fear. It was an indescribable epiphany. It was not fear of punishment or chastisement, but of sheer power and grandeur. It was like standing near an erupting volcano or watching a great tidal wave approach the shore. Closeness to such power is humbling and elevating at the same time. I felt like a tiny gnat being swept away by an immense wind. It is this kind of awe-inspired reverence that Nanak speaks of in this line of verse. Once we taste this experience, we are moved to make great effort on the spiritual path. We begin to see it as our holy duty and the purpose for which we have been created.

If we truly experience the power of God then our entire life will be transformed. The secret is to apply the second principle of spiritual transformation: prioritize. In other words, we must set up an ideal and live by it. The next step is to apply the third basic principle: put in a quality effort to realize our goal. This means that we must work for it with all our heart and soul. In every walk of life we see that life rewards action.

The student who puts in quality effort will succeed more quickly than others. On many occasions my master would ask, plead, and cajole us to apply ourselves toward our goals. I remember one incident when he questioned a particular disciple. The disciple then replied, "I will *try* to do it." He replied back forcefully, "Trying means half-hearted effort. Either you do it or you don't. Where there is a will there is a way. The world impossible is found in the dictionary of fools."[18] When we truly want something, our language reflects our intention. Most of us simply create excuses for not getting the job done. We say that we are too weak, too old, too this or that, but these are no more than limiting belief systems or self-fulfilling prophecies; they have no basis in reality. As my master would say, a strong man revels in his strength and a weak man wonders how he got it.

There is a story told of the French impressionist painter Monet, who suffered from extreme arthritis during the last part of his life. The pain was so great that even holding up the brush to paint was excruciatingly painful. When asked why he still continued to paint he replied, "The pain eventually fades, but the beauty remains."[19] As we struggle to deepen our spirituality we realize that the mystery of a beautiful life is a love that never fades. As we come to understand that divine love is the ultimate purpose of our existence, we gradually make greater and greater efforts to realize the Truth. In the end, we learn to transform every situation into an opportunity for spiritual growth and utilize every second to increase our love. Or, as Sant Rajinder Singh has said, "As the silken bonds of God's love tighten, chains to the physical world loosen."[20]

Rise to Universal Brotherhood and Consider All Beings Your Equals

Nanak continues:

And in the crucible of Love melt the nectar divine.

Like every great teacher, Nanak embodied the realization that love of God and love of all creation have been the cornerstones of every great religion. Wherever he went he brought a message of reconciliation and fellowship. True Religion, as Nanak preached, was founded on devotion, compassion, good deeds, and a direct connection to God's divine word, or Naam. He spread this message not only throughout India but to the north across the snow-capped Himalayas to Tibet and China, eastward into the modern states of Bengal and Burma, west to the Middle-Eastern countries of Baluchistan, Afghanistan, Persia, Arabia, and as far as Mecca, Jerusalem, Egypt, and Turkey.

During one of his travels to the north Nanak was imprisoned for preaching unity and reconciliation between the two prevailing religions, Hinduism and Islam. Barbur, who was the Mogul ruler at the time, is said to have had great reverence for all men of God, and when he came to know that Nanak had been imprisoned he ordered his immediate release. He then proceeded to question Nanak on a variety of issues. Nanak, in turn, counseled Barbur and offered him his sage counsel and a way out of the madness of inter-religious hatred. "Worship God everyday," he told the ruler, "be just and kind to everyone. He told him that Sat Naam, the Holy Word of God or *Kalma*, was a panacea for all ills of life here and in the hereafter." Finally he said, "Be pure and truth will reveal itself to thee. Have love of God uppermost in thy heart and hurt not the feelings of His creatures."[21]

Love alone has the power to purify us completely from the dross of the world. The message of divine love is the cornerstone of every major religion, and yet we have seen almost every major religion persecute and wage war in the name of God. What is true love? The great teachers answer that it is complete selflessness. Examples of this love do exist, but they are rare. Such love consumes everything except the object of our love. Sant Darshan Singh tells us:

The intensity of love
Melts life itself.
It is a candle, O Darshan
Which is consumed by its own flame.[22]

Love in its sublimity is ineffable and beyond description. If God is unlimited then so, too, is the experience of divine love, for God is love. In the game of love it is said that two is a crowd. The following story illustrates this point beautifully:

Once, a lover knocked at a friend's door.

The friend replied, "Who is there? Oh trusted one?"

The lover replied, "It's me."

The friend replied, "Leave, there no room for the likes of you."

So, the lover wandered in the wilderness of longing. As each day passed, his heart burned brighter and brighter in the fire of love's passion. Love is such a fire that leaves nothing left but the beloved. A year passed and he returned to the friend's door. With each approaching step he covered himself more tightly with the cloak of modesty and self-effacement.

He knocked on the door. The friend answered, "Who is there?"

The lover replied, "It's You, oh heart-ravisher."

The friend answered, "Since it is me, come in my Self"[23]

Truly, selfless love admits no ego and no "I-ness." But although we would all like an easy and effortless ride on the spiritual path, the true aspirant soon realizes that love is not as easy as it may appear to be. There is a story of a man who came to Socrates and asked to receive wisdom. Socrates told the young man to walk with him to the edge of the river, and once they had reached its banks he told the man to look into the water and describe what he saw.

"I see nothing," said the man.

"Look closer," Socrates instructed.

As the man leaned over to get a closer look, Socrates pushed his head under the water and held it there for some time. At first the man did nothing; but as his need for air increased, he began to violently shake and tried to escape. Finally, after great struggle, when the man was about to drown, Socrates released him and let him up for air. Coughing and gasping for air the man replied, "Why are trying to do kill me?"

"When I was holding you under the water what did you want more than anything else?" Socrates asked.

"I wanted to breathe. I wanted air."

"When your desire for truth is as great as your desire for air you will find the truth." Socrates replied.[24]

We would all love to have wonderful experiences of unconditional love, beauty, bliss, and joy, but somehow or another it doesn't really work out for us that way. Think about the last time you asked someone how they were doing and they said, "I have been feeling completely at peace for the last six months without interruption and unconditional love for everyone I met. Nothing makes any difference." When is the last time we heard that? Most of the time we can't go for even ten minutes without experiencing some unpleasantness, pain, difficulty, or strife. So there is a price to pay. The sad thing is that few realize the important fact that we must give up our old ways. This is especially ironic because the price we pay is actually nothing, for all we give up are transitory phenomena, a passing charade and deceptive illusion. In the end nothing real is lost because *love alone is real.*

What is real is never lost and never destroyed. Nevertheless, we experience pain. Why? Because we have developed attachments to our desires. When we look deeply at the inner spiritual journey, we see that it is filled with pathos, yearning, and intense longing. But this pain is different from the loss of worldly attachments. When we experience the loss of the sacred in our lives, all illusions disappear. How can we understand this from our present awareness? It is akin to being with the most loving and beautiful person imaginable...and then you have to leave. All of a sudden, your heartstrings are pulled and you start thinking of them all the time. You can't let the thought of them go. This is similar to what it's like once we have tasted something of the reality of love within us. No other experience can match the majesty of divine love. We want reality, but we can't have it until we are completely purified of all that is not reality. My master summarized this purifying process of love in the following verse:

> *Love is the flame which when it blazes,*
> *consumes everything other than the Beloved.*[25]

All different spiritual traditions have described the purifying journey of love. In the end, nothing but love remains. How can we understand this? It means every atom of ill will, revenge, unkindness, irreverence, insensitivity, and selfishness must go. All of these emotions are foreign to the essence of love.

In the field of mineralogy, gold is both incredibly durable and highly valuable. But it is rarely found it its pristine state in nature. Rather, it is often mixed with many other minerals in varying amounts. Unless the other substances are removed, the gold has little value. However, by heating gold to extreme temperatures these foreign minerals melt away; what remains is pure gold, which can last for thousands of years. In the same manner, divine love already exists within us but is mixed with our animal ego and desires. Until we remove the foreign substances our soul cannot ascend to its original home. How is this process accomplished? The alchemy of converting our base desires and animal ego into the pristine super substance of love is accomplished through intense longing, constant remembrance, incessant vigils, and selfless and compassionate actions. What is left at the end of this journey is neither lover nor beloved—only love. Having purified himself of all that is not God, the lover becomes an embodiment of all that is God. Until we are completely pure we cannot experience the unending ecstasy of God's love.

There is a famous story about the meeting between a great yogi named Swami Vedvyasanand and Sant Kirpal Singh. The yogi had been unwilling to meet with Sant Kirpal Singh because he considered him a householder and, therefore, beneath him in spiritual status. Sant Kirpal Singh was unconcerned about these matters and decided to visit the swami anyway in the interests of establishing fellowship between the different religions. The Swami was shocked to see that Sant Kirpal Singh had ignored his refusal; but he was even more shocked when Sant Kirpal gave him a huge hug. He later said that it felt "like a current of 8000 volts going through his body."[26] At that moment he recognized that the spiritual power working through Sant Kirpal Singh was far greater than he had ever imagined. From then on he worked side by side with him to help foster unity and fellowship between many faiths. If we can raise our level of receptivity then we can become conduits for this tremendous energy of love. But first we have to purify our inner being in order to receive that transmission.

Nanak continues:

Only in such a mint can man be cast into the Word.

One of the greatest mysteries of the spiritual path is the mystery of divine love. The more we love, the more we are called to sacrifice. Yet the more we sacrifice the greater our experience of complete joy and bliss. What does the symbol of the cross signify in the life of a true Christian? It is the sacrificing of the small, selfish, petty ego at the altar of divine love. This sacrifice produces pain at first, but deeper inside lays an experience of perfect peace.

In contemporary times, another votary of the gospel of love echoed the same message. "True love is love that causes us pain that hurts, and yet brings us joy," said Mother Teresa. "That is why we must pray to God and ask Him to give us the courage to love."[27] For her the very essence of Jesus' teachings is love: "The whole Gospel is very very simple. Do you love me? Obey my commandments. He (Christ) is turning and twisting just to get around to one thing. Love one another."[28] If there is one message that sums up the essence of all spiritual traditions it is summed up in what St. Paul called *agape*: altruistic, self-giving love. "Let all that you do be done in love."[29]

Take Refuge in God Alone

Nanak continues:

But they alone who are favored by him can take unto this path.

The spiritual journey is very long, but it is joyous. It is the work of lifetimes of searching, purification, and spiritual practice. In the Hindu tradition there is a well-known aphorism that the guru appears when the disciple is ready. That inner power is aware of our every move and is ready to assist us at every step. At the appropriate moment we are guided to the inner path and a competent teacher appears to help us. These events are not haphazard or by accident, but unfold according to divine plan.

My own spiritual master saw the inner radiant form of his teacher seven years before he met him in the physical form. During those years he thought it was the form of Guru Nanak that he was seeing inside. When he finally met his master on the banks of the river Beas, he asked him, "Maharaj, Why this delay in meeting thee?" His teacher replied, "This is the most opportune time."[30]

In the field of mysticism it is often said that love emanates from the heart of the beloved. Our love for God is only a response to God's love for us. It is the mother who first loves the child; the child's love is only reciprocal. The lost sheep cannot find the shepherd; it is the shepherd who finds the lost sheep. How can the spiritually deaf and blind find one who has spiritual sight and hearing? Nanak reaffirms the supremacy of God's will over our singular efforts that ultimately brings us to truth:

> *By His Will the pious obtain salvation,*
> *By His Will the impious wander in endless transmigration.*
> *All exists under His Will*
> *And nothing stands outside.*
> *One attuned with His Will, O Nanak, is wholly freed from ego.*[31]

In the summer of 1973, I had the great good fortune of spending three ecstatic months with Sant Kirpal Singh in India. I had arrived in Delhi in early June and, as the weather was exceedingly hot, he gathered the few Westerners visiting from abroad and some of his immediate family and traveled to the Kashmere, where the temperatures were much cooler. It was a blessed filled time overflowing with intimate and heartfelt moments with Sant Kirpal Singh. As per his instructions, our routine consisted of about eight to ten hours a day of meditation and two darshan sessions with him per day, one in the evening and one in the morning. On occasion we would travel with him to pristine natural parks, where we would enjoy the exquisite countryside, silence of nature, and the even greater blessings of Sant Kirpal Singh's majestic physical presence.

One afternoon, while we were all gathered in a circle, Darshan Singh's son and soon-to-be successor was telling stories about the Master. At one point, he remarked that is a great blessing to have a living master. Sant Kirpal Singh immediately sweetly interrupted him, and interjected, "No it is the greatest blessing to have a real master in one's life."[32] The air was filled with profound stillness as we watched Sant Kirpal Singh remember his own spiritual master, Hazur Baba Sawan Singh. A tear welled up in his eye and delicately rolled off his cheek. It was a magical moment filled with indescribable pathos and unbearable yearning. Suddenly all of us could feel a gush love of pouring through our hearts, ripping us open with an unquenchable longing for God. It was only a thimbleful's taste of our master's love, but it was beyond our frail human capacity to fathom. Within a few minutes every eye was moist with the pearls of longing and every heart beating in unison with his heart.

To be in the presence of such love is to experience firsthand the true meaning of God's unconditional love. I have thought about this incident many times, and each time the love wound grows deeper and more painful. But the pain is paradoxically filled with immense bliss. I still have not fathomed the value of a true master or the gift of love from such a being, but I do know that to have had that experience even for a moment is a blessing of ineffable beauty. It is a gift of grace, which cannot be earned.

Love Is the Ultimate Gift

It is this grace of which Nanak speaks in the final lines of the stanza:

> On whom he looks with grace,
> He fills with everlasting peace.

Over the years, I have pondered again and again the meaning of this verse. In the end, I have concluded that everything is a gift of grace. Even the cry for help is a response to God's love for us, for the hard of heart cannot cry out to God at all. Love is a gift. It cannot be earned, bartered, or bought. We must, of course, do our part and put in a sincere effort in our search for truth. But nothing we can do can ever even remotely equal the gift of love. Love—in its sublimity, majesty, and perfection—is peerless, priceless, and ineffable.

The ultimate secret of spiritual attainment was revealed in a question asked of Sant Kirpal Singh: "What made you acceptable in the eyes of your master, and how did you get from him all the instructions you are following?" His reply tells the story. "The only words I can say are, it was love—love that he gave me for himself. And that taught me everything."[33]

Grace is always unconditional. But grace is always present; it pours down upon us seven days a week, twenty-four hours a day. The real question is: are we receptive enough to be able to receive it?

A Life of Sacrifice

In order to receive grace we must live a life of compassion and service. But what does a life of compassionate service entail? First and foremost, it is a life of sacrifice. Nanak spent nearly half his life spreading the gospel of unity. Leaving his family, relations, and community, he traveled the length and breadth of India as well as the Middle East, Kashmere, and Sri Lanka. While in Mecca and Medina, he lay down weary and fatigued in a mosque with his feet pointing toward the Kaaba. When the local Mullah saw this act of sacrilege he kicked him and said, "Knowest thou not this is the House of God, and thou sleepest, with thy feet towards the holy Kaaba." Nanak, whose vision of God was unlimited, answered humbly, "Turn my feet in whichever direction God's House is not. The Mullah, who was well versed in the Qur'an, could not but agree, as it says in the Qur'an that God's house is everywhere, in the north as in the south, in the east as in the west."

Upon hearing that a man of God had entered the mosque, people gathered round and asked, "Who is the greater of the two, a Hindu or a Musalman?' The Guru replied, "Without good deeds, both will come to grief." Then they asked, "Of what religion are thou?' The Guru replied, "I am a mere man, made up of five elements, a puppet in the hands of God."[34]

Claiming allegiance to one religion or another does not absolve us of our evil actions. It is not what religion we claim, but our actions that claim us. Knowing the truth is not the same as living it. Nanak's message was simple: "Truth is High, but Higher still is true living."[35] We may profess truth, proclaim it from the mountaintops, but unless we are living examples of truth we are mere hypocrites. We must live the message of truth.

I can think of no better message for the world today, torn as it is by religious strife, hypocrisy, and fanaticism. To serve the poor, the orphans, the homeless and the sick—this is our real work. In the final analysis we will be judged by our actions, not whether we are Christian, Jew, Muslim, or Hindu. In my travels I have observed that many Americans are beginning to understand that what is important is not the religion we are born into or profess, but whether we practice the faith in our lives. In the end what matters is not our religious label but the love enshrined in our hearts. The acid test of all spirituality is the degree to which we live it.

In its day, Nalanda University, the first Buddhist university, promoted the essence of spiritual knowledge. It is said that one day Shil Bhadra, the head of Nalanda University, was asked what knowledge is. He replied, "My child, knowledge is perception of the principles or laws of life. And the best principle of life is fellow feeling—sharing with others what you have."[36] All knowledge is a gift to be shared with others. What good is knowledge if not shared for others' benefit? This is what is meant by generosity of spirit. If we look carefully at our own lives we will see that most of what we have achieved is the result of someone's generosity.

The mother sacrifices everything for the child's welfare. All of this is done selflessly, out of love for the child. Our knowledge is the gift of our teachers, who offered their time and attention to help us acquire the skills necessary to succeed. Often our material comforts are the result of someone else's financial assistance or sacrifice.

Without the loving sacrifice and generosity of others, where would we be in life? We are all the products of someone's gifts. To return those gifts is the essence of spirituality. Nanak recognized that out of this generosity of spirit a universal brotherhood and sisterhood could emerge. He said: "The highest Religion is to rise to universal brotherhood, aye to consider all creation as your equal."[37]

All great teachers tell us that true spirituality is based upon seeing all creation as our equal. There should be no high or low. Nanak considered that there was no greater sin than the spirit of separateness. In reality what separates us from one another is what separates us from God. Once we recognize the same light shinning in all, how can we reject any part of God's creation? Since everyone has arisen from the same source, all have the same privileges and rights from God. To respect those rights is the first principle of true compassion and generosity. If we cannot rise above the superficial differences of race, religion, nationality, and gender, then we can never recognize the universal ground of spirit in all. Nanak emphasized that we should all study together as likeminded students and experience in full consciousness the living presence of God.

The question is, how do we practice this in our own lives? How can we expand to see everyone as part of our own self? This is true community and true generosity. So long as we continue to see distinctions and divisions, we cannot rise to universal brotherhood. Nanak gave the substance of all life in a beautiful song:

> *I have turned my heart into a boat;*
> *I have searched in every sea;*
> *I have dwelt by rivers and streams;*
> *I have bathed at places of pilgrimage;*
> *I have eaten bitter and sweet;*
> *I have seen the remotest regions;*
> *And this I have learnt that he is the True Man*
> *Who loveth God and loveth man,*
> *And serving all abideth in eternal Love.*[38]

To be truly human, each of us must realize the love that is already within us. To imbibe that love two qualities are necessary: service and sacrifice. Once, while I was sitting with my master in India, he commented on the real task in front of us. "Who is a true human?" he said. "To serve others, to live for others, is really a criterion to know who is a man." What is at the bottom of this? It is to learn that "to serve others, to live for others, is really a criterion to know who is a man. We are all beasts in men."[39] When we realize that our own happiness is totally contingent upon the happiness of others, a radical shift takes place. The little "I" becomes a servant of the divine in each and every being. This is the essence of the path of compassionate service.

The Four Categories of Humans

It has been said that humanity can be divided into four distinct groups of people by seeing how we relate to each other. In the first category we have the people who believe that *what is mine is mine and what is yours is also mine.* These are the kind of people who want it all for themselves. No matter what these people receive, it will never be enough. They are always scheming and usurping the rights of others. Such people live only for themselves. They spend their time amassing possessions, power, and position at the expense of others. Sadly, the world is populated with far too many people of this variety.

The second category of people believes that *what is mine is mine and what is yours is yours.* These people are just in all their actions and dealings with others. They try to live by the golden rule: treat others as you wish to be treated. The vast majority of people fall into this group. You will often hear people like this say, "I have worked hard for everything and nobody is going to take it away. I deserve what I have been given." Such people respect others' rights and expect others to respect their rights. They do not covet others' possessions or try to usurp the rights of others. However, this is not really an expression of generosity, as it is still rooted in the realm of duality. Those of us who fall into this category have not seen beyond our little corner of the universe. Still it is much better than the previous view.

At the level of the third category, people believe that *what is mine is yours, and what is yours is also yours*. This attitude reflects real generosity of spirit. Those of us at this stage are able to see something beyond ourselves and recognize that we are all connected. The soul that understands this knows that we never loose anything when we give. Why? Because whatever we do to others, we ultimately do to ourselves. Jesus reminds us beautifully that, "Verily, I say unto you in as much as ye have done it to the least of these ye have done it unto me."[40] We are all connected. At this level, we realize that it is only by sharing with others that we can receive more ourselves. One of my teachers once said that love is the only commodity that, when given away, is never lessened. Ironically, we find that we have an even greater capacity to give than before. People in this third category never worry about receiving, but instead seek to constantly give to others. They have moved out of the realm of duality and operate under a higher law: the law of generosity born of love.

The fourth and highest category is characterized by an attitude that says: *What is mine is not mine and what is yours is not yours. It is all God's.* At this stage, duality has been fully transcended. There no longer exist any notions of "I" and "thou." We realize that only God and God alone exists. Therefore, any notion of individual ownership is absurd. Everything belongs to God and to Him are we all returning. This is the realm of the saints and mystics. It is the domain of perfect giving and true generosity.

Nanak and True Abundance

As a youth, Nanak was given the job of storekeeper in a local farmhouse. As a part of his job he was to sell wheat and other farm supplies to the local farmers. One day, it is said, Nanak was weighing the wheat on the scale for one of his customers when he came to the number thirteen. The word *tera* means thirteen, but it also means *Thine* or *God's*. As soon as Nanak repeated the word tera he went into a divine trance and lost himself in God. While in a state of divine intoxication he continued to repeat the word tera again and again. "I am thine, I am thine, I am thine." As he weighed out more and more wheat, the customer realized that Nanak's bounty was endless. When we understand that everything belongs to God, true generosity arises. It is only our limited ego that creates division and separation. Nanak saw that everything belonged to God because everything is God's.[41]

At this point it would be helpful to pause and review where we stand in our own journey. The following exercises may be useful tools in developing generosity.

Exercises in Developing Compassion

In reviewing the fundamental strategies for developing greater generosity, let us first be mindful that generosity arises from our hearts. Therefore, cultivating an attitude of inner charity precedes all true giving. If we can open our hearts to the boundless source from which all generosity arises, we can go a long way in awakening this quality in our daily lives. True service to others is a quality of giving characterized by grace and graciousness. When awakened it flows through us like a river, permeating everything we do and everyone we meet. The following four exercises may be useful tools in releasing the grace, which allows the spirit of giving to flow unimpeded.

Exercise One: Reviewing Our Life

In keeping with the spiritual principle of flexibility and adjustment, our first act of generosity is to make room for change in our lives. Let us be willing to review our life and see what changes we can make in order to incorporate a spirit of generosity and service.

Let us take a moment and review our life from the perspective of the four simple principles already mentioned above. First, take a moment and answer these questions on a separate sheet of paper or in a journal:

- In what areas in my life do I covet others' possessions, attainments, position, or power?

- In what areas of my life do I have an attitude of justice? In other words, in which areas will I respect others' rights so long as they respect mine?

- In what areas of my life do I become upset and eager to seek justice?

- Where do I give, but only if it does not really require much sacrifice?

- Where do I give, but with a certain level of expectation of return or compensation?

- Where do I give without expecting anything in return?

- In what areas of my life do I wish to share with others without a desire for acknowledgment?

Exercise Two: Seeing Beyond Boundaries

We have all had moments of transcendent giving, in which we see beyond boundaries, beyond me and mine, and reach to "thine." This is the sacred ground where we don't see ourselves as the giver or others as the receiver. We become conduits for the inner river of grace and giving that comes directly from the infinite source — God. Ask yourself the following questions:

- When do I give, share, or offer without awareness of the needs, expectations, or desires of my individual self?

- When do I spontaneously sacrifice myself for others without thinking of myself as a separate individual?

- How often do I allow my heart to feel the boundless happiness of giving joyously to others?

- How often do I see my acts as arising from the source of all giving within me and within others?

- How often do I see God alone as the source of all goodness, blessings, and grace in me and in others?

Exercise Three: Expanding Our Sense of Giving

After taking this initial inventory, many of us may find that we are far from our highest aspirations and goals. We may even find that we have barely begun. But in the next step, reflect a little more deeply on when you have given selflessly. Think of a moment when you gave without any desire for reward, purely for the joy of giving. Describe that incident. While you do so think about:

- How do you expand the notion of self?

- How do you learn to deepen your sense of community?

- Where are you called to express your unique gifts and understanding?

- Where are you challenged or blocked from expressing deeper levels of fellowship, commitment, and love?

As we learn to expand our sense of self, our practice of giving expands as well. In this exercise it is useful to note in a journal all the times in which you were called to serve or give in some way, but did not. What is important here is not how much you gave but, ultimately, how much loving you put into the giving.

Review these guidelines to see in what manner the giving was done:

- Was the giving done with a smile on your face?

- Was it offered with joy in your heart?

- Was it given without desire for any reward, inner or outer?

- Did you serve others to the best of your ability?

- Did you serve or give to completion and with attention to detail?

- Did you serve or give without concern for how others received it?

Exercise Four: Creating a Blueprint for Compassionate Service

Keeping all the above in mind, let us review Nanak's simple outline for cultivating a daily practice of compassionate service:

1. **Seek the highest knowledge.** Prioritize your life's goals and put spirituality and selfless giving as one of the highest purposes in your life's journey.

2. **Kindle a spirit of holy dedication.** Once you have understood your life's true purpose, do not waste a single moment before putting in a sincere and quality effort that reflects the importance of this goal in your life. Start today.

3. **Remember god continuously.** Every day, every hour, and every moment cultivate the inner remembrance of God. This can be done by selecting any name of God with which you resonate (Jehovah, God, Allah, Rahem, Ram, Krishna, and Sat Naam).

   - Begin a simple, daily, inner invocation of this name, gradually invoking the presence of God through his heartfelt deep remembrance.

4. **Rise to universal brotherhood and sisterhood.** The goal of universal brotherhood and sisterhood is not a hopeless dream of starry-eyed idealists; it is an essential inner practice to be cultivated on a daily basis. True generosity begins by recognizing the intrinsic and essential equality of all humanity and, indeed, all sentient life.

- Begin by treating all beings as equals, no matter their station, education, wealth, power, or prestige.

5. **Love is letting go of what is not real.** If we can recognize that only love lasts in the end, letting go of what is impermanent and non-essential becomes much easier and, indeed, joyous. If we can see that everything ultimately belongs to God, then we can become conduits for his boundless generosity. Since everything must be relinquished one day, why not start today?

   - Each day, release first mentally and then physically one of the non-essentials in your life. By letting go continuously, you will open the floodgates of grace and generosity to flow through you. With this in mind, try to relinquish something every day.

6. **Attune yourself to the divine will.** To see God's will wrought in our daily lives is an act of true giving. We have to give over our limited version of events and meaning to see the Creator's greater wisdom in all things. How can this be done?

   - Begin a practice of meditation. Start your day with at least fifteen minutes of meditation. This is your gift to the Creator. Meditation opens the heart to see the transcendent in the ordinary and the will of the Creator wrought in every detail of life.

7. **Give Continuously to Others.** Shape your life around the realization that generosity is essential for our spiritual health.

   - Make it a habit to do something for someone each day, no matter how small or large. Keep in mind that it is not how much you give that matters, but how much love you put into the giving.

We find in the Buddhist Bodhisattva vow a perfect illustration of this ultimate stage of boundless inner charity or infinite generosity. This vow declares that as long as there is a single sentient being who has not attained salvation, the Bodhisattva will remain in this world to help them reach the other side. Of course, reaching this stage may appear overly idealistic and beyond the realm of ordinary humans. But let me suggest that only when all beings are free from suffering are we truly free ourselves. The highest form of liberation is the liberation of all. We are all part of the cosmic body of Christ, the all-encompassing Buddha nature; the microcosm is ultimately in the macrocosm. When one suffers, we all suffer. This is secret to creating a true global community.

Darshan Singh

Chapter Seven
Darshan Singh: The Path of Self-effacement and Positive Mysticism

What does it Matter if I am called a man
In truth I am the very soul of Love
The entire earth is my home
And the universe my country.[1]
—Sant Darshan Singh

aised from birth in the august presence of two great twentieth-century saints, Sant Darshan Singh often credited his early spiritual propensities to being born into a family immersed in the spirit. Each morning when we awoke he would see his mother and father sitting in meditation and, although he had no knowledge of what they were doing, squat down beside them to imitate. Then, at the tender age of five, he gathered the courage "in both hands," as Sant Darshan would say, and approached the illustrious sage of Beas, Hazur Baba Sawan Singh Ji Maharaj. With childlike reverence, he asked Hazur to be initiated into *Naam*. The great sage smiled and handed him some sweets, saying, "Here is your *enaam*." Enaam is an Urdu word for reward or prize.

The young boy scampered off with what he thought was the same gift his father had been given—the Naam that, centuries early, Kabir had called *Shabda*, Nanak had called *Sat Naam*, and

Rumi and Hafez had called the Ancient Word (*Kalam i Qadim*), Light of God (*Nur Allah*), or Sound from the Heaven (*Bang i Asmani*). Soon, however, he realized that the sweets were not what he was seeking. He went back to Hazur and asked him again for Naam. When he reached out to give the young boy some more sweets, Darshan pleaded, "I want the same Naam which you given to my Bauji (father)." On hearing his reply, Hazur said, "All right, you come back in the afternoon."

When he returned, Hazur was sitting in his room with his usual regal demeanor. He motioned for young Darshan to sit before him. Gently placing his thumb on the boy's forehead, he told him to concentrate within. Darshan quickly rose above body consciousness and began describing the different mystical lights that he was witnessing within. When he reached the level of the *inner stars* Hazur remarked, "That is sufficient for the time being. You can have the rest later."

Darshan, as he later recalled, was so elated that when he saw his father coming he cried out in jubilation, "Father, father, how far have you got Naam? I have got it up to the stars."[2]

For the next four decades he dedicated himself both inwardly and outwardly to the perfection of his spiritual life. He found the luminous revelation of the great poets-saints, including Nanak, Kabir, Rumi, Hafiz, Khwaja Mir Dard, St. Teresa of Avila, and St. John of the Cross, and, following humbly in the footprints of his illustrious teachers, he later became a living fountain of the great spiritual current of the Sant Tradition. In time he was honored as one of India's most revered mystic poets and saints. Through his scintillating Sufi verses, he offered a new emanation from the fountain of pre-eternal divine light. But although he was acclaimed as one of the foremost Urdu mystic poets, his teachings were accessible to all.

Sant Darshan, as he was later addressed, embodied a remarkable living presence. Through the simple touch of his hand or with a glance he could awaken the dormant spirituality in each of us. Revered as one of India's most beloved saints, he mixed freely with the masses and acted like an ordinary man. But he was far from ordinary.

I often visited India in the early days of Sant Darshan's mission and attended many large-scale events. One particular event, however, not only captivated me personally but gave me a glimpse into the irresistible humanity of this saint. Once, while Sant Darshan Singh was sitting in front of a crowd of over ten thousand people, he abruptly walked off the stage. He moved stealthily through the immense crowd to a man who was being held against his will at the back of the congregation. Incoherent and ranting wildly, the man's presence threatened the peace and tranquility of the near pin-drop silence of the gathering. Sant Darshan Singh approached the two security guards who held him forcibly, and instructed them to release the struggling man immediately. The guards cautioned the Master that he was out of control and threatened his safety. But Sant Darshan insisted, so they released him.

As he held the man gently yet firmly on the arm, Sant Darshan told him, "Look into my eyes." Within minutes the man's violent movements subsided and he started to calm down. Sant Darshan requested a cup of water and then gently fed the man himself. Only five or ten minutes had passed, but the once raving man had now calmed down completely. As the man continued to gaze into Sant Darshan's eyes, his face went through a miraculous transformation. The frenzy and fear departed and a new serenity now radiated from his face.

Soon the man returned to normal, but something wonderful had transpired beyond the obvious visible signs of his physical relief. Master Darshan walked quietly back to the dais, where he resumed his discourse where he left off. I stood wonderstruck at both the power and accessibility of this man, and many of us left that day wondering what had *really* happened. To me, nothing more aptly describes the accessibility, openness, and extraordinary graciousness of Sant Darshan Singh, or the immediacy of his teaching.

Positive Mysticism: Becoming Fully Human

Like his illustrious predecessors, Hazur Baba Sawan Singh and Param Sant Kirpal Singh, Sant Darshan brought a modern perspective to the exacting traditional disciplines of mysticism. In his poetry the reader will find subjects ranging from personal relationships to spiritual practices, work, play, healing, and service. One of his most profound innovations was the call for *positive mysticism,* a term he coined to encourage the pursuit of spirituality while proactively engaged in the world. This included not only fulfilling the normal responsibilities of an adult life, including earning an honest livelihood and raising a family, but also taking an active interest in the local, national, and international issues that we as global citizens all face. It was this new approach, which wedded the age-old traditions of mysticism with the exacting demands and difficulties of living in today's modern world, for which he may well be remembered.

Master Darshan was unconcerned with national affiliation or religious background, professing that all human beings are endowed with the same spark of divine consciousness. As such he attracted seekers from all religions, cultures, ethnicities, and nations. Tens of thousands came to hear his illuminating discourses and receive the *darshan,* or glance of a living saint. An enchanting storyteller and master of metaphor, he drew upon common events, myth, and folktales to capture the imagination of his audiences. He unhesitatingly poured out the cup of divine love to all souls regardless of religious affiliation, social status, or background. Most of all, like all truly great human beings he offered "the way of the heart," a path stripped of dogma and artifice that led to inner illumination through the perfection of our humanity. As such, it was a path uniquely suited to bridge the world of work and career with silence and meditation.

His approach was simple and universal. He embraced the goals that all spiritual traditions share and the ideals that all religions espouse. He sought to ignite the embers of peace within each individual and embraced each as a literal member of his own family. His profound knowledge of both the Abrahamic and Vedic religions, combined with his mastery of Urdu, Persian, English, and Punjabi languages, allowed him to see the spiritual horizons from a multi-religious, multi-cultural perspective and make each person feel spiritually at home.

Sant Darshan's poetry illuminates the stages of the inner journey in startling simplicity and detail. Like that of Hafiz, his poetry provides us with a precise inner mapping of the stages and states of the inner journey, often referred to as *hal* (state) and *muqam* (stage) in Sufism. This universal inner roadmap provides a steady light and sure guidance on the path — regardless of our background, religion, or stage of evolution.

First Steps on the Path

From the moment he was initiated into the mysteries of the beyond by Hazur Baba Sawan Singh Ji Maharaj, at the age of five, Master Darshan passionately dedicated all his energies to treading the spiritual path inwardly and outwardly. When his own Master passed on in 1948, he continued his spiritual growth under the compassionate guidance of his father, His Holiness Param Sant Kirpal Singh Ji, who took over the work of Hazur Baba Sawan Singh.

In one of his own works, *A Tear and Star*, Sant Darshan begins with a reflection on the paradoxical nature of our first steps on the mystic path:

> *I started alone on the journey of love, filled with faith and zeal*
> *At every step, travelers joined me and soon we were a caravan.*[3]

In this opening verse he explains that though we start alone on the spiritual journey, our initial steps on the path are often filled with seemingly boundless joy and limitless vistas of hope. Once we taste even a single drop of the unconditional love of God, we experience a powerful urge to return to our Source. We are not the same again and our life now turns irresistibly to God.

However, we may also find as we move forward that few family members or friends share our newfound aspirations and yearnings. They may even be critical or disrespectful of our new direction. At these moments we should remember that the seed of spirituality ripens in each one of us at its own time. There is no imposition in spirituality, and we cannot force our spiritual longings on others. It is during these times that our faith is often tested and we begin to see how deep our aspirations really are.

In time, as we mature in love and become seasoned, we are not affected by the approval or disapproval, praise or blame of family, friends, or the world. We stand firm and solid in our convictions. We realize that everyone is on his or her own journey and each must go their own way. As we move forward we find new friends who share our aspirations. If we are true to our inner principles the seed of spirituality begins to grow and our light begins to shine. Jesus tells us, "You shall know them by their fruits. Do men gather grapes of thorns or figs of thistles? Even so every good tree bringeth forth good fruit."[4] If our lives begin to reflect our values, people will automatically become attracted to our way of life. In my own experience as a teacher I have noticed that people pay little attention to what we say but watch closely how we act.

We see that early in the history of Christianity Christ's followers were mocked and jeered, but that later they were hailed and praised. If we truly walk the talk, our lives will impact others. Slowly, without us ever having to say a thing, other people will begin to see how we have changed for the better. My master called this the *spiritual revolution*. First we change ourselves and then we change others through radiation. This message has ignited thousands to become the change we seek, as Gandhi put it. The real life of the spirit is not about converting others but about converting ourselves first. If we can become pure conduits for the love, compassion, and mercy of God then we can transform the world. But we can only do so by becoming true human beings ourselves.

Positive Mysticism: Becoming Fully Human

What is the hallmark of a true spiritual giant? They build loving community and fellowship wherever they are. They make a concerted effort to strengthen the silken threads of love in all arenas of life—at work, at home, and especially in their spiritual communities. Sant Darshan skillfully guided us to become ideal spouses, loving parents, and responsible colleagues. He showed us how we can balance the demands of home and career life successfully. Most importantly, he taught us how to become fully human in the midst of all our pressing outer demands and duties.

Continuing *A Tear and a Star*, Sant Darshan writes:

> *O Cupbearer, let those long divided embrace one another,*
> *And through the intoxication of your love make all mankind*
> *   truly human.*[5]

This verse echoes the universal theme of all great masters, which is the development of our humanness. He made it clear that a life of solitude may be conducive to prolonged meditation, but the daily challenges of work, marriage, and family life afforded their own unique opportunities leading to accelerated spiritual growth. Monastic life could not be for everyone and, indeed, few these days are attracted to a solitary life in some remote hermitage. Today's seekers need a more accessible approach, one that can be achieved by living in the here and now. Positive mysticism emphasizes that spirituality is best achieved by fulfilling our role in society with joy and dedication, while remaining detached from the results of our efforts. Inner renunciation is required and is best achieved while living in the midst of life. Each of us has been placed in circumstances that will afford us the maximum spiritual progress. Viewed from this perspective, *life itself is our monastery and the night is our jungle.*

Sant Darshan Singh stressed that work is a kind of worship, in the sense that honest work is a training ground for leading an ethical life. If we cannot support ourselves through honest means, we have little hope of leading a Godly life. Positive mysticism is more than leading a balanced life; it requires a complete metamorphosis and change of heart. But how are all our imperfections to be removed? How can we convert anger into forgiveness and lust into divine love? How can one sinking in the quagmire of ego save oneself by one's own efforts alone? Master Darshan advised us to take firm hold of the hem of someone who had achieved this transformation and follow his advice implicitly. Spiritual adepts teach us to rest our hopes in a Higher Power and not to rely on our own efforts alone. Still, many of us ignore this wisdom and realize its truth only later, by trial and error.

The Art of Alchemy

The development of our humanness can be likened to the art of alchemy—a process by which the iron of ego is turned into the gold of God-consciousness. The work of the master teacher is the transformation of the disciple into a God-conscious soul while he or she is living responsibly in the world. There is no need to retreat to the jungles, forests, or mountaintops; yet many seekers often fail to grasp this simple fact. The true Master does not give us anything we do not already possess, because each of us is already divine in nature. That glory is now hidden. As Sant Rajinder Singh says, "The spiritual Master shows us how to tap within ourselves. He teaches a method by which each person can contact the divine love already within. He is a *catalyst* that lights the fire of divine love within. A true spiritual Master is one who gives us the key to open our own heart to the divine love."[6]

Sant Darshan understood that spirituality is not a spectator sport. It requires full participation in the processes of self-discovery and self-mastery. Each of us needs to exercise and develop our own inner muscles of truthfulness, insight, and detachment. With an awakened heart and insightful mind we can gradually plant the seeds of forgiveness and contentment, which eventually grow into the fruit of unselfish love and compassion. The path of positive mysticism encourages people to speak openly about their problems and not engage in negative thinking, self-deception, or self-condemnation. One incident in my own life helped awaken me to this reality and brought home to me the necessity of both self-mastery and self-honesty.

In early October 1980, I had decided to visit Sant Darshan Singh in India. However, I had left my home in the United States with a somewhat ambivalent attitude. While I sincerely longed to spend time in meditation, certain unresolved problems with my wife were eating away at my heart. Nevertheless, against my better judgment I decided to go to India in the hopes of clarifying and resolving those problems.

When I arrived I quickly fell into the daily-required routine of sitting for eight to ten hours per day. For the first few days, I was immersed in the bliss of prolonged meditation and the unfathomable joy of basking in a spiritual Master's presence.

While my routine seemed effortless, however, it also may have helped to mask some of the inner turmoil I was experiencing. Not long after I arrived I came down with a mild cold. It was nothing serious and, in fact, nothing unusual, for many Westerners often came down with colds when they came to India. The weather could get cold in the evening and, since there was no heating in the rooms, mild colds, flu, and other ailments were not unusual. It was, however, unusual for me. I rarely got colds and usually acclimated myself well to the Delhi's inclement weather. One day, while was sitting for my mid-morning meditation, I heard a knock at the door. At first I decided to ignore it, as I assumed it must have been a mistake. I knew that my roommate had the key, and I figured that anyone else could wait until I came down for lunch. However, a second a third knock followed in quick succession. I decided that I needed to attend to it, whoever it was.

When I opened the door there stood Sant Darshan Singh starring me straight in the face. Behind him was a group of over fifteen smiling disciples. I was wonderstruck. This was most unusual. Rarely if ever did he visit disciples in their rooms unless there was something seriously wrong. As I stood there a thousand thoughts rushed through my head. He was smiling and had a most mischievous look on his face. The sun shone brightly and the sky was perfectly blue. He beamed joyously, and with a twinkle in his eye he asked, "Are your sick?"

I replied, "No master," then I thought for a second and said, "I don't think so."

He then looked at me with a most enchanting and delightful smile and asked, "Are you sure you are not homesick?"

The play on the words "home" and "sick" brought an instant round of laughter from everyone. I didn't know what to say. My mind blanked and I tried to compose myself. But I was struck dumb. As I stood awkwardly at the door, Sant Darshan himself broke out into a thunderous laughter. Soon everyone joined in. I said nothing but inwardly blushed.

Then he paused briefly and said, with great mirth, "Don't' worry it doesn't hurt to tell the truth sometimes." Again, everyone broke out in spontaneous laughter. As I stood there trying to figure everything out, the Master turned around and left. I was left wondering what had happened.

At first I didn't get it. Then, minutes later, I it struck me like a bolt of lightening. It was too perfect for words. Indeed, I was sick. I was sick with regret over my unresolved problems and with worry over the future. My body may have been in India, but my heart was at home with my problems. Shortly afterward, I realized an even deeper truth — a painful truth that I had not been able to admit to myself or anyone else. The Master had hit the bulls' eye. The ultimate, capital t Truth was that I was hiding from myself. I was hiding from any truth that was unpleasant or painful and, in fact, hiding from a deeply held fear of being wrong or less than the image I wanted others to see.

This realization was devastating and completely turned my world upside down. The more I looked at it, the more deeply it resonated. I realized that this was the process of real transformation and the path of positive mysticism. Real change requires brutal self-honesty and fearlessness — not once in a while, but from moment to moment. How can we follow this powerful teaching? Sant Darshan outlined the path in four unique stages and three cardinal practices.

The Four Stages of Spiritual Development

The entire spiritual journey can be divided into four distinct stages. The first of these can be compared to the exoteric side of religion. Here the aspirant learns how to follow the outer rites, rituals, and moral code of his or her particular faith or religious tradition. These tenets include instruction for how to perform specific ceremonies, the celebration of certain holidays, and a basic understanding of our religious scriptures. In essence, this stage lays down the outer aspect of how we should conduct our life.

The second stage is entering into a mystical path (*Tariqat*) via initiation by a competent spiritual Master. In this stage the seeker gains knowledge of the inner life and tastes his or her first experiences of the mysteries of the beyond. Here begins the long journey of inner purification and cultivation of the spiritual qualities of love, compassion, truth, and humility. This process has been termed the "dark night of the soul" by St John of the Cross and other Christian mystics. This is really the path of developing our full humanity and the ennobling attributes that are prerequisites for the next stage.

The third stage is gaining knowledge of the inner reality or higher self (*Ma'rifat*, or *gnosis*) and the ultimate merger in one's own spiritual Master, known as *fana-fil-shaykh*. In this stage the soul gains full knowledge of whence it has come and where it will go at the moment of death. It now recognizes itself as soul and of the same essence as its Creator. The soul that has awakened to it true nature clearly sees the causes that have set its life in motion and how the intricate system of cause and effect is administered. Here the seeker sees with light of God the unity in the apparent multiplicity of phenomena, and becomes a true seer of the hidden dimensions of the universe.

The fourth stage is direct experience of the ultimate Truth (*Haqiqat, Sat*, or *Theosis*). *Haq* in Sufism and *Sat* in Sant Mat, which also means God, indicate that we have merged our individual essence with that of our Creator. This fourth and final stage begins only after we have crossed all the higher stages, where we ultimately become submerged in the ocean of all consciousness. This is the stage where our final objective is reached and we become one with our Creator, or *fana-fil-Allah*. This is the stage in which Jesus declares unambiguously, "I and my Father are One."[7]

The Three Essential Practices

This entire journey can be accomplished through three core practices: 1) *Self-Knowledge* and the development of ethical qualities through a system of self- introspection and self-analysis; 2) *Meditation*, or the science of withdrawal of the consciousness, also known as "dying while living"; and 3), *Satsang*, or association with Truth. "Sat" literally means truth and "sang" the company of truth.

Taken together it refers to the outer association with a Master Soul, or *Satguru,* who is the living embodiment of truth, or, where this is not possible, the association with the words of a Master soul instead.

Pillar One: Becoming a True Human Being

Let us review in more detail how this first pillar of ethical development is actually practiced. Ethical perfection can be defined as an inner cleansing of all the blemishes or impurities adhering to our soul. Most great spiritual traditions have incorporated some system to attain this requisite state of inner purity. In Judaism, Moses gave out the Ten Commandments; in Christianity, Jesus gave out the 10 beatitudes. Likewise, Buddha taught the eight-fold path, and Prophet Muhammad the practice of *Shariat,* or moral codes. The great Sant Saints understood the profound similarity between religious and spiritual traditions and, to this end, offer a systematic and scientific method of personal transformation that anyone can practice, regardless of religious or spiritual traditions. In this way they not only remove any cultural barriers to approaching the divine but also provide a sound, scientific basis for ethical development. After centuries of critical, first-person experimentation and firsthand experience they have developed an inner science or technology of spiritual-realization.

It is interesting to note that in recent years a field of academic inquiry has developed called Contemplative Studies, which seeks to understand this inner science. This new field has sought to study the "inner technology" of inquiry through third-person critical investigation along with internal first-person experiences. In essence, this age-old mystical science attempts to analyze the soul from mind, matter from spirit, and to understand the pristine nature of consciousness itself. This simple system frees the "embodied" consciousness from its self-created, self-imposed prison of habituated, reactive, and conditioned thinking patterns. These patterns, developed over hundreds of lifetimes, form the basis of our *pralabhð karma*, or destiny.

According to Sant Mat, spirituality can be approached in an objective and scientific manner. If we analyze the situation we see that four factors affect our spiritual progress: 1) our background, 2) the amount of time regularly allotted for contemplative practices (i.e. prayer and meditation), 3) the degree of inner yearning and one-pointed focus, and 4) the energetic boost (grace) of a living master. Since we cannot control what has happened in the past (*pralabhð karma*), we should not worry about that. What we can control is our present actions (*kriyaman karma*). Speaking to this theme, Sant Kirpal said, "There are those who come with very good past background but do little in this life. Others, who come with little or no background but practice regularly, will progress faster than those with good background."[8]

The secret to success lies in our present actions in three areas: 1) self-knowledge, 2) meditation, and 3) association with a true master. Let us remember principle number four: life rewards action. The details of this practice can be summarized as follows.

Step One: Self-knowledge — Keep a Spiritual Journal

The first step in our journey toward self-knowledge is to keep a detailed, ongoing spiritual journal or record of our failures in thought, word, or deed in seven categories: truth, non-violence, love and compassion, selfless service, chastity, humility, and spiritual practice. The purpose of this spiritual journal is to analyze or separate truth from falsehood, consciousness from matter, and reality from illusion. Many of the great traditions have stated that unless we know who we are, we cannot know our Creator. Self-knowledge precedes God-knowledge.

Western mysticism is based on a deep search for self-understanding. The early Greek philosophers predicated the entire search for wisdom on the dictum "Man Know Thyself," or *Anthrop gnothie seauton*. Plato tells us, "I must first know myself," and as the Delphic inscription says, "to be curious about that which is not my concern, while I am still in ignorance of my own self, would be ridiculous."[9] St. Augustine, the great theologian of the early Byzantine Church, also used to pray, "Let me know myself, Lord, and I shall know you."[10] Similarly, in a famous Hadith, a disciple asked Prophet Mohammed, "What am I to do so that I do not waste time." He replied, "Learn to know yourself."[11]

In this first step the goal is to realize experientially that we are a tri-partite being composed of a body, mind, and soul. Without knowing our true self, how can we know God? The great Vedic sages reaffirmed this same truth when they declared unhesitatingly, "What is that, the knowledge of which makes everything else known?" and in the same breath replied, "Knowledge of the higher self—the true man."

This process can be divided into four phases:

1. Knowledge of our physical characteristics, mental habits and emotions, and the nature of the physical mind.

2. Knowledge of our subtle emotional body and the astral world in which it exists.

3. Knowledge of our casual or seed body, which represent our latent tendencies going back thousands of lifetimes.

4. Knowledge of Higher Self, which is consciousness itself.

The fundamental principle or purpose behind the recording of one's inner thoughts, words, and deeds is to discern this higher Self within us. This practice is done on a daily basis, free from self-pity, self-condemnation, or self-loathing. It can be likened to the actions of a conscientious gardener who inspects his garden each day, carefully pulls up the weeds, waters the flowers, and provides the necessary nutrients for the plants to grow abundantly. In the same way, each day an aspirant must first record diligently his or her shortcomings in nonviolence, truthfulness, greed, and ego. Next, he or she must dispassionately but insightfully weed out the failures in each category, and lastly, replace negative tendencies and actions with positive ones. In this metaphor, our mind is the garden, the gardener is our higher consciousness, and the weeds are negative thoughts, words, and deeds.

The first step in this process is acknowledging the weeds of anger, falsehood, vanity, greed, and lust, as well as the inner tendencies, negative mental loops, habituated thinking patterns, and reactive thinking patterns. As easy as this may sound, it is in fact very difficult. Most of us are not prepared to admit our mistakes even to ourselves. Yet our tendency to cover up or overlook our mistakes is overcome over time through painstaking self-honesty and thorough examination of our flaws. When we do finally admit our mistake there is an inner delight and an exhilarating sense of liberation. It is as if we have been released from the thought prison of our own making.

Step Two: Locate the Error

Acknowledging our errors and mistakes is a powerful step in the right direction, but not enough by itself. A good gardener does more than just notice the weeds; he must take steps to remove them. Removing these blemishes upon the soul can be greatly aided by further identifying the specific situations, environments, or moods in which these negative thoughts, words, and deeds arise. To isolate the root cause of our errors, we should search our life history for clues to the originating circumstance.

Sant Kirpal Singh has said that if we can identify where these negative impulses and tendencies are mostly likely to occur we go to the root of the problem. As we delve deeply into our inner life we find that certain situations provoke or engender negative responses. Someone may say something which irritates us or annoys us and we respond with unkindness or impatience. The important thing to understand is that this is a learned response, which has become habituated over time. We no longer think through our reactions but, instead, simply react. In her ground breaking book *Minding the Body, Mending the Mind,* Joan Borysenko called these habituated patterns "dirty tricks department of the mind,"[12] because they manage to fool us into repeating these patterns again and again.

The good news is that all these kinds of reactive thinking patterns can be unlearned. But it is not enough to just watch the mind; after identifying the root cause, we must then reprogram the mind by *re-scripting* our response in the light of our higher aspirations. This is accomplished by internally visualizing our new response, and then practicing it until it becomes a habit. This is an entirely rational process in which we simply replace one behavior for another. Naturally, this may take some time.

Even this step, however, is not sufficient to overcome deeply ingrained habits and tendencies that have become embedded in our character. Such habits develop into the equivalent of automatic software systems that run subliminally in the computer of our mind. I use the word sub-liminal because they operate below the threshold of our conscious awareness. The first step is to de-install them. To do that there must be a high level of internal sincerity.

Step Three: Self-honesty

Real transformation at the deepest levels can only occur if it is motivated by a deep and sincere desire for change. How many of us profess we want to change to our friends or family but inwardly continue to desire and think about those very things? It is as if we are praying, "Oh God please remove this terrible defect from me…but not quite yet." We cannot fool God or our higher Self. After all, why should God bother to help us if we have no real desire to help ourselves?

Here we must bring into practice the third principle of self-transformation: one-pointed concentration and quality effort. All the great teachers of humanity speak in one voice on this subject.

Even re-scripting how we will act in the future will fail if it is not accompanied by a profound commitment and one-pointed concentration on our goal. Here is where many seekers stumble and fall: We do not seek real change, but deceive ourselves. We act, but more out of ritual, mechanical habit or outer necessity than sincere desire for change. In so doing our actions—though outwardly correct—are out of sync with our real intentions. It is no wonder, then, why our behavior does not change. Sant Rajinder Singh told a humorous story that brings this point home.

Once, a deaf man was advised that a friend had taken ill. He realized that he was obligated to make a visit, but because he was quite hard of hearing it would be hard to communicate with the sick man—especially as his friend was ill and his voice was weak. So, he devised a plan.

When I see his lips move, the deaf man thought to himself, I will assume a logical answer based on what I would say if I were in his situation. When I say, "How are you, my friend?" he will probably reply, "I am fine," or "I am doing well." Then, I will naturally reply back, "Great. Thank God. What remedy have you been taking?" He will most likely say, "A mixture of various pills and ointments," to which I will reply, "That's great. I am glad you're in good health. By the way who is your doctor?" Then he'll tell me "so and so," and I will respond by saying, "I have heard that he is a wonderful doctor. I'm sure he will bring you back to health."

In this way, based on his seemingly logical conjectures, the deaf man prepared to visit his friend. When he reached the house he asked, "How are you?"

The sick man said, "I am at the point of death."

"Oh thank God", cried the deaf man. When the sick man heard this he naturally became indignant. Inwardly he thought to himself: What possible cause for thanksgiving is this? He seems more like my enemy than my friend!

Unbeknownst to the deaf man, his conjecture had turned out to be folly. Unfortunately, he continued on, asking his friend what he had drunk.

"Poison" said the sick man.

"That's wonderful," replied the deaf man. "I am sure it will bring you good health!"

Upon hearing these senseless remarks the sick man was barely able to contain his anger.

But the deaf man inquired again, "Which doctor is seeing you?"

His friend replied, "The angel of death is coming. Get out of here."

The deaf man nodded and smiled. "Thank God for that," he said. "May his arrival bring you good health. And now please excuse me for I must leave."

As the two parted ways for what would be the last time, the sick man said in horror, "My God, he is not a friend, but my worst enemy!"[13]

This wonderful story hints at the subtle nature of self-deception and inner duplicity. It is also a fierce reminder of the dangers of making assumptions about what others think or how they might respond to us. In reality, many people who do works of charity are more concerned with being approved of and rewarded for their so-called pious actions than they are with the joy of service. For this reason all their actions are fruitless. In the same way that the deaf man thought he was being kind and dutiful, in reality his words had the opposite effect. The deaf man (in all of us) has a high opinion of his own actions and says to himself "I have paid my respects, I have performed what was due to my neighbor"; but in reality all we have done is kindle a fire of resentment and anger. While we may publicly admit our wrongdoing, we seldom question our actions in private. The truth is, however, that we often unintentionally hurt others and inflict more pain than we ever care to admit or even imagine. Our seeming righteousness is little more than filthy rags.

Correcting our errors requires an honest and thorough self-assessment followed by a sincere desire to change. The aspiration must come from the deepest core of our being. From this wellspring we can then ask ourselves, "What can I do differently to change my thoughts, words, and deeds?" For me, admitting that I was afraid to tell the truth because it portrayed me in a bad light was not an easy step. Here Shakespeare's famous adage rings true, "This above all; to thine own self be true, and it must follow as the night the day, thou canst not then be false to any man."[14]

Of course, it is the ego that blinds us to our own faults and paints a rosy picture of who we are. If we can take the first step, which is honesty and sincere self-assessment, then the inspiration and true aspiration to change will open up. The reality is that God gives us what we really want anyway. So who are we fooling? Jesus sums this spiritual truth up when he tells us, "For where your treasure is there will be your heart."[15]

Step Four: Inner Detachment and Resolve

Once our desire for real change is sincere, we need to cultivate a deep inner resolve to make the necessary changes in our lives. Then we have to stick to it. This resolve should be so strong that it does not allow us to be influenced by any form hypocrisy, insincerity, or desire for recognition. The example of the lotus flower, which floats on top of the pond but is never soiled by the muddy water, expresses the concept that we should live in the world but be not of it. Ultimately, through this steady process of inner purification, the soul empties itself of all that is not God. But we must remember that the process of self-purification is the work of a lifetime. Spiritual transformation rarely occurs suddenly or overnight.

Here the principles of regularity, patience, and perseverance come into play. There are many who start on the spiritual path but then, after making some progress, once again fall back into their old habits. Unless they are completely rooted out, our old tendencies come back to haunt us or catch us at our weakest moments. Life is filled with hundreds of distractions and diversions that leap before us when we least expect them. Most seekers tend to give in to worldly desires and temptations after two or three years of sincere effort. It is a rare soul that, once having stepped forward on the journey, has such strong inner resolve that he or she never looks back.

In order to avoid such a cycle, we must be totally focused on our spiritual goals. Spirituality cannot take a second seat to anything; it is an all-or-nothing approach. By understanding how great the stakes really are we will be willing to make the necessary sacrifices. Each day that we commit ourselves wholeheartedly we will find ourselves moving steadily closer to our goal. The American Aviator Elinor Smith once said, "It has long since come to my attention that people of accomplishment rarely sat back and let things happen to them. They went out and made things happen."[16] Spiritual progress requires total commitment, and nothing short of total focus will give us the desired results.

There is an illuminating story in the life of the famous explorer Hernán Cortés. In the year 1519, on his first expedition to Mexico, Cortés landed on the coast of Yucatan with over five hundred men and eleven ships. After arriving on the land he made a decision that, perhaps, few before him had ever made: he burned all of his ships, leaving no means of return. This decision committed himself and his men by closing all doors behind them. Imagine the power of such commitment to harness the inner resources necessary to be successful. But we don't have to burn our ships in the literal sense; we have to develop true *inner* renunciation.

There is a story told in the East of a great renunciate:

Raja Janak was not only a king but also a great mystic. At that time Sukh Dev, son of the famous sage Ved Vyas, was just young ascetic of spiritual bent. But his father realized that his son needed a master to help him advance further in his spiritual journey. One day the sage told Sukh Dev, "If you want complete enlightenment, you should go to Raja Janak and take him as your Guru."

Sukh Dev was at first reluctant because he wondered what a sadhu like himself, who had renounced the entire world, could learn from a King who possessed everything. But holding his father in high esteem he decided to go and visit the king. Carrying only a tiny knapsack he entered the sumptuous palace of the King. On either side the court was lined with great sculptures, beautiful paintings, and many beautiful women. Everywhere his eye turned he saw gold and precious jewels. And there, at the end of the long hall-way, was Raja Janak seated on a royal throne with the most beautiful handmaidens attending to him.

As Sukh Dev walked down the hallway he wondered, "How can this man, who is obviously lost in the world of the senses, guide me?" Reading Sukh Dev's mind, Raja Janak perceived the young man's doubts as to his competence, yet he greeted him warmly.

"I hope you have seen all of the sights of the magnificent capital," said the king.

Sukh Dev replied, in the negative.

Raja Janak then invited him to take a tour of the pal-ace in the company of his guards. Sukh Dev was quite pleased—but before he proceeded, the king offered him a bowl filled to the brim with milk. "Carry this with you while going around the palace," the king told the young seeker. "If even a single drop should spill, I have given orders to my guards to behead you instantly."

Sukh Dev was shocked and trembled with fright, but there was no escaping the commandment of the king. Accepting the challenge, Suk Dev took the bowl and went off with the guards.

A few hours later he returned, tired but still alive. Raja Janak greeted him warmly and asked, "Which of the wonderful sights of the city did you like best?"

Sukh Dev answered honestly, "My attention was completely riveted to the bowl of milk. How could I enjoy any of the sights while your sword was hanging over my head?"

The great King then replied, "Look here, my son, I carry on these kingly duties because my spiritual mentor commanded me to do so. But amidst all the grandeur of the court, my attention is focused on God. I know in my heart of hearts that all worldly pleasure and possessions are transitory. I know that the sword of time hangs over my head."

Sukh Dev immediately understood his error and bowed down in all humility to Raja Janak, accepting him as his Guru.[17]

There are two very profound lessons in this story. First, we are all like Suk Dev with our attention attached to the world. Second, if we can remember that the sword of time hangs over our head at all times, we will not forget God, even for a moment. Real resolve is born out of a powerful renunciation and inner detachment of all that is not God in our lives. Our real mantra is an affirmation that God alone exists.

Pillar Two: Meditation

To underscore and illuminate the profound importance of meditation, Sant Darshan Singh Ji drew within his orbit a diverse constellation of spiritual traditions. He might, for example, cite a parable from the Christian New Testament or the Muslim Qur'an to help illustrate an anecdote from the Sikh scripture, the *Guru Granth Sahib*; or, he might take a tale from the Hindu Upanishads and use it to clarify the meaning of a modern teaching. The result was a tapestry of rare beauty and wisdom on the universality of meditation.

As in the case of the spiritual diary, Sant Darshan revealed meditation to be an inner science with its own unique methodology. In referring to the science of meditation, he quoted Christ: "If therefore thine eye be single, thy whole body shall be full of Light."[18] Further elaborating, he would ask rhetorically, "But what does it mean to make the eye single? How can two eyes become one?" Some biblical scholars often translate this particular verse in a metaphorical sense, but Sant Darshan Singh Ji explained that the *single eye* is the inner spiritual faculty that lies between the two eyebrows—the point of entry between the physical and spiritual worlds.

Hundreds of years before Christ, Plato exclaimed, "There is an eye of the soul which is more precious that ten thousand bodily eyes, for by it alone is truth seen."[19] Master Eckhart spoke of this also, when he turned his attention inward and said, "The soul has two eyes—one looking inwards and the outer outwards. It is the inner eye of the soul that looks into essence and takes being directly from God."[20] He realized that it is with the interior eye that truth is seen. The Sufis have referred to this aperture as the *Nuqta Sweda*, eye of wisdom, or *kursi*. This inner spiritual eye is not a figment of one's imagination, but conclusively spoken about in the testimonies of literally hundreds of mystics in all times, cultures, and epochs. Rumi tells us about "the eye of the heart, which is seventy fold and of which these two sensible eyes are only the gleaners."[21] In more explicit terms, it is written in the *Sophic Hydorlith* that, "He would gain a golden understanding of the word of truth, should have the eyes of the his soul opened and his mind illumined by the inward light of which God has kindled in our hearts from the beginning."[22] This inner spiritual eye has also been referred to as the *agna chakra* in Hinduism, the tenth door by the Theosophists, and the *Tisra til* in the Sant Tradition.

Defining meditation in its most simple form, Sant Darshan Singh would say that meditation is the practice of concentration. By concentrating our attention wholly and solely at this seat of the soul in the body, we eventually transcend body consciousness and enter into higher spiritual realms of bliss and light.

The practice of meditation was the sine qua non of the spiritual path. In fact, it is the core teaching of every spiritual and religious tradition, though often spoken of in different ways or by different terms. For example it might be known as contemplation or silent prayer within Christianity. But whatever terminology we may use to describe it, it is essentially the same—the science of inner withdrawal of the spirit, culminating in the merger of our soul with the higher reality within us.

Sant Darshan Singh Ji insisted that mediation had a beneficial and remedial effect on all aspects of life. When someone asked, "How can I control my anger?" He would often say, "Meditate more." If a person lacked concentration or functioned poorly in the workplace, he suggested more meditation. Likewise, it was the key to achieving more harmony and peace within the family and the world. He stressed, however, that the most profound benefit of meditation, the highest goal, was self-and God-realization. At the practical level, his replies to questions about the practice and technique of meditation were astoundingly simple yet profound in depth. Even the most difficult questions were often resolved with a simple story or parable. The entire process could be divided into three distinct phases, each with its own specifics and guidelines.

Phase One: Physical Stillness
Accompanied by Deep Relaxation and Heightened Awareness

In this first phase the practitioner chooses any position in which he or she can sit for long periods of time without any physical movement. Any position is fine so long as there is no tension in any part of the body, including the neck, eyes, and forehead. Deep relaxation is a prerequisite for physical stillness, for as long as there is any kind of tension or tightness in the body, physical stillness cannot be achieved. Hence, rigid or difficult hatha yoga postures may not be suitable for most aspirants, as they would not be able to hold the posture for very long without moving. Likewise, positions in which the body is twisted, turned, or not aligned properly would also cause tension and, hence, be unsuitable. The aspirant is asked to completely release all physical tension, not only in the body but also mentally and emotionally. The general rule is that unless there is deep relaxation, the body will not be able to remain still for long periods.

Since the goal of meditation is to withdraw the soul or spirit from the body, any movement or disturbance to the body would cause the process of withdrawal to stop. In our normal waking condition the soul, or consciousness, is dispersed in every cell of the body. Its animating rays enliven the five senses and give life to the entire body. For the withdrawal process to work, physical stillness is a prerequisite. These two simple guidelines will, in time, produce relaxation accompanied by heightened awareness at the spiritual eye or seat of the soul. As soon as these conditions are met, concentration at the seat of the soul begins and withdrawal of the soul commences.

Phase Two: Mental Stillness Leading to One-pointed Concentration

In the second phase, the practitioner is asked to still the mind or reduce the thinking process—in simple terms, to *stop the mind*. This is, of course, a daunting and seemingly impossible task for those first attempting to meditate. Most aspirants find when they first sit down that they are bombarded with thoughts from every direction. In the beginning phases the mind often acts like a restless monkey, flitting about restlessly about from one branch to another. Any attempt to control it results in resistance and restlessness. Since our mind has been running wild in the sense pleasures and worldly passions for eons, it automatically resists being controlled. Most of us find our initial attempts to control our mind disappointing and frustrating. However, with proper training and discipline we can gradually bring the mind under our conscious control. As we develop still further we can even still it altogether. Sadly, many aspirants mistakenly believe that because of their initial disappointing efforts the task is unattainable and give up or lessen their higher aspirations.

The process of withdrawal cannot be achieved until there is a certain degree of mental quiet. In the same way that water will not turn to steam until a certain temperature is reached, inner access cannot be achieved until the mind is under the aspirant's control. Until the mind is adequately controlled the second component, one-pointed concentration, will be impossible. Hence the general rule: Without control of the mind, inner one-pointed concentration is impossible; and without one pointed concentration, entry into the higher worlds of spirit is difficult. Each is predicated upon the other.

In order to accomplish this task, masters from all traditions have recommended the use of inner invocation of God's names to help still and control the mind. This inner invocation has been called *mantra* in Hinduism and Buddhism. In Christianity it is known as a litany or rosary, in Islam as *∂hikr*, and in Sant Mat as *simran*. The great law of the universe known to all Masters is *"As you think, so you become."* Thus the use of inner silent repetition of the names of God acts as an inner restraint upon the mind of the aspirant. The mind, like the wild horse will continue to wander around unless tethered properly. Once the horse is tethered it can only go as far as the length of the rope and then it is pulled back. Similarly, the mantra tethers or links the mind to the name of God and prevents it from running aimlessly in every direction. Gradually the mind, like the horse, learns that it cannot run away and settles down to concentrate. In due course, through the continued repetition of the inner names of God, the mind becomes completely pure and begins to reflect the divine light of the soul. As the light of the soul becomes more and more luminous, one-pointed concentration now propels our soul into the higher spiritual regions. By changing the content of our thoughts, we also change its direction. Hence, by directing our thought process to God, our inner direction becomes Godly.

Phase Three: Contemplation Leading to Absorption

In this last phase, the aspirant enters into higher spiritual realms through one-pointed concentration and comes into contact with the higher expressions of the celestial light and ringing radiance. The practitioner gradually absorbs himself or herself into the inner reality of this Word, or Naam, to reach the final destination. After entering into the realms of spirit, the radiant or light form of the spiritual master appears and guides the soul on its further journey. As this phase develops, the practitioner learns the art of contemplation on the inner form of his spiritual master. The art of contemplation can be compared to the art of alchemy, in which iron or copper is transmuted into gold. As the aspirant contemplates upon the light form of the master, he takes on all the qualities of the *inner master.* Light merges into light and becomes greater light.

To explain this process more fully, we know that a piece of iron must be heated to extreme temperatures before it can be molded or shaped. Once heated, its chemical properties change and it begins to radiate both light and heat. In the same way, once our attention reaches the zenith of concentration it becomes absorbed into the light form of the inner master and continues its journey through the realms of spirit as pure spirit, separated from the mind and body. Jesus referred to this when he exhorted his disciples that, "God is a Spirit: and they that worship him must worship him in spirit and truth."[23] This means that the small self has merged into the greater self, the ray of consciousness has merged into the sun of consciousness, the soul has merged into the over-soul, and the light of our souls has merged into the greater Light of all Consciousness. In short, where there was once an object and subject there is now only one consciousness. The seer has become the seen; the drop has merged into the ocean.

Pillar Three: Satsang or Association With Truth

The last practice, called *satsang*, literally means keeping the association (sang) with Truth (sat). This has two phases or aspects. The first phase is outward association with truth by keeping the company of someone who is truth personified, or a *Satguru*. The second phase is indirect association with truth by listening to the discourses of a realized being while not in their physical presence. On one level the entire path is a path of association. First, we associate with someone who is a living embodiment of truth or word made flesh. Sant Darshan expressed the invaluable necessity of a living guide in the following verse:

> *With every breath I must bow to my friend,*
> *For I owe my life to his grace.*[24]

For the spiritual aspirant, association with an authentic spiritual guide has no equivalent. Here Sant Darshan suggests that his life itself is a gift of his friend. If life itself is a gift, then every other blessing is also a result of this original gift. In every religious and spiritual tradition the value of a master soul has been stressed repeatedly. At some point we must ask why such importance is given to the spiritual master. Shams i Tabriz, considered the spiritual master of Rumi, described the *shaykh's*, or Master's, importance as follows: "Find a Pir (spiritual Master), for without a Pir the way is beset with dangers, difficulties, and tribulations "[25] Likewise, the farther we are from their presence, the further we are from God. Rumi guides us again "Take rest under the shelter of an accepted One, for the proximity of a liberated soul shall liberate thee as well."[26] How is this possible? Since they are in close proximity to God, God's energy is transmuted directly to us through the power of their radiation.

We can understand this more completely by taking a scientific example. Newton's law of thermodynamics tells us one charged body passes its charge on to another. For example, when one moving billiard ball strikes another it passes its energy on to the ball it hit. That ball now begins to move with the force of the colliding object. In the same way, by keeping the company of a master soul we automatically become the beneficiary of their spiritual energy.

There is a wonderful story about the effect of a saint's words:

A thief on his deathbed called his only son to his side and gave him two pieces of advice: "First, my son," said the dying man, "do not go to any temple to hear the sermon of a saint. And second, if you are ever caught stealing, do not confess—even if you are hanged."

Sometime later, while the man was returning from breaking into a home, he saw a policeman coming. There was an alley nearby, so he quickly ran there to save his life. There he found a temple, and inside the temple a sermon was being delivered. Immediately the thief remembered his father's dying words, but before he could put his fingers in his ears heard one sentence: *the angels, gods, and goddesses do not have shadows.*

It wasn't long before the man was caught as a suspect in the robbery. When he was presented before the king and asked if he had committed the crime, however, he recalled his father's second piece of advice. "No sire," he said, "I did not steal anything." The man was then beaten, and when he still would not confess he was thrown into a prison house.

One woman on the king's police force was very clever, and she came up with a plan to make the man confess. The king agreed that it was a fine idea and gave her the assignment. That night the policewoman disguised herself as the goddess Durga. She got two artificial arms and fixed them to two burning torches in her hands. She walked with an artificial lion by her side and made a horrible commotion. The doors of the jail were flung wide open, and in the darkness the light of the candles shown brilliantly. When the poor thief saw the apparition he leaped up and prostrated himself at her feet. The self-made goddess gave him her blessings and said, "Behold, son. I, Durga, have come to remove your misery. If you have committed a theft and tell the truth, I will help you to be released."

The thief was almost ready to confess when he saw the shadow of the fake goddess. He instantly recalled the words of the saint at the temple: gods and goddesses do not have shadows. In a flash he understood that it was all a deception. The thief said, "Mother! I did not commit the thief, and the king is punishing me unjustly."

The next day the clever woman told the king that the young man was not the culprit. The king in turn ordered the man to be set free. The thief was naturally very pleased with the bizarre turn of events. He then thought to himself how wonderful it was that by hearing only one sentence from the satsang, he had been released from prison. Imagine, he thought to himself, if I could hear all the words of satsang, it would surely transform my life. As the story goes he began attending satsang and, in time, left his life of thievery and became a great devotee.[27]

This simple and humorous tale illustrates the deep significance of attending to the words of an inspired teacher. Satsang, or the association with someone who speaks and lives truth, is a cardinal principle in all religious traditions. It is based on the simple, scientific principle that there is a spiritual charge to the words of a realized teacher. It is not merely the words that have the power to transform, but the charge behind them. Let us examine a bit more closely how this principle works.

Every thought has a radiation based on its frequency level. That means that each of us radiates who we are at all times. Some people call this radiating energy a person's aura. The more spiritual the person, the more purified the frequency and the greater the aura. Indeed, the aura of a truly spiritual person can extend even miles up. By being in that aura we experience the effects of that person's purified radiation. Even if they say nothing, their presence still affects us. However, when they do speak their words are filled with their spiritual radiation. By hearing their words we are affected at the deepest core of our being. There words have the power to transform us because they resonate with our deepest inner consciousness. This, in fact, is the secret of how true masters work. Those who become more receptive to them can feel that power or current anywhere in the world.

For example, we know that we can pick up radio waves from thousands of miles away if we tune our radio to the right wavelength. Similarly, when we are receptive to the radiation of a realized teacher we will receive the same benefit as if we were in their physical presence. The question then becomes how to develop receptivity to that divine power, which is omnipresent and omnipotent.

Receptivity is developed when nothing stands between that power and us. In other words, it arises when our attention is constantly riveted on that inner power. Two qualities help develop this inner receptivity: yearning and sincere aspiration born of love.

These twin qualities create the inner condition necessary for receptivity to the spiritual charging of God.

The Path of Yearning:
Spiritual Need and Sincere Love

Both East and West, the great traditions of mysticism are built upon the pillars of intense yearning, passionate love, and complete surrender. Unless the heart is open and there is true spiritual need for God, little else can occur. Out of this intense inner passion an overwhelming yearning to return to our source captivates the soul. Paradoxically, each step toward the Beloved produces greater and greater yearning. This, in turn, leads to greater and greater surrender of the old self. Sant Darshan spoke often and eloquently on the need for yearning and the effect of separation on the soul. In the following verse he expresses the unique predicament of the soul as it ascends to its source:

> *O restless heart, come let us weep,*
> *Let us toss in pain,*
> *Why think now of sleep?*
> *We have a night that knows no dawn.*[28]

In this verse, Sant Darshan expresses the soul's intense longing to be one with God. Out of its profound longing the heart weeps tears of love and keeps vigil all night, pinning restlessly for a glimpse of the divine Beloved. In this state sleep is banished from the eyes of the lover. There can be no rest until the soul finds consummation in union. Sant Darshan continues, "The suffering caused by the pangs of separation can become so intense that we find some lovers have not been able to bear the separation; they have given up the body, they have succumbed to the unrequited torment."[29]

Despite the seemingly tragic predicament of the soul in this state of separation, there is a silver lining to it. Sant Rajinder Singh Ji Maharaj explains that, "A disciple not only wants to be with the master, but also cannot bear separation from yearning for the master. This strange condition one finds on the spiritual path. If one is not with the master, one wants to have yearning to be with the master. Thus the pain has its own charms."[30] The yearning to be reunited with our divine source has been referred to by many great spiritual masters as the pangs of separation. And while the experience of final union with God is no doubt one of endless joy, bliss, and ecstasy, readers may wonder whether the path of spirituality is one of unending pain and separation. However, those lovers who have experienced even one moment of God's transcendent bliss and peace know that it is compensation enough. As the soul begins to experience the bliss of the higher spiritual regions, it naturally longs to return to its source with increasing intensity. Likewise, the soul loves the spiritual master with an ever-increasing intensity because the master soul is the vehicle for the transmission of God's love, light, and life. Speaking of this bond of intimacy with the spiritual master, Sant Darshan tells us:

> *That one night spent in your assembly,*
> *Has been the fulfillment of a lifetime of longing.*[31]

Here the poet speaks of the mystical communion of his soul with the divine master after a lifetime of intense longing and separation. The gift of final consummation of the soul with the oversoul is entirely in the hands of the master soul. Like an orchestral maestro, a spiritual master draws forth the notes of longing and yearning from deep within his disciple. Every step the disciple takes toward his master is, in fact, a gift from the master himself. This remarkable ability to respond to the heartfelt cries of the disciple wherever she or he may be stems from the omniscient God-consciousness operating through the spiritual guide. A master soul is not the body, but the God-consciousness working through it. That power is in tune with the hearts and souls of all disciples; the master is aware of each sincere cry and responds in accordance to each soul's capacity and need. Wherever there is fire, oxygen comes by itself. Likewise, progress on the spiritual path is a result of our spiritual need. When God causes anyone to weep, His mercy is aroused and that seeker then drinks of God's bounty.

There is an illuminating story about the life of two disciples of Hazur Baba Sawan Singh:

> There once were two simple farmers who made their living off the land. Each month, their fields would receive a certain allotment of water from the local water irrigation system. It so happened that the season had been excessively hot and their fields were in desperate need of water. But it was their habit to sit continuously for meditation until they saw the inner radiant form of the guru, a rare phenomena attained by only the most devoted of lovers.
>
> As usual, the morning when they were to receive their allotment they were sitting for meditation. After a long time one brother opened his eyes and said, "I have not seen the form of our Master within. Have you seen the Master?"
>
> The other brother replied, "No I have not seen the Master either. But it is time to go and receive our allotment of water or our crops will surely die."
>
> The first brother replied, "This is God's field and God's water and we are in God's hands. I am not prepared to leave until I see the inner form of our Master."
>
> The first brother then agreed and they both returned to their meditation. After a short while the inner Master appeared to both of them.[32]

This story addresses two aspects of the spiritual thirst. The first aspect is that spiritual growth is contingent upon inner need and deep yearning for God. As in the case of the two disciples, communing with the inner radiant form of their Master was a greater compensation than their entire livelihood. Second, they were willing to sacrifice everything for a mere glimpse of their spiritual friend.

It is impossible for most of us to really comprehend the depths of this kind of love. We do have parallels in the history of romantic love that, to a certain extent, mirror true spiritual love. But they cannot give us a true picture of its sublimity. This inner need cannot be created artificially, but arises out of the depths of one's heart. Only true need arouses God's mercy and opens up the gates of his loving kindness.

Bulleh Shah was a mystic poet of the Punjab and disciple of Hazrat Inayat Shah. He spent many years of his life in separation from his Master, which caused him great pain and suffering. He described his state in the following manner:

> *Because of this intense longing for Thee my heart has broken.*
> *What should I do?*
> *I cannot live, I cannot die.*
> *Please listen to my sighs.*
> *There is no rest for me, either day or night,*
> *Without seeing my beloved, my eyes do not close even for a*
> *second.*[33]

Guru Amar Das, the fifth Guru of the Sikhs, echoes the same sentiments in reflecting on his love for his Beloved:

> *Without seeing the Beloved sleep does not come*
> *This separation has now become unbearable.*[34]

How can an aspirant feel such intense, heartbreaking longing for God? The answer is simple: increase your spiritual need. And how can we increase our need? The answer is to control the ego. It is the ego that separates us from God, and it is the ego that, at every juncture, seeks to turn our face from our Beloved. For this reason every spiritual tradition agrees on the need to control the ego as a prerequisite for spiritual growth. Perhaps no saint in history has given so explicit a teaching on controlling the ego—both in theory and practice—as Sant Darshan Singh Ji Maharaj. Let us reflect for a moment on some of the cornerstones of a life lived in and founded on true humility and modesty.

The Path of Controlling the Ego

Sant Darshan explained that the thickest veil between us and our creator is the ego. In fact, ego is the root cause of all our other failings. By ego he did not mean the traditional Freudian notion of the healthy sense of self necessary to function effectively in the world, but one's s false identity with body and mind. Over time, this false identity gives rise to individuality based on the illusion that we are separate from each other and from God, our source. This is the greatest of illusions. The reality is that we are souls, drops in the ocean of all consciousness, or God. We—as soul, as consciousness—are already united and have our very being in God. *Divine unity already exits, we have only forgotten it.* The reality is divine oneness.

Out of the false sense of individuality, however, all illusion, forgetfulness, and discord arise. To forget our connection with our creator is the very essence of original sin. It is this original forget-fulness that has caused us to return again and again into this world of illusion and suffering. We suffer from a massive identity crisis; we have forgotten who we really are. Regardless of our religious or spiritual tradition, when seen from this angle it becomes clear that the entire path depends on controlling our ego. Unless and until we can control our ego, progress on the path is merely a figment of our imagination. To this end Sant Darshan laid out one of the most significant teachings on the development of humility. Let us review the essentials of this powerful teaching.

1. Avoid the trap of self-satisfaction.

First and foremost, we must never allow ourselves to fall into the trap of self-satisfaction. By self-satisfaction I mean the feeling

that we have achieved something by our own efforts and, therefore, are somehow better or more important than others. Often a
feeling subtly arises that we are "good disciples" or "good people."
We come to believe that though we are not perfect, we are decent
people and have achieved many worthwhile things in our life. This
is the ego speaking. It is a subtle form of self-congratulation or self-
cherishing. The same condition may arise if we are given a special
role, position, or title and as a result we begin to think we have special privileges or authority over others. The minute this occurs we
start to look down on others and our ego gets inflated. This is a very
subtle point. Inwardly we lose respect for others even if outwardly
we behave the same way toward them that we always have.

As seekers we should always consider ourselves to be beginners on the path. It says in the book of Isaiah, "But we are all as an
unclean thing, and all our righteousness are as filthy rags."[35] Again
in the Jewish Tradition it states, "The Lord is nigh unto them that
are of a broken heart; and saveth such as be of a contrite spirit."[36] In
other words, we should never claim success for ourselves. We must
never imagine even in our wildest dreams that we have achieved
anything by our own merit or ability. In the Sikh scriptures it
is written:

> *Where egotism exits, Thou are not experienced,*
> *Where Thou art, is not egotism,*
> *You who are learned, expound in your mind*
> *This inexpressible proposition.*[37]

To avoid this insidious trap we should always see ourselves as
falling short of our goal. Ironically, the more dissatisfied we are
with ourselves the happier God is with us. Dissatisfaction, however,
does not mean shame, self-loathing, or unrelenting guilt; rather, it
is understanding that no matter what we have achieved, the final
horizon is still very far away. We should be able to drink the seven
oceans of spirituality but still have parched lips.

2. Pass all credit on to God.

One of the easiest snares we fall into on the spiritual path is to assume credit for our good actions. People may praise us or see some good quality in us, and in our heart of hearts we pat ourselves on the back (even if we don't acknowledge it outwardly). The result is that our ego gets inflated. We should recognize that spirituality is a gift of God and his messengers and saints. As a gift, it does not belong to us; we cannot claim it, own it, or wear it as a label to make ourselves feel good.

Sant Darshan has said, "True saints never claim anything for themselves or by themselves. They know everything belongs to God and is from God."[38] Whoever thinks he has attained anything has attained nothing, because spirituality cannot be claimed by our ego. When Jesus was once called "good" by an observant onlooker, he replied, "Why callest thou me good? There is none good but one, that is God; but if thou wilt enter into life keep the commandments."[39] This is not false humility but the highest truth.

The minute we seek recognition, applause, or special attention we assume that we have done something. The reality is that nothing happens without the will of God. Without God's help we are help-less. Instead, we should always acknowledge God and the help of others in every success we have. The basic principle is that all success comes from God. God is the real doer. Sant Darshan addressed this point most emphatically when he said, "It is a path on which no one can ever speak in terms of himself. Nobody can use the 'I.' It is a path in which everybody says, 'That is my master's work.' And actually it is the Master's work. Once we begin to see the hand of our Master working in everything he blesses us. We are nothing. We are just mortals, we are nothing of ourselves. Nobody can claim any credit for himself. Nobody can claim he can do a bit on the path by himself; this is not a path of 'I-ness.'"[40]

When Sant Kirpal Singh passed from this world in 1972 he entrusted Sant Darshan Singh with the mantle of spirituality. Through his grace I had come to know inwardly that he was the successor of my master. Consequently, I left Dehra Dun, where I had been meditating, and traveled to Delhi to see him. The excruciating pain of missing my own spiritual Master was only mitigated by the hope of seeing my spiritual friend in the new form in which he was working. After a long, bumpy ride filled with great anticipation and trepidation, I made my way up a small staircase to a simple concrete apartment building. This was one of many identical government apartments that stretched on for some distance. I knocked on the door meekly and was met by a middle-aged Indian woman with a kind smile. She graciously invited me to sit down on the floor with several others who were also waiting for Sant Darshan Singh to come out and greet us. No one spoke except in soft whispers, and a feeling of reverence and deep peace permeated the room.

Sant Darshan entered through a side door and quickly sat down within a few feet of those already seated. After greeting everyone politely, he bowed his head and remained so for what seemed like an eternity, but was probably only about thirty minutes. His head occasionally moved back and forth or tilted upward while his soul seemed drowned in an ocean of unfathomable mysteries. He gave out an expression of such utter remoteness and yet a blanket of warmth and affection filled the room. Paradoxically, he stood out as the most human of all humans and the most perfect expression of the divine.

After a long period of time he slowly began to raise his head as if from a very far away place. He looked directly into my face and said; "Let us sit in sweet remembrance of Sant Kirpal Singh." He once again turned his head down and disappeared into an infinite vastness. About twenty minutes later, he opened his eyes and gazed steadily into mine for some time. Our faces were only a foot or so apart and his eyes, like two glaring headlights, seemed to penetrate all things seeing in their essence the same everlasting oneness. Then a luminous, crystalline light poured from his from his deeply set eyes and permeated my entire body with a scintillating infusion.

As the evening came to a close, the Master turned to me and said, "I am nothing. I am absolutely nothing. It is all the grace of God and the grace of my master."[41] As I walked out I bowed to touch his feet…and as I glanced up to say goodbye it was no longer Sant Darshan Singh but the form of Sant Kirpal Singh, my own Master. My heart was ripped open. Never in my life had I experienced such total humility and self-effacement. Sant Darshan was not there. Nothing was there except that light. It was God who was speaking, radiating, resonating. The mystery of his presence continues to haunt me like a moon drifting across pitch-black night. Whatever I had thought God was, as the sun rose early the next morning I now saw in the impenetrable silence of His total self-effacement. Words fail miserably to convey this experience.

3. **All criticism is born of ego. Seek first to understand then be understood.**

The reality is that God is in everyone. And if God is in everyone, then we should treat others as respectfully as we would honor God himself. Reiterating this message in speaking of the tendency to criticize and gossip others, Sant Darshan Singh said, "Criticizing others is born out of the ego. I can only criticize someone if I am myself above criticism. But we only have to peep into our own hearts to see that we are full of failings. And if we are full of failings, what right have we to judge anyone, let alone indulge in criticism?"[42]

Finding fault with others has become so pernicious and pervasive a practice in our society that it is now deeply ingrained in our culture. On the television, radio talk shows, in print media, and in movies, everyone is putting each other down. We are a put down culture. It is not only socially acceptable; it has become a pernicious form of entertainment in our society. Recently I read that one of the growing problems in our secondary school system is bullying.

Statistics show that it has become so pervasive that millions of dollars yearly are being devoted to correcting this problem. All this is born out of ego. Basic respect for our family, teachers, or elders is rarely found and everyone has become a target for criticism. In this kind of atmosphere our children learn that making fun of others, putting them down, and judging them is a normal adult behavior. Our children—our most precious inheritance—are losing faith in their peers, parents, elders, and finally in themselves. The final price we pay is the loss of the sacred in our lives.

When people came to India to be with Sant Darshan Singh, often the first task he embarked on was reuniting children with their parents and healing the wounds of broken homes. Once, while giving a discourse on the importance of respecting our parents, a disciple from the West asked the Master, "Why should I respect my parents when they don't respect me? I haven't seen them and they don't care about me. They have no interest in my life."

Sant Darshan became visibly moved and replied, "We must respect our parents, for they have given us our life."

To this the young man responded, "But what have they done from me?"

"What have they done for you?" Sant Darshan asked. "For how many years did they care for you when you were incapable of even walking? When you were helpless, they cared for your every need. Your attitude reflects your ingratitude and selfishness."

The young man's expression softened somewhat, moved by Master's simple explanation. Yet still not quite convinced he said, "But why should I try to see them if they are not concerned about me?"

Becoming animated, the Master said, "We all owe our parents a debt of gratitude, which we can never repay." He added, "Do you know what it is like to be pregnant, to carry a child in one's womb for nine months? And be in physical discomfort for nine months?

Do you have any idea what sacrifice your mother made for you?" Then Sant Darshan called out to an Indian sevadar, "Get me a bag and fill it with weights. Our young friend will soon now what it is like himself."

The sevadar returned shortly and brought Sant Darshan Singh Ji a bag with weights in it. He instructed the person to tie it around the young man's waist. The mood of the room changed to laughter as the Master seemed to have found a new way to reach the young man.

Sant Darshan smiled sweetly and said, "Spend the rest of the day with this around your waist and we'll see tonight whether you have more respect for you parents."

The young man complied and spent the rest of the day carrying around the bag. He returned convinced and was warmly welcomed by Sant Darshan Singh.[43]

The spiritual path begins and ends with reverence and respect for others. Criticism of others is a reflection of ego and has no place on the spiritual path.

4. Apologize quickly and seek forgiveness.

One of the subtlest traps of the ego is our inability to admit our mistakes. We may commit numerous errors, but how many of us apologize quickly and seek forgiveness for our wrongs? Sometimes we wait years before we seek forgiveness for our mistakes. The greatest tragedy is that many of us never even see the suffering we have inflicted on others. What is the result? We suffer and cause others to suffer as well. The rule of the illuminated masters of spirituality is to seek forgiveness quickly and not let hurts fester or deepen. Most of the time, we focus on trying to rationalize our own behavior and finding fault with others' actions. It is rare to find someone who admits his or her mistakes and does not lay the blame on others.

On one occasion Sant Darshan Singh was summoned along with a group of other disciples into the presence of his Master. When he arrived, Master Kirpal was asking for a certain man, "Where is he? This is all wrong. Who is responsible for all this?" There were many people present. Master Darshan was standing at the back, but he immediately said, "Master, we are sorry. This mistake will not be repeated again. We are very sorry for it. Please forgive us. We are very, very sorry." Great Master Kirpal said, "All right."

After all the people had left, Master Kirpal called for Darshan and, when he came in, he asked, "Darshan, you were not the one who made that mistake. Why did you ask for pardon? Why did you say to me, 'I am sorry?'"

Master Darshan replied, "All right, that is true. But whoever did it is my brother or sister. I don't know what the mistake was, but anyhow, I thought it well to beg forgiveness on his or her behalf."[44] Such humility is the hallmark of the saints. They not only take responsibility for their own mistakes, but for those of others as well.

5.   Do not trust the ego; put faith in God and spiritual guides.

Spirituality and ego cannot coexist. Spirituality is an affirmation of the inherent unity of all life and the divine oneness. Ego, on the other hand, negates that unity and creates separation between the divine presence and us. The little ego creates a false sense of separation through our identification with our body and mind. If this premise is true, then we need to be ever vigilant against our ego, which seeks to justify itself and its actions at all times. The great masters of the East and West have understood how quickly we can be caught in the throes of our ego. This is important if we are to seek the greater good. In one of the Hadith, the Prophet he prays, "Whosoever has in his heart even so much as a rice grain of pride Mohammad cannot enter into paradise."[45] Why? Because pride is a negation of others and of the principle of God's unity. Putting our faith and trust in God and our spiritual Master is the first step in controlling our ego.

On many occasions Sant Darshan would reiterate the words of his Master, saying the love of a Master for his disciples is hundreds and thousands of times the love of a selfless mother for her children. In fact, to receive the love of a true Master is beyond any experience of love we can have in this world. It is this example of selfless love that awakens in us a deeper recognition of our true identity as love itself.

During the early 1980s Sant Darshan had invited a group of Westerners to accompany him on a tour to the town of Rhotak in India. One afternoon while on tour, we pulled over on the roadside by a canal. We were informed that we would have a surprise picnic lunch. There was a high railroad trestle over the canal with no handrails and only space between the railway ties. Master Darshan got out of his car and started across the trestle, gesturing for the others to follow him.

Two ladies were following right behind the Master and keeping their eyes on him, fool-heartedly skipping from tie to tie without fear and telling each other that they were "walking in the Master's footsteps." The others were crossing more slowly and cautiously. As Master Darshan proceeded forward, the two girls walked a little way up the canal and then turned to watch the others crossing the trestle. Looking across to the other side, they saw Mata Harbhajan Kaur, Master's wife, gesturing and shaking her head that she did not want to cross the trestle. Master Darshan instructed the two girls to stay where they were and that he was going back across to assist his wife. Taking her gently by the hand, he led her across the trestle while the rest of the group watched intently.

Once on the other side, Master Darshan let go of his wife's hand, and leaving her with the others, walked very quickly past everyone further up the canal. One of the girls decided to catch up with Master Darshan and follow him. When she got close to him she noticed that he was holding his sandals and walking bare footed.

She got excited to see this because she loved to go bare footed. So, she slipped off one of her sandals and stepped onto the ground with the intention of removing the other sandal and carrying them. However, when her foot hit the ground she yelped in pain.

"Master," she cried out, "There are thorns all over the ground!"

Master Darshan turned to look at her with a sweet smile on his face. "Daughter," he said, "these thorns are just little thorns, compared to the Thorns of Life."

She quickly put her sandals back on and watched in astonishment as Master Darshan walked quickly to and fro through the thorns, showing no sign of distress. He seemed to be looking for something. Suddenly he stopped, and gesturing to some sevadars that were following at a distance, he indicated where to lay the thick blankets they were carrying on their heads.[46]

When she saw all this, the young woman realized that Master was using his bare feet to find a place without thorns for us to have our picnic. His actions were a perfect metaphor for the self-sacrificing love a true Master has for his disciples. A true Master considers it his or her special joy and pleasure to lovingly remove all the "thorns" and problems from our paths in order to make our journey easier. These selfless acts awaken in us our own latent love and inspire the same selflessness in us.

6. **Recognize that we should seek all guidance and grace from God and the Master souls who are His messengers.**

As we mature on the path we come to recognize that all goodness and grace comes from God and God alone. Hence, we should seek intimacy and closeness to God or those who are close to God.

This may sound overly simplistic or even naïve; nevertheless God is the transcendent cause of all that is good in our lives.

This does not mean that we should not seek guidance and counsel from others. Seeking assistance from others is always a good thing. It expands our sense of vision, deepens our insight, and provides support and encouragement along the way. Trusted friends are a rare and special blessing in life and we should always avail ourselves of their help and guidance. The error occurs when we place too much hope, trust, and confidence in the advice of those whose vision is limited and shortsighted. We find in the end that the "wisdom of the world" is a limited and fallible.

Conversely, the wisdom of the sages and saints is based upon the unlimited vision of God, which will never leave us disappointed or disillusioned. We come to recognize that, while we may seek the help and support of others, we should place our trust in God alone. This is a subtle distinction. Our vision is limited and subject to error. God's vision is unlimited and perfect. Therefore, we should seek God's guidance directly or through one of his messengers. In this way we will never become disappointed with others and never rely on our own egos. Both are subject to error.

Breaking the Cup of Ego

There is a beautiful story from the life of Laila and Majnu, two celebrated lovers in Persian literature. On one occasion, Laila was distributing milk to many people who waited in long lines holding earthenware cups in their hands. When he heard about this, Majnu, who was madly in love with Laila, came to stand in line also. He held his cup in hand waiting for his beloved Laila to fill it with milk.

Laila sweetly and quietly filled the cups of all. When she came to Majnu, he stretched out his hand with the cup in it. But instead of pouring the mile, Laila hit Majnu's hand from below and the cup flew into the air, fell down on the ground, and was smashed to pieces.

A friend of Majnu's, in whom he had confided his love for Laila, ridiculed him. "What kind of beloved do you have?" he laughed. "She has given milk to all, but in your case she has broken your cup."

But Majnu said, "You do not understand. I brought a limited cup to my beloved. By her gesture of breaking my cup she is telling me that what she wants to give me is unlimited."

Unless we can see with the eyes of a Majnu, how will we arrive at an interpretation like this? God almighty and the great teachers of all traditions have unbounded treasures of divinity to give us. They are oceans of divinity without beginning or end. How can this infinite ocean be contained in the limited cup of our ego? Sant Darshan Singh explains, "The ego creates the smallest, most limited vessel, where there is only room for the small self to enter. Our Beloved needs a vessel without limits, without walls, without stops. We must break the cup of ego to receive the unending flow of His bountiful gifts."[47]

To fully receive their unlimited grace and guidance we must break the cup of ego, which means we must never rely on our own version or limited understanding of events or people. The Masters have come to resurrect the spirit—to release us from the cage of "I, me, and mine." In giving up our limited, selfish existence we receive an unlimited, everlasting life. What are we afraid of losing?

What steps might we take in order to solidify our inner progress? Unless we are willing to sublimate our limited ego we can never hope to attain true spirituality, which is a denial of all the limitations born of the separate ego self. While this may at first seem like a daunting task, each day can bring little successes that can, in turn, inspire us on our way.

The following are a few simple, practical steps that, if adhered to, can radically alter our lives.

Six Exercises in Controlling Our Egos

1. **Avoid self-superiority.** We can define self-superiority as the little voice of ego that seeks superiority over others. It sometimes appears as subtle assertions that "I have achieved something special" and I am therefore better than others. The feeling of superiority may manifest as a feeling of superior intelligence, greater wealth, or the feeling of power over others as a result of one's position or job. The sad result is that instead of treating others as equals, with love and compassion, we seek our own selfish ends and cherish our little self with its accomplishments and opinions.

    *   One simple step we can all take is to make a daily habit of listing our errors in thought, word, and deed. In this way we are constantly reminded of our need to improve and of how far we really are from achieving perfection.

2. **Never claim credit or recognition for our accomplishments or ourselves.** Claiming credit for our good actions or accomplishments has another negative side to it. The minute the little self claims credit for our successes, we become the agent for our actions. These actions then become a barrier between God and us. The reality is that God alone should be credited with true doer-ship, for it is by the will of God that all things transpire. By seeking recognition we seek to subtly separate ourselves from others and, in so doing, from God. In some cases we even place ourselves above God by failing to acknowledge His presence in all things. In both ways we deny the reality of God's omnipotence and affirm our own little self.

    *   One simple step we can all practice is to hide whatever good may come out of our actions.

- The second is that, if praise or acknowledgement happens to come our way, we should make a point of sharing that praise with others and inwardly passing it onto God, where it truly belongs.

3. **Apologize quickly for our mistakes.** Apologizing for our mistakes may seem like an insignificant gesture in the larger scheme of things, but I can assure you that it is one of the most powerful acts anyone can offer. Not only does it go a long way in healing the day-to-day rifts and arguments, but by learning to apologize quickly we do not give the petty ego a chance to simmer in the stew of self-pity or cast aspersion and blame on others. The longer we wait to apologize for our mistakes, the easier it is for the ego to harden and eventually create division and discord. Once again, the ego is ever ready to assert its superiority over others. In apologizing we affirm our own humanity by recognizing our own mistakes and the humanity of the other, whom we have intentionally or unintentionally mistreated. Apologizing may be one of the hardest things in life to do, but it is also one of the most important.

   - As a simple first step we can begin by inwardly saying we are sorry. Once we have done this, our little ego softens and it becomes easier to say we are sorry out loud. In time, we learn to apologize quickly and sincerely for our errors.

4. **Treat others as we would like to be treated.** The golden rule is as simple as it sounds. If all of us actually practiced this principle in our daily lives, the world would be transformed overnight. The reality behind this principle is that God resides in everyone and, therefore, we should treat everyone with the same respect and reverence we give to God and expect for our own self. Thank God we all have the capacity to give and receive respect naturally. What we need to do, however, is make it a daily habit.

- One simple thing we can start with is allowing others to go first when waiting in line. It sounds so simple, but it really pays off. Try it.

- Offer basic courtesy to everyone, but especially to strangers and elders. This means greeting others, acknowledging them, and showing respect to their presence.

- Perhaps a little more difficult is offering the same respect to others who may not share our religion, culture, language, or belief system. This can be especially challenging when we openly disagree with them or what they may be saying. Honoring their humanity, however, does not imply that we sanction their actions or belief systems. It means that we give respect to God, who has created them, and to their divine presence.

5. **Never trust our own egos, and recognize how quickly each of us can err.** One of the big errors all of us make is placing too much trust in our own opinions and beliefs. We almost automatically assume that our beliefs, culture, or way of life are better than others. When we do this we place our limited vision above others and, ultimately, above God. Too often we fail to question our own motives and desires, allowing ourselves to be lured into negative thinking and distrustful actions. Learning to trust God means that we have to give up our limited vision. In reality, we should trust God and distrust our own ego. The latter more often than not seeks its own singular benefit and rarely has the welfare of others in mind.

- One powerful first step is to seek others' happiness before our own. This can be done in numerous ways, from small to grandiose. For starters, wake up in the morning and start your day with a conscious act of kindness to someone you love.

- The next step is to consciously sacrifice something for others in order to bring them happiness. This could be as simple as not buying the next fancy piece technology and instead helping out a friend with his or her personal needs.

6. **Seek Guidance from God, His messengers, saints, and prophets.** In many ways this entire book has been a call to seek wisdom continuously and from all sources possible. We should be so open that we can take guidance from even a stone or running brook. But most importantly, let us seek assistance from those who have mastered the mystery of life and death and who have known their true Self. Let us not forget the wisdom of the great spirit of Nazareth, who told us, "And if the blind lead the blind both shall fall into the ditch."[48] Here are three simple starters:

- Seek out wisdom wherever you can and from whoever comes into your orbit of relationships.

- Don't hesitate to keep the company of those who are avidly seeking God and have devoted themselves to a life of spirit.

Actively seek the company of awakened beings, inspired spirits, and realized souls, and truly listen with an open heart to their message. Better yet, put it into practice today.

Sant Rajinder Singh

Chapter Eight
The Tale of the Sands

Being in the presence of a highly evolved being not only provides us with the essence of spiritual wisdom and transformation, but, more importantly, connects us with the living current of light of a spiritual lineage. It is said in Greek mythology that the hand of Pygmalion molded his ideal love, Galatea, from chiseled marble. Then, with a mere touch from Aphrodite–the Goddess of love — Galetea sprang to life. In similar fashion, the guiding touch of the living Master can mold personalities and bring to life their latent divinity. Using praise and correction, seeming indifference and compassion, great teachers chisel our egos while uplifting our souls. With a single word or a simple glance great teachers give us the needed insight to help solve the knottiest of problems. How often have I gone to see my Masters laden with worries and fears and found myself inexplicably uplifted, delightfully perplexed by their unseen magic, wondering what the problem was in the first place?

In the spring of 2005 Sant Rajinder Singh Ji visited Long Island, New York and, as poet Sant Darshan Singh Ji says in one of his verses, "A single glance of the divine Cupbearer produced a metamorphosis, entering his tavern, old ascetics are transformed into bubbling youths."[1] The experience of being in his presence could not be better described. A single solitary glance from the Cupbearer, or spiritual Master, sends a beam of pure light into the depths of our being. Suddenly, magically, even miraculously we find ourselves bubbling over with new life, as if waking up from a long, long dream.

That day, Sant Rajinder Singh told a wonderful story. As I listened to his words, his face receded and all I saw was a continuous flow of super-sensory golden light pouring into my own eyes and face. Wave after wave of this scintillating love-wine permeated every particle of my being, fanning the dormant embers of light of my own soul. Every pore of my being was in love with His light. I invite you to enter the love-tavern to be transformed and transfigured by this same love-light.

The story Sant Rajinder Singh told that day was this:

> Once upon a time, a stream traveling from its source in the far-off mountains found itself flowing into the sands of a great desert. Throughout its long journey through the countryside the stream had brazenly passed through every kind of obstacle, and just as it had crossed every other barrier, it assumed that it would cross this one by force of will. So, the stream pressed on; but, to its dismay, it found that as quickly as it ran into the sand, its water evaporated and disappeared.
>
> The stream was convinced that it must cross this desert, and yet there was no apparent way to do so. As it ruminated its fate, a hidden voice whispered from the desert sands: "The wind crosses the desert, and so can the stream."
>
> The stream doubted the voice and saw no purpose in dashing itself repeatedly against the pitiless desert sands — after all, each attempt had ended in futility and exhaustion.

How could it possibly cross over like the wind, which could fly effortlessly?

The ancient voice of the sands replied, "By hurtling yourself in your own accustomed way you will never succeed in getting across. You will either disappear completely or become nothing more than a marsh. You must allow the wind to carry you over to your destination."

"But how could this happen?" thought the stream, who had little faith or knowledge of the wind. "What nonsense. How could I be absorbed in the wind?"

This idea was difficult for the stream to grasp. After all, it had never been absorbed before; and besides, it feared the loss of its individuality. Once having lost it, could it ever be regained?

"The wind," said to the sand, "has a special inner power. It gathers up the water in its inner embrace and then carries it over the desert, where it then lets it fall again. Falling as rain, the water once again becomes a river."

"How can I know that this is true? What is the proof?" asked the stream.

"It is so. Believe it or do not; but by continuing in your habitual way you will never become more than a giant marsh—and even that could take many, many years. Whatever the case, a marsh is certainly not the same as a stream."

"But can I not remain the same stream that I am today?' inquired the stream.

"You cannot remain the same," came the whisper. "Your essential part is carried away and forms a stream again. Remember, the reason why you are called water is because you contain two separate gases—two parts hydrogen and one part oxygen."

When the stream heard this, it began to recognize what its original essence really was. Dimly, the stream remembered a state in which it had been held in the arms of a wind. It also began to vaguely remember that this process of transformation was the real journey of his life, though not necessarily the easy or obvious thing to do.

Finally, the stream raised his vapor into the welcoming arms of the wind, which gently and easily bore it upward. It reached higher and higher and was carried for many miles, and then the wind released it to fall softly down the side of a mountain.

Because the stream had had its doubts, it now remembered vividly all the details of the experience. After the long journey it pondered, "Yes, now I have learned my true identity." The stream was learning. But the sands whispered, "We *know*, because we see it happen day after day; and because we extend from the riverside all the way to the mountain."[2]

As the discourse ended I knew that the real journey was far from over. Every day we are faced with the challenge of remembering our true identity and not getting caught up in the petty controversies and arguments of the world. One of the most beautiful aspects of being in the presence of Sant Rajinder Singh Ji, however, is that he knows the inner condition of our heart, and yet his awakened heart accepts all without judgment or conditions. He understands the power of the forces of anger, greed, and ego and how they so easily influence our thoughts, words, and deeds; but he also sees beyond the false identities we have forged for ourselves and recognizes the immaculate jewel of light that resides in each of us. This process of awakening is made all the easier as he guides us to recall our true identities as light through the gift of his light-bearing presence.

In the marvelous tale of the flowing stream, Sant Rajinder Singh likened our spiritual transformation to the process of water's evaporation into the air. Truly, the work of an authentic Master is akin to the alchemical process of converting one substance into another. In the story, the stream represents our inner essence, our life force or soul, which is eternal and immortal. As it journeys through life it flows downhill, pulled by the force of gravity. Because of the force of the stream's momentum and its ability to flow around any impediment, no obstacle can stand in its way. This forceful and willful movement represents our ego and its self-assertive nature. In the course of life, we often act according to our own selfish ends and pay little heed to the needs and interests of others. In due course, our life comes to a crossroads, which is symbolized in the story by the stream reaching the desert sands. This crossroads is the realization of our own death. Having reached the desert, the stream quickly realizes that simply dashing itself madly against the sands will not get it anywhere. We, too, learn that we cannot cross over to the other side by merely willing it. The self-assertive ego and the conventions of everyday life leave us confused and bewildered on the disappearing sands of time.

At present, we are all like the stream: in a state of gross ignorance with no clue as to our own true nature. We have become so identified with our body and mind that we doubt even the existence of our own soul. However, through gentle and gradual guidance, we begin to see that we have little choice; our own way cannot take us to the other side. Although we fear for our own individuality, we realize that we must find a way out of the self-centered prison of the mind and a new perspective on the unity of being.

The whisper from the sands is the voice of guidance coming from those who have already crossed over. These are the Masters of the mystery of life and death, who have learned the alchemy of inner transformation—the illuminated souls who daily cross to the other side and know the means to achieve that end. Just as the stream realizes that by separating itself into its two component parts, hydrogen and oxygen, it can become vapor and traverse over the sands with the aid of the wind, so, too, our spiritual guides instruct us to look to our essential inner nature. They teach us the method of inner alchemy, whereby we separate the kernel from the shell, matter from spirit, and body and mind from consciousness. This is the technology of meditation.

When Sant Rajinder Singh finished the story we all sat for meditation. It is a very special boon to be able to mediate in a Masters company, for his life-sustaining radiation has a quickening and purifying effect on our souls. His very presence fuels our modest efforts into sustained fires of zeal and passion. He unleashed the necessary boost to produce a new view of the way toward spiritual realization that years of solitary meditation couldn't have achieved.

What, then, is meditation? It is the separation of the mind and body from consciousness. As we see that our essential part is not lost, we begin to dimly remember that we have traversed this journey many times and there is nothing to fear. Our memory begins to expand and the once-cloudy and obscure past comes into full view. We now eagerly seek the completion of the transformation process.

As we are gathered up into spirit we soar over the mountain of the body through the portal of death, and come to see that this process is natural and blissful. In fact, it is filled with "the peace of God which passeth understanding,"[3] as the New Testament declares. We come to realize that our true existence as soul and the secrets of life itself are carried along on the journey of the current of spirit, passed on from generation to generation through the medium of the saints who are its unseen guides and caretakers.

Epilogue

Whenever we want to learn something new, we inevitably turn to a teacher. Isn't this why we go to school, train with coaches, hire consultants, and value mentors? An expert teacher can take us further, faster, and with better results than we can achieve on our own. As with every other field of inquiry, spirituality is no exception to this rule.

The development of our spiritual life transcends mere theoretical knowledge. We may learn a great deal from scriptures, but knowledge of our higher self and of God, as we have already mentioned, is born of direct inner revelation. There is no substitute for one own inner communion with God. As we enter into spiritual realms, however, we need a competent guide who has already traversed these regions. A guide who daily traverses these inner regions can show us the fastest, easiest way to our goal. It is really just common sense—why waste time when we don't have to?

Let us remember that spiritual Masters do not teach us anything; rather they come to awaken us to what we already possess. Although the light is latent, each of us already contains the spark of divine consciousness within us. As Sant Rajinder Singh Ji Maharaj says, "The spiritual Master shows us how to tap within ourselves. He teaches a method by which each person can contact the divine love already within. He is a catalyst that lights the fire of divine love within us. A true spiritual Master is one who gives us the key to open our own heart to the divine love."

The role of a spiritual Master, then, is not only to provide guidance and inspiration, but also to life the soul into the spiritual realms within through a powerful infusion of *spiritual consciousness*. This is the gift of divine light and ringing radiance, our baptism into the beyond or second birth, which assists the aspirant to pierce through the layers of illusions now covering the soul and experience God within.

Spiritual Masters never bind us to themselves, but to the God who is already within us. Furthermore, authentic guides never ask us to take anything on blind faith, but rather to explore the inner realms through our own direct, subjective experiences. Spirituality can be practiced as a verifiable inner science through our own first-person critical investigation. Like all other gifts of nature, it has no price tag or cost and is always given freely to one and all regardless of religion, race, or background. For those seeking a next step in their spiritual journey, Sant Rajinder Singh Ji Maharaj can help.

About Science of Spirituality

Science of Spirituality is a multi-faith international organization under the guidance of Sant Rajinder Singh Ji Maharaj. Science of Spirituality provides a forum for people to learn mediation, experience personal transformation, and grow spirituality. We are a global, non-profit spiritual organization. But we are much more than that. We are hundreds of thousands of individuals—of all nationalities, races, and faiths—who are deeply committed to bettering ourselves and our world through a spiritual way of living based on meditation, ethical values, and regard for all life. If we were to summarize our organization in three words they would be: peace, service, and spirituality. Science of Spirituality has meditation groups and centers worldwide, with national and headquarters in Naperville, Illinois.

About Sant Rajinder Singh Ji Maharaj

Sant Rajinder Singh Ji Maharaj is respected by the international community of spiritual and interfaith leaders as one of the great spiritual Masters of our time. He teaches meditation on the inner light and sound, the core of which is personal inner experience. Through his numerous tours, television appearances, radio interviews, books, and magazine articles he has brought the message of spirituality to people all over the globe. He is author of many popular books, including *Inner and Outer Peace through Mediation* (with a Foreword by His Holiness the Dalai Lama) and *Empowering Your Soul through Meditation and Spiritual Peals for Enlightened Living,* available in bookstores or from internet booksellers. His numerous books, DVDs, and CDs are available through S. K. Publication, 4s 175 Naperville Rd., Naperville, IL 60563.

Appendix One:
Meditation Instructions According to
Sant Rajinder Singh Ji Maharaji

The key to a successful meditation is the withdrawal of the sensory currents to the eye focus or the third eye. Once there, it requires a constant gaze into the middle of whatever is lying in front of us without any distractions of thought. On one hand it is an easy process, as it does not require any difficult poses, or *asanas*. It does not require breathing exercises or any austerities. Although it is simple, however, it takes a lot of practice to do it accurately.

Let us begin with finding a time to meditate. Do you pick a time in which there are no distractions? Do you pick a time in which you are wide awake? If the time we choose is not proper, then we can find our concentration disturbed by outer interruptions. There may be telephones or doorbells ringing, children requiring attention, obligations that can intervene, and any number of dis¬tractions. So let us think through the time we select for meditation and pick one that will grant us uninterrupted time. Why? Once the withdrawal starts, if we are interrupted, the sensory currents return to the body. Then we have to start all over again. Each time the practice is aborted we have to try again. If it takes us half an hour to be concentrated enough to withdraw, then an interruption will mean we have to put in another half an hour to return to the same spot, rather than continuing on from that first withdrawal point. In this way, one will not have sat long enough to have full withdrawal.

Another thing is that in seeking to avoid distractions we may select a time when we are sleepy. This may be either because it is too late in the night, or we wake up too early and have not had enough sleep during the night. If we are sleepy, then falling asleep will interrupt our attention. So, the first thing to analyze is the time we choose.

Then we need to look at where we sit. Are we comfortable? Is our pose comfortable enough to sit in that position for the longest possible time? If we are always wiggling and readjusting ourselves then each movement will cause a break in our concentration and our attention will again return to the body. We want a pose that is comfortable, but not so comfortable that we fall asleep. For example, if you meditate in bed, chances are that falling asleep will break your concentration.

Next we need to look at whether we can repeat the names. In order to keep the mind still, we need to repeat the names of God. The charged names (for initiates), or *simran,* are also a powerful help in withdrawing the attention. A blockage may be caused if we stop the repetition. When this happens, thoughts have a chance to intervene and our concentration is disturbed. We need to make sure the repetition of the names goes on continually during the simran practice. If you find you are having trouble with this, spend fifteen minutes a day just saying the names/mantra until they become automatic. Then when you sit for meditation each day, the practice you did will transfer over into the meditation session.

If we are experiencing a blockage it could be that we are not keeping a constant gaze. Our job is to go on looking sweetly and lovingly into the middle of whatever is lying in front of us. That may be darkness, it may be colors, and it may be flashes of light. The thing to remember is to stay conscious of whatever we see. We should be able to say: "I saw this or that or even blackness." If we cannot remember what we saw it means that we were not looking. We stopped looking and got absorbed in our thoughts. No matter what we see, our job is to gaze constantly into the middle. If we start to see colors and it stops, it means something intervened to take our attention away. Maybe our body moved, maybe our mind had a thought, maybe we stopped repeating the names, or maybe we stopped looking. Even if it is a split-second break, it is a break nonetheless. That gives the sensory currents a chance to descend back down. It does not take much for the sensory currents to return to the body. That means the withdrawal process has to begin again. Remember, it is not the colors that are going away; it is our attention that is going away.

Another tricky thing to watch for is that even the desire to see a particular sight is a thought. Thus, desire to have one thing or another, or clutching, also interferes with the process. So your very question about not breaking through the colors indicates that you may not be gazing at the colors, but thinking about what you wish to come up beyond the colors. Therein can be the cause of your distraction. That is why surrender to what comes in meditation is an important part of meditation. Desire for anything should not intervene. Just go on sitting, accept lovingly what comes, wait, and watch what unfolds.

If we can focus on improving in all these areas, then we will be able to analyze for ourselves why we are having difficulty in meditation. If we work like a spiritual athlete on our areas of weaknesses, then day by day, like a physical athlete, we will surely be able to jump over all hurdles and obstacles and win the marathon.

Appendix Two:
Spiritual Diary Developed by
Sant Kirpal Singh

Spiritual Diary

Name: _____

For the month / year of: _____

Please print or type all information

Observe	Failures	1	2	3	4	5	6	7	8	9	10	11	12	13	14	15	16	17	18	19	20	21	22	23	24	25	26	27	28	29	30	31	Total
Non-violence	In thought																																
	In word																																
	In deed																																
Truthfulness	In thought																																
	In word																																
	In deed																																
Love for all / compassion	In thought																																
	In word																																
	In deed																																
Humility	In thought																																
	In word																																
	In deed																																
Diet	Wrong Food																																
	Drugs																																
	Alcohol																																
Selfless service	Physically																																
	Financially																																
Time devoted to	Meditation																																
	Total																																

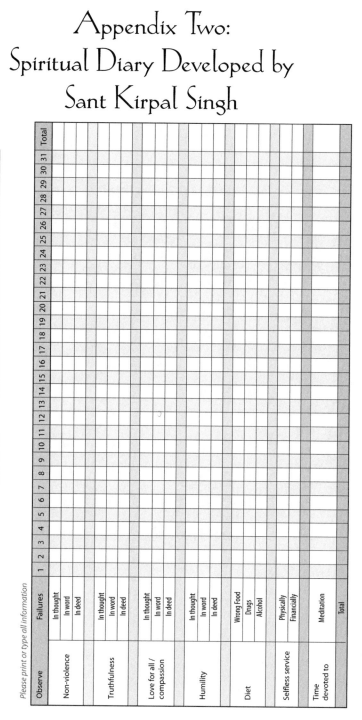

Endnotes

Introduction

1. Singh, Sant Kirpal, *Portrait of Perfection, A Pictorial Biography of Kirpal Singh*, Delhi, India, S. K. Publications: 1981, p. 5.

2. *Ibid.*

3   John 3:3.

4. Singh, Kirpal, personal interview, Delhi, India, August, 1973.

5. Singh, Kirpal, *The Teachings of Kirpal Singh*, S. K. Publications, Bowling Green, VA: Volume 3, p. 7. 1985.

Chapter One

1. Singh, Kirpal, personal dairy Delhi India, July, 1973.

2. Plato's analogy of the cave, Sant Rajinder Singh; *Glimpses of Divinity*, video tape.

3. Oral Tradition of Sat Mat and *Mathnawi* of Rumi, *Mathnawi* Book I, p. 153, verse 2835.

4. Matthew 16:26.

5. Singh, Darshan (trans. D. Singh), "A Tear and a Star," *Love at Every Step*, S. K. Publications, Bowling Green, VA: 1989 p. 30.

6. Oral Tradition. Sant Rajinder Singh, Chicago Illinois. A similar version is found in Rumi's Mathnawi, as well as Indris Shaw's *Tales of the Dervishes*, Dutton: 1970 p 25.

7. Singh, Kirpal, *Satsandesh*, October, 1970, p. 3.

8. Retold from: Kirpal Singh, *Night Is a Jungle*, S. K. Publications, Bowling Green, VA: 1975, p. 58.

9. Guru Nanak, quoted in Sant Kirpal Singh. *Crown of Life* S. K. Publications, Bowling Green, VA: 1985, p. 42.

10. Singh, Darshan, from collection of stories about Sant Darshan Singh, *Soul of Love*, collected and edited by Dr. Andrew Vidich and Dr. Art Stein, unpublished.

11. Singh, Kirpal, personal diary, Delhi, India, July, 1973. A very similar version may be found in the *Mathnawi* of Rumi as well.

12. Vidich, Andrew, personal diary, Delhi, India, 1973.

13. Singh, Darshan, *The Wonders of Inner Space*, S. K. Publications, Bowling Green, VA: p. 148.

14. Dhammapada 1:1–2.

15. Bayazad al Bistami quoted in Sant Kirpal Singh, *Simran*, Ruhani Satsang, Delhi, India, pp. 25–26.

16. Singh, Darshan (trans. by D. Singh), *Love at Every Step*, S. K. Publications, Bowling Green, VA: 1989, p. 16.

17. Singh, Kirpal, *The Teachings of Kirpal Singh*, edited by Ruth Seader, S. K. Publications, Bowling Green, VA: 1985, Volume 3, p. 54.

18. Singh, Kirpal, personal diary, Kashmir, India, June, 1973.

19. Singh, Darshan (trans. by D. Singh), *Love at Every Step*, S. K. Publications, Bowling Green, VA: 1989, p. 78.

Chapter Two

1. Singh, Rajinder, from Talk: *Spiritual Love: How to Find It*. This version is taken from a talk given by Sant Rajinder Singh in Delhi India on his world tour in 1994. A version of this story is found in *The Divine Book* of Attar and Rumi's *Mathnawi*, Book VI, verse 4205.

2. Qur'an 15:29.

3. Genesis 1:26.

4. Kena Upanishad 1:1–2.

5. Matthew 6:21.

6. *The Teachings of Kirpal Singh*, edited by Ruth Seader., Volume 1, p. 57. Also Sant Kirpal Singh, personal interview, Delhi, India, July 1973.

7. Singh, Kirpal, *The Teachings of Kirpal Singh*, S. K. Publications, Bowling Green, VA: Volume II, p. 8.

8. *The Enneads* (trans. by Stephen MacKenna), Faber and Faber, London: Part 1, Vol. 1, p. 6.

9. Indris, Shah, *Tales of Dervishes*, Dutton, NY: 1970, p. 77. Also Sant Darshan Singh, *Wonders of Inner Space*, S. K. Publications, Bowling Green, VA: p. 17.

10. Covey, Sean, *Seven Habits of Highly Effective Teens*, Simon and Schuster, NYC, NY: 1988, p. 8.

11. Singh, Kirpal, personal diary—question and answer session, Delhi, India, July, 1973.

12. Matthew 7:7.

13. From Oral tradition of Sant Lineage. This story was told by Sant Rajinder Singh at a talk in Chicago on Dec. 2, 2007. Slight adaptations made.

14. Rumi, Jalalu'ddin (trans. by A. J. Arberry), *Discourses of Rumi (Fiha Mi Fiha)*, Samuel Weiser, New York: 1961, p. 242.

15. Singh, Kirpal, personal diary, Delhi, India, 1973.

16. Singh, Darshan (trans. by D. Singh), *Love at Every Step*, S. K. Publications, Bowling Green, VA: 1989, p. 62.

Chapter Three

1. Kabir (trans. and quoted by Sant Kirpal Singh), *Naam* or *Word*, Ruhani Satsang, Delhi, India, 1981 p, 189.

2. *Kabir Bijak, Shabda 103* (Kabir 1972: 145) Kabir *Parachai*. Ananta-das version from manuscript corrected edition by David Lorenzen. pp. 40–41 and 126–128. The two main recessions used were the *Niranjan Panthi* and the 1693 V. S. manuscript of Dadu Panthi (trans. by D. Lorenzen).

3. *Ibid.*

4. Kabir's work survives in three main collections written in the vernacular Bhorg dialect and collected in three separate regions of India; the modern states of Punjab in the West, Rajasthan in the Midwest, and Uttar Pradesh/Bihar in the East. The oldest is the Guru Granth or *Adi Granth*, which has been present since 1603 and is the sacred scripture of the Sikhs. The less old, but still revered, Rajasthani collection is called the *Pancvani* and the *Bijak*, which is the sacred scripture of the Kabir Panths. The legends and stories survive in several versions of which two are most notable: Ananta Das's *Kabir Parachai*, the *Kabir Manshur* and Nabha-das's *Bhaktirasa Bhaktamal*. (see footnote p. 20, D. Lorenzen). His iconoclastic, and sometimes stringent verse, though relatively small in number, continues to exert a profound influence today as they have over countless generations up to the present era.

5. Quoted by Kirpal Singh in *Naam* or *Word*, Sant Bani Press, Sanborton, NH: 4th printing, 1974, p.134.

6. *Adi Granth*, Bibhas Prabhati Kabirji, p. 1285. Also translated by Kirpal Singh and Rajinder Singh in a talk given July 27, 1985 in Vancouver, Canada.

7. John 1:1–4.

8. *Adi Granth*, (trans, by Dr. Gopal), Vol. 1, p. 317, verse Gauri kabirji 7.

9. Plato (trans. by Benjanim Jowett), *The Dialogues of Plato* (Apology, 21 D, 23 a), Clarendon Press, Oxford: 4th edition, 1953.

10. Singh, Kirpal, personal interview, Delhi, India, 1973.

11. *Adi Granth* (trans. by Dr. Gopal Singh), Volume 1, p. 329, Sloka 9.

12. Singh, Rajinder, unpublished public talk, NYC, NY, 1996.

13. Singh, Kirpal, personal darshan, Delhi, India, 1973.

14. *Adi Granth*, (trans, by Dr. Gopal), p. 324, Guari 4-25-3.

15. Robinson, John (ed.), *The Nag Hammadi Library*, Harper and Row, New York: 1981, p. 108.

16. Modern Edition, Matthew 13:4.

17. Kabir (trans. by Kirpal Singh), *Simran*, Ruhani Satsang, Delhi, India,. 1973, p. 2023.

18. Singh, Sawan, *Unpublished Letters*, Beas, India, pp. 140–141.

19. Rabia Basri Farid ud din Attar, *Tadhkirat Al Awiliya, Memorial of the Saints*, R. Nicholoson (trans. by Pavet de Courteille), 1889, Demengehm Vies., Chapter on Rabia Basra.

20. Singh, Darshan, *Satsandesh*, S. K.. Publications, Bowling Green, VA: June, 1984, pp. 2–3.

21. *Adi Granth*, (trans, by Dr. Gopal), Vol.1., Guari, p. 325.

22. Matthew 6:21.

23. For the most complete version, see the Brahmalinamuni version in *Saduru shrikavira-charitam*. For other versions, see also Paramananda-das's *Kabir Manshur*, the *Janmavali Dharam Das ki*, and a recent semi-scholarly study published by the patronage of the former head of the Damakheda faction, Grindhamuni Nam Sahab (David Lorezen, *Kabir Parachai*, pp. 58–59). This particular version is adapted from Sant Darshan Singh Ji, *Streams of Nectar*, S. K. Publications, Bowling Green, VA, pp.112–114. It is also found in a talk by Sant Rajinder Singh called Spiritual Love: How to Find It given in Delhi, India and on his world 1994 world tour.

24. Matthew 19:24.

25. Matthew 17: 26.

26. Mother Teresa, *No Greater Love*, New World Library, CA: 1997, p. 56.

27. *Adi Granth*, (trans, by Dr. Gopal), p. 325, 4-1-5, 56.

28. This legendary king lived in Balk Bokara sometime in the later half of the 7th century. How this story has become associated with Kabir is still unknown as the dates and times don't correspond. This story is taken from *The Memorial of Saints* by Farid ud Din Attar. Found in the oral tradition of Sant Mat lineage as well.

29. Romans 13:7.

30. Farid ud din Attar, *Tadhkirat Al Awiliya, Memorial of the Saints*, R. Nicholson (trans. by Pavet de Courteille) 1889 Demengehm Vies. Chapter on Ebrahim ibn Adham, pp. 63 –71. Also appears in *Mathnawi* of Rumi as well.

31. Kabir, *Adi Granth* (trans. by Dr. Gopal Singh), Guari, p. 324.

32. John 14:21.

33. John 12:50.

Chapter Four

1. Rumi, Jalalu'ddin (trans. by Vidich), *Mathnawi* (Book One, verse 1794). All translations of Rumi, unless otherwise noted, are taken from *The Mathnawi of Jalalu'ddin Rumi*, Books 1–6, edited and translated by Reynold A. Nicholson. Published and distributed by the Trustees of The E. J. W. Gibb Memorial, 1926, current edition 2006.

2. Marks, Alexandra, *Christian Science Monitor*, November 25, 1997.

3. For a more complete discussion of Rumi's ubiquitous presence in America and around the world, see *Rumi: East and West Past and Present* by Franklin D. Lewis. Introduction, One World Publications, 2000.

4. From the Oral tradition of the Masters. See also Rajinder Singh, *Spiritual Pearls for Enlightened Living*, Radiance Publications, 2006, pp. 96

5. Rumi, Jalalu'ddin, *Mathnawi*, Book 2, verse 1525 (trans. by Nicholson).

6. Quoted by Kirpal Singh, *Satsandesh* (trans. by K. Singh), S. K. Publications, Bowling Green, VA: April 1971, p. 25.

7. Rumi, Jalalu'ddin, *Mathnawi*, Book 2, verse 3410 (trans. by Nicholson).

8. Singh, Kirpal, personal diary, Delhi, India, 1973.

9. Quoted in Kirpal Singh, *The Teaching of Sant Kirpal Singh*, S. K. Publications, Bowling Green, VA: Vol. 1, p. 64.

10. *Divani I Shams-e Tabrizi*, version by Badi al Zaman Foruzanfar Kolliyate-e Shams ya Divan-e Kabir, 10 volumes (University of Tehran Press, Tehran: 1957–67, Ghazal number 1526).

11. Walad, Sultan, *Waladnama*, ed. Jalal Huma i. Tehran, 1315 sh/1936 (trans. by Schimmel in *Rumi's World*, p. 19. (*Rumi, Waladnama*).

12. Galatians 2:20.

13. Rumi, Jalalu'ddin, *Mathnawi*, Book 3, verse 3480 (trans. by Nicholson).

14. Singh, Kirpal, *Morning Talks*, Ruhani Satsang, Delhi, India, 1970, p. 18.

15. Singh, Kirpal, personal meeting, Delhi, India, August 10, 1973.

16. Medical Study, *Behavior Medicine*, 1997, Winter: 22 (4);174–177.

17. Rumi, Jalalu'ddin, *Discourses of Rumi (Fihi ma Fihi)*, trans. by A. J. Arberry. Weiser Publications, NY, NYC: 1961, p. 239.

18. *Ibid*.

19. Rumi, Jalalu'ddin, *Mathnawi*, Book 3, verse 3480 (trans. by Nicholson and M. Fard).

20. Rumi, Jalalu'ddin, *Mathnawi*, Book IV, verse 794 (trans. by Nicholson and M. Fard).

21. *Ibid.*, verse 772.

22. Mark 3:28.

23. Singh, Darshan, *The Wonders of Inner Space*, S. K. Publications, Bowling Green, VA: 1988, p. 168.

24. *Forty Hadith Qudsi* (trans. by Ezzeddin Ibraham and Denny Johnson Davies Hadith 34. Dar Al Koran Al Kareen, The Holy Koran publishing House, Beirut Lebanon), 1981, p. 126.

25. Luke 23:34.

26. Rumi, Jalalu'ddin, *Discourses of Rumi (Fihi ma Fihi)* (trans. by A, J. Arberry), Weiser Publications, 1961, p. 209.

27. Singh, Darshan, *Secret of Secrets*, S. K. Publications, Bowling Green VA: 1987, p. 48.

28. Rumi, Jalalu'ddin, *Mathnawi*, Book IV, verse 1489 (trans. by Nicholson).

29. Singh, Darshan, *A Tear and A Star* (trans. by D. Singh).

30. Sant Exupery, *Little Prince*, quoted in *Spiritual Awakening* by Sant Darshan Singh, S. K. Publications, Bowling Green, VA: 1986, p. 134.

31. Matthew 5:44.

32. Matthew 5:39.

33. Mother Teresa, *No Greater Love*, New World Library, Novato CA: 1989, p. 108.

34. *Ibid*. p. 53.

35. Myers, David, *The Pursuit of Happiness*, 1992, p. 194.

36. Singh, Hazur Baba Sawan, *Portrait of Perfection*, S. K. Publications, Delhi, India, 1981, p. 37.

37. Seyed, *Thus Spake the Prophet*, Sri Ramakrishna Math, Madras, India: 1962, p. 51.

38. Rumi, Jalalu'ddin, *Discourses of Rumi (Fihi ma Fihi)* (trans. by A, J. Arberry), Weiser Publications, 1961, p. 14.

39. Quoted by Shems Friedlander, in *Submission, Sayings of the Prophet*, Harper Collins, New York: 1977, p. 117.

40. Singh, Darshan, Talk given July 4, 1983, Hayden Hall. See S. K. Reference Library, p. 1 of Talk.

41. *Satsandesh*, Feb–Mar, 1985, p. 21.

42. Rumi, Jalalu'ddin, *Mystical Poems of Rumi*, A. J. Arberry, University of Chicago Press, London: 1974, Ghazzal 111, p. 96.

43. Rumi, Jalalu'ddin, *Mathnawi* (trans. by Nicholson and M. Fard), Book 1, verse 3009.

44. Bunyan, John, *Pilgrims Progress*, quoted by Kirpal Singh in his Pamphlet on Humility, S. K. pPublications, Bowling Green, VA. Also found in *Pilgrims Progress, Simplified and Abridged by Mary Godophin*, McLoughlin Brothers, New York: 1884, p. 104; J. B. Lippincott Company, 1967 Retold.

45. Rumi, Jalalu'ddin, *Mathnawi* (trans. by Nicholson), Book I, verse 2351. Also found in Badi uzzaman Furuzanfar, *Mathnawi-yi ma'naw* (Mahtab, Tehran University, trans. 1980).

46. Abdullah, Ansari, *The Persian Mystic, The Invocations of Sheikh Abdulah Ansari of Herat* (trans. by Sardar Sir Jegendra Singh), John Murray, London: 1939, p. 39.

47. Rumi, Jalalu'ddin, *Mathnawi* (trans. by Nicholson), Book II, verse 3353.

48. *Ibid*., verse 895.

49. *Ibid*., verse 897.

50. Singh, Kirpal, personal interview, Delhi, India, June, 1973.

51. *Beloved Master*, Ruhani Satsang, Delhi, India, p. 11, and Darshan Singh, *Wonders of Inner Space*, S. K. Publications, Bowling Green, VA: Ch. 13.

52. Rumi, Jalalu'ddin, *Mathnawi* (trans. by Nicholson), Book II, verse 783.

53. Singh, Kirpal, personal diary, Delhi, India, July 9, 1973.

54. Singh, Kirpal, *Spiritual Elixir*, Volume 11, chapter 1, p. 1.

55. Singh, Ji Maharaj, Rajinder, *Fragrance of the Divine*, S. K. Publications, Bowling Green, VA: 2003, pages not available in book.

56. Singh, Kirpal, *Satsandesh*, S. K. Publications, Bowling Green, VA: May, 1970, p. 11.

Chapter Five

1. Hafiz, *The Green Sea of Heaven* (trans. by Daryush Shayegan), White Cloud Press, Ashland OR: 2002, p. 19.

2. Hafiz, *The Gift: Poems by Hafiz* (trans. by Daniel Ladinsky), Penguin Press: 1999, p. 12.

   Note: Variations of this story are found in several sources including one of the earlier translations by Wilberforce-Clarke (1891). In his version the damsel he falls in love with is Shakh-Nabat ("branch of candy"), and on the fortieth morning he meets *Khizr*, or the green one, the hidden guide referred to in the *Qur'an* who gives him a cup of the water of immortality. *Divan i Hafez*, translated by Wilberforce-Clarke with introduction by Michael C. Hillman, Ibex Publishers, Iranbooks Inc., Bethesda, MD, 1998.

3. Bell, Gertrude, *Teachings of Hafiz*, Octagon Press, London, UK: 1979, p. 44.

4. Hafiz (trans. by Elizabeth Gray), *The Green Sea of Heaven*, White Cloud Press, Ashland, OR: 2002, p. 18.

5. Singh, Darshan, *Secret of Secrets*, S. K. Publications, Bowling Green, VA: 1978, pp. 47–49.

6. *Ibid*. pp. 47–48.

7. *Ibid*. p. 47.

8. Hafiz (trans. by Elizabeth Gray), *The Green Sea of Heaven*, White Cloud Press, Ashland, OR: 2002, p.19.

9. Qur'an 7:172.

10. Hafiz quoted by Sant Darshan Singh, *The Wonders of Inner Space*, S. K. Publications, Bowling Green, VA: p. 32.

11. Rumi, Jalalu'ddin (trans. by Kirpal Singh), *Mathnawi*, Book III, verse 3900–3907, translated by Kirpal Singh.

12. Hafiz (trans. by Elizabeth Gray), *The Green Sea of Heaven*, White Cloud Press, Ashland, OR: 2002, p. 37.

13. Personal darshan, May 3, 2005.

14. Hafiz (trans. by Elizabeth Gray), *The Green Sea of Heaven*, White Cloud Press, Ashland, OR: 2002, p. 37.

15. *Ibid*. p. 37.

16. By 1380 when Hafiz was in his sixties, Timur Lang (known in the West as Tamerlane) had consolidated power in central Asia north of the Oxus River and turned his attention to the territories of the old Il Khanid Empire. Not long after in 1387, Hafiz witnessed the sacking of Isfahan where Timur looted the entire city and massacred its entire population. See Gertrude Bell. *Teachings of Hafiz*, Octagon Press, London UK, 1979, pp. 45–51.

17. Bell, Gertrude, *Teachings of Hafiz*, Octagon Press, London UK: 1979, pp. 45–51.

18. Singh, Darshan, *Spiritual Awakening*, S. K.Publications, Bowling Green, VA: 1986, pp. 235–246.

19. Hafiz (trans. by Elizabeth Gray), *The Green Sea of Heaven*, White Cloud Press, Ashland, OR: 2002, p. 37.

20. Farid ud din Attar, *Tadhkirat Al Awiliya Memorial of the Saints*, R. Nicholson, trans. by Pavet de Courteille, 1889, Demengehm Vies, Chapter on Ebrahim ibn Adham, p. 62.

21. Hafiz (trans. by Elizabeth Gray), *The Green Sea of Heaven*, White Cloud Press, Ashland, OR: 2002, p. 37.

22 Matthew 16:26.

23. Qur'an 2:152.

24. Qur'an 3:41.

25. Singh, Kirpal, *Simran*, Ruhani Satsang, Sawan Ashram, Delhi 7, India, 1973, p. 20.

26. Singh, Darshan, *The Wonders of Inner Space*, S. K. Publications, Bowling Green, VA: 1988, p. 24.

27. Hafiz (trans. by Elizabeth Gray), *The Green Sea of Heaven*, White Cloud Press, Ashland OR: 2002, p. 20.

28. Singh, Kirpal, *Morning Talks*, Ruhani Satsang, Delhi, India, 1970, p. 257.

29. Singh, Darshan, *The Wonders of Inner Space*, S. K. Publications, Bowling Green, VA: 1988, pp. 160–161.

30. John 15:12.

31. John 15:9.

32. Singh, Darshan, *A Tear and A Star*, S. K. Publications, Bowling Green, VA: 1986, p. 2.

33. Quoted in Sant Darshan Singh, *Secret of Secrets*, S. K. Publications, Bowling Green, VA: 1978, p. 52.

Chapter Six

1. Singh, Kirpal, *The Jap Ji: The Message of Guru Nanak*, trans., introduction and commentary by Kirpal Singh, S. K. Publications, Bowling Green, VA: 1981, p. 143.

2. Duggal, K. S., *Sikh Gurus: Their Lives and Teachings*, The Himalayan Int. Institute, Honesdale, PA: 1987, p. 14. Also *Sri Guru Granth Sahib* (trans. by Dr. Gopal Singh), Allied Publishers, Delhi, India: 2002.

3. *Adi Granth* (trans. by Gopal Singh), p. xxxvi. Also *Guru Granth Sahib* (trans. by Gopal Singh), p. xxxvi, Var of Majh, M. 1.

4. Singh, Kirpal, *The Jap Ji: The Message of Guru Nanak*, trans., introduction and commentary by Kirpal Singh, S. K. Publications, Bowling Green, VA: 1981, p. 127.

5. Duggal, K. S., *Sikh Gurus: Their Lives and Teachings*, The Himalayan Int. Institute, Honesdale, PA: 1987. p. 32.

6. *Sri Guru Granth* (trans. by K. S. Duggal). Also *Sikh Gurus: Their Lives and Teachings*, The Himalayan Int. Institute, Honesdale, PA: 1987, p. 10.

7. Duggal, K. S., *Sikh Gurus: Their Lives and Teachings*, Himalayan Int. Institute, Honesdale PA:1989, pp. 4–5.

8. Singh, Kirpal, *The Jap Ji: The Message of Guru Nanak*, S. K. Publications, Bowling Green, VA: 1981, p.128.

9. *Ibid.*, p.132.

10. *Ibid.*, p. 129.

11. *Ibid.*, p. 123.

12. Part of Kirpal Singh's most repeated sayings. From His 1972 birthday message, *Spiritual Elixir*, Volume II, Ruhani Satsang, Delhi, India, p. 56.

13. Quoted in *Simran* by Kirpal Singh, Ruhani Satsang, Delhi, India, 1973, p. 22.

14. Matthew 5:8.

15. Addas, Claude, *Quest for Red Sulphur: The Life of Ibn Arabi*, Islamic Texts Society, Cambridge, 1993. A story quoted by Sant Rajinder Singh, Naperville, IL.

16. *Aesop's Fables*, quoted in Sant Rajinder Singh's *Spiritual Pearls for Enlightened Living*, Radiance Publications, Naperville, IL: 2006, p. 48.

17. Singh, Kirpal, personal diary, Delhi, India, 1973.

18. Singh, Kirpal, *The Jap Ji: The Message of Guru Nanak*, S. K. Publications, Bowling Green, VA: 1981, p. 123.

19. Monet, Claude, quoted by Darshan Singh in *Wonders of Inner Space*, S. K. Publications, Bowling Green, VA..

20. Singh, Rajinder, *Echos of the Divine*, S. K. Publications, Naperville, IL: 2004.

21. Singh, Kirpal, trans. and commentary, *The Jap Ji: The Message of Guru Nanak*, S. K. Publications, Bowling Green, VA: 1981, p.123.

22. Singh, Darshan, *Love at Every Step*, S. K. Publications, Bowling Green, VA, 1989, p. 50.

23. Rumi, Jalalu'ddin, *Mathnawi*, Book 1, verse 3056, translated by M. Fard and A. Vidich. A similar story has been told by Rajinder Singh in Chicago, Dec. 2005.

24. Covey, Sean, *Seven Habits of Highly Effective Teens*, Simon and Schuster, New York: 1998, p. 216.

25. Singh, Kirpal, personal diary, Delhi, India, 1973.

26. Singh, Rajinder, Chicago, Public discourse, 2003.

27. Mother Teresa, *No Greater Love*, New World Library, Novato, CA: 1995, p. 27.

28. *Ibid.* p. 21.

29. Corinthians 16:14.

30. Singh, Kirpal, *Portrait of Perfection*, S. K. Publications, Bowling Green, VA: 1981, p. 12.

31. Singh, Kirpal, *The Jap Ji: The Message of Guru Nanak*, S. K. Publications, Bowling Green, VA: 1981, p. 89.

32. Singh, Kirpal, personal diary, Kashmere, India, June 1973.

33. Singh, Kirpal, *Portrait of Perfection*, S. K. Publications, Bowling Green, VA: 1981, p. 17.

34. *Sri Guru Granth*, trans. and commentary by Dr. Gopal Singh, Allied Publishers Limited, New Delhi, India: 2002, p. xxxix.

35. Singh, Kirpal, *Canon*. Well-known verse of Guru Nanak.

36. Singh, Kirpal, *Satsandesh*, S. K. Publications, Bowling Green, VA: Sept. 1972, pp. 5–6.

37. Guru Nanak quoted by Kirpal Singh, *The Jap Ji: The Message of Guru Nanak*, S. K. Publications, Bowling Green, VA: 1981, p. 113.

38. Quoted in Kirpal Singh, *Spiritual Elixir*, Part II, Ruhani Satsang, Delhi India, 1967, p. 35.

39. Singh, Kirpal, *Morning Talks*, Ruhani Satsang, Delhi, India, 1970, p. 3.

40. Matthew 25:45.

41. Singh, Kirpal, *Morning Talks*, Ruhani Satsang, Delhi, India, 1970, p. 127.

Chapter Seven

1. Singh, Darshan, *A Tear and A Star*, S. K. Publications, Bowling Green, VA: 1986, p. 55.

2. Story of Sant Darshan Singh's initiation. This story is told over and over in the writings of Sant Darshan Singh. One reference is in *Love has only a Beginning — The Autobiography of Darshan Singh*, S. K. Publications, Bowling Green VA, 1996, p. 3.

3. Singh, Darshan, *A Tear and A Star*, S. K. Publications, Bowling Green, VA: 1986, p. 50.

4. Matthew 7:17.

5. Singh, Darshan, *A Tear and A Star*, S. K. Publications, Bowling Green, VA: 1986, p. 57.

6. Singh, Rajinder, Pamphlet *The Role of a Living Master*, S. K. Publications, Bowling Green, VA: 1986 p. 2.

7. John 10:30.

8 Singh, Kirpal, personal diary, Delhi, India, July, 1973.

9. Plato, *The Dialogues of Plato* (trans. by Benjamin Jowett), Oxford Clarendon Press, 4th edition, 1953, *Phaedrus* 299E.

10. *St. Augustine's Soliloquies*, cited by St. John of the Cross in E. Allison Peers: *Complete Works*, Westminster, MD, Newman Bookshop, 1945, Vol. II, p. xii.

11. Aziz ibn Muhammad al Nasafi in Palmer, E. H., *Oriental Mysticism*, Cambridge: 1868, Part V, pp. 50–51.

12. Borysenko, Joan, *Minding the Body Mending the Mind*, Toronto, Canada: 1987, p. 112.

13. Rumi, Jalalu'ddin, *Mathnawi* (trans. by M. Fard and A. Vidich), Book 1, verse 3360, This story has been adapted by Sant Rajinder Singh.

14. Shakespeare, William, Hamlet, I:iii.

15. Matthew 6:21.

16. Covey, Sean, *The Seven Habits of Highly Effective Teens*, Simon and Schuster, New York, p. 63.

17. Singh, Darshan, *The Wonders of Inner Space*, S. K. Publications, Bowling Green, VA: 1988, p. 93.

18. Luke 11:34.

19 *The Dialogues of Plato* (trans. by Benjamin Jowett), Oxford Clarendon Press, 4th edition, 1953, Republic, p. vii 527E.

20. Blakney, Raymond Bernard, *Master Eckhart, A Modern Translation*, Harper and Brothers, NY: 1941, p. 206

21. *Mathnawi*, Book IV, verse 338, (trans. by Reynold Nicholson), Gibb Memorial Series.

22. *Sophic Hydrolith* (or *Water Stone of the Wise*) by an anonymous European author forming part of the Hermetic Museum, Vol. I, pp. 95–96.

23. John 4:24.

24. Singh, Darshan, *A Tear and A Star*, S. K. Publications, Bowling Green, VA: 1986, p. 48.

25. Singh, Kirpal, *Godman*, S. K. Publications, Bowling Green, VA: 1979, pp. 48–50.

26. *Ibid*.

27. From the oral Sat tradition, recorded from a Discourse of Sant Rajinder Singh, Chicago, 2003. Also found in *Satsandesh*, November 1971, p. 14.

28. Singh, Darshan, *Tear and a Star*, S. K. Publications, Bowling Green, VA: p. 27.

29. Singh, Darshan, *Secrets of Secrets*, S. K. Publications, Bowling Green, VA: 1979, p. 106.

30. Singh, Rajinder, *Satsandesh*, S. K. Publications, Bowling Green, VA: September, 2003, p. 7.

31. Singh, Darshan, *A Tear and A Star*, S. K. Publications, Bowling Green, VA: 1986, p. 12.

32. This story told originally by Sawan Singh appears many places in the Sant writings. I have recollected it from Sant Rajinder Singh Ji's personal darshan session in Chicago, May, 2006.

33. Quoted in *Secret of Secrets* by Sant Darshan Singh, S. K. Publications, Bowling Green, VA: 1979, p. 102.

34. Quoted by Sant Kirpal Singh, *The Teachings of Kirpal Singh*, S. K. Publications, Bowling Green, VA: Volume 3, p. 102.

35 Isaiah 64:6.

36 Psalm xxxiv:18.

37 Singh, Gopal (tr.), *Adi Granth*, Maru-Ki-Var, M. 1, p. 1092.

38. Singh, Darshan, *The Alchemy of Love*. S. K. Publications, Bowling Green, VA, *Satsandesh*, April, 1979, p. 26.

39. Matthew 19:17.

40. Singh, Darshan, S. K. Publications, Bowling Green, VA, *Satsandesh*, December, 1977, p. 21.

41. Singh, Darshan, personal meeting, November, 1974, Delhi, India.

42. Singh, Darshan, S. K. Publications, Bowling Green, VA, *Satsandesh*, December, 1977, p. 21.

43. Singh, Darshan, private interview with Linda Bagga, Vancouver, British Columbia, Canada, 1990.

44. Quoted from Sant Darshan Singh, *Ruhani Newsletter*, Sept–Oct, 1976, Volume 2, Number 5, p. 13.

45. Schuon, Frithjof, *Perspectives Spirituelles et Faits Hamains*, Paris, Cahiers du Sud, 1953 p. 267.

46. Bagga, Linda, private interview, Vancouver, British Columbia, Canada, 1990.

47. Singh, Darshan, *Break the Cup of Ego*, S. K. Publications, Bowling Green, VA: *Satsandesh*, Nov. 1979, p. 32.

48. Matthew 15:14.

Chapter Eight

1. Singh, Darshan, *A Tear and A Star*, S. K. Publications, Bowling Green, VA: 1986, p. 16.

2. This story has circulated in many traditions but this particular version was adapted from the Sant lineage through the oral tradition of Sant Rajinder Singh. It was recorded by me in a talk given by Sant Rajinder Singh in NYC, NY, in 2004. A version of this appears in *Tales of the Dervishes* by Indris Shah, E. P. Dutton, New York, NY: 1970. p. 23.

3. Philippians 4:7.

Bibliography

Sacred Texts

Dhammapada, Buddhist Canon, famous utterances ascribed to the Buddha: Part of the *Sutta Pitaka,* trans. by F. Max Muller, *The Sacred Books Series of the East,* Vol. X, Part I. Oxford, UK: Clarendon Press, 1898.

Sri Guru Granth Sahib, Sikh Canon (Adi Granth): Trans. and annotated by Dr. Gopal Singh, New Delhi: Allied Publishers PVT. Limited 1960. Current edition 2002.

Qur'an; Sacred scripture of Muslims: Trans. and published by Tahrike Tarsile Qur'an, Elmhurst, New York, NY 22373, 7th edition, 1999.

Holy Bible, Christian Canon, King James Version, Reference Edition. Camden, New Jersey: Thomas Nelson Inc., 1972.

Forty Hadith Qudsi: Trans. by Ezzeddin Ibraham and Denny Johnson Davies Dar Al Koran Al Kareen. Beirut, Lebanon: The Holy Koran publishing House, 1981.

Mathnawi of Jalalu'ddin Rumi, Books 1–6: Edited and trans. by Reynold A. Nicholson, published and distributed by the Trustees of The E. J. W. Gibb Memorial, current edition 2006, 1926.

Kabir, *Sri Guru Granth Sahib, Sikh Canon* (Adi Granth): Trans. and annotated by Dr. Gopal Singh. New Delhi: Allied Publishers PVT. Limited, 1960. Current edition 2002.

Scholars may want to see the other editions below:

See the most complete Brahmalinamuni version in *Saduru shrikavira-charitam.* For other versions see also Paramananda-das's *Kabir Manshur,* the *Janmavali Dharam Das ki,* and a recent semi-scholarly study published by the patronage of the former head of the Damakheda faction, Grindhamuni Nam Sahab.

Kabir Legends and Ananta-Das's *Kabir Parachai,* with a translation of the Kabir Parachai prepared in collaboration with Jagdish and Kumar and Uma Thukra, and with an Edition of the Niranjan Panthi Recension of this work. *Note:* Ananta-das version from manuscript corrected edition by David Lorenzen. The two main recessions used were *Niranjan Panthi* and the 1693 V. S. manuscript of Dadu Panthi. The first two stories are referenced here in State University of New York Press. Albany, 1991

Books, Journals, and Articles

Addas, Claude, *Quest for Red Sulphur: The Life of Ibn 'Arabi.* Cambridge: Islamic Texts Society, 1993.

Aesop's Fables, Quoted in Sant Rajinder Singh's *Spiritual Pearls for Enlightened Living*. Naperville IL: Radiance Publications, 2006.

Arberry, A. J., *Hafiz and His English Translators*, Islamic Culture 20 (1946).

Attar, Farid ud din, *Tadhkirat Al Awiliya Memorial of the Saints*, trans by R. Nicholson. Pavet de Courteille Demengehm Vies. Chapter on Ebrahim ibn Adham, 1889.

Aziz ibn Muhammad al Nasafi in Palmer, E. H., *Oriental Mysticism*. Cambridge Press, Part V, 1868.

Behavior Medicine, Journal of, 1997, Winter: 22 (4); 174–177.

Bell, Gertrude, *Teachings of Hafiz*. Octagon Press, 1979.

Blakney, R. Bernard, trans., *Master Eckhart, A Modern Translation*, New York, NY: Harper and Brothers, 1941.

Borysenko, Joan, *Minding the Body, Mending the Mind*. Toronto: Bantam Books, 1987.

Cloutier, David, trans., *Hafiz of Shiraz, News of Love; Poems of Separation and Union*. Greensboro, NC: Unicorn Press, 1984.

Covey, Sean, *The Seven Habits of Highly Effective Teens*. New York: Fireside Book, Simon and Schuster, 1988.

Divan i Hafiz. Trans. by Wilberforce-Clarke with introduction by Michael C. Hillman. Bethseda Maryland: Ibex Publishers, Iranbooks, Inc., 1998.

Duggal, K. S., *Sikh Gurus: Their Lives and Teachings*. Honesdale, PA: The Himalayan Int. Institute, 1989.

Friedlander, Shems, *Submission, Sayings of the Prophet*. New York, NY: Harper Collins, 1977.

Godophin, Mary, *Pilgrims Progress, Simplified and Abridged*. New York, NY: McLoughlin Brothers, 1884, J. B. Lippincott Company, 1967 retold.

Gray, Elizabeth, trans., *The Green Sea of Heaven*. Ashland, OR: White Cloud Press, 2002.

Hillman, Michael, *Unity in the Ghazals of Hafez*. Minneapolis, MN; Bibliotheca Islamica, 1976.

Jowett, Benjanim, trans., *The Dialogues of Plato*. Oxford, UK: Clarendon Press, 4th edition, 1953.

Ladinsky, Daniel, trans., *The Gift: Poems by Hafiz*. Penguin Press, 1999.

Lewis, Franklin D., *Rumi: East and West, Past and Present*. NYC, NY: One World Publications, 2000.

MacKenna, Stephen, trans., *The Enneads*, Part. 1, Vol. 1. London, UK: Faber and Faber.

Marks, Alexandra, In *Christian Science Monitor*. November 25, 1997.

Pursglove, Parvin, *Translations of Hafiz and Their Influence on English Poetry since 1771; A Study and Critical Bibliography*. PhD. Diss. University College of Swansea, 1983.

Radha Krishnan Khanna and Sahai, B. M., *The Saint and His Master*. Delhi, India: Ruhani Satsang, 1968.

Rehder, Robert, versions in *Classics of Islamic Literature*. New York, NY: Mentor Classic, 1969.

Robinson, John, ed., *The Nag Hammadi Library*. New York NY: Harper and Row, 1981.

Ruhani Newsletter. Sept.–Oct, 1976. Volume 2, Number 5, p. 13.

Rumi, Jalalu'ddin, *The Discourses of Rumi (Fihi ma Fihi)*, trans. by A. J. Arberry. NYC, NY: Weiser Pub., 1961.

Rumi, Jalalu'ddin. *Mystical Poems of Rumi*. Trans. by A. J. Arberry. London, UK: University of Chicago Press, 1968.

St. Augustine Soliloquies cited by St. John of the Cross in E. Allison Peers: *Complete Works*, Westminster, MD, Newman Bookshop, Vol. II, p. xii, 1945.

Schuon, Frithjof, *Perspectives Spirituelles et Faits Hamains*. Paris, France: Cahiers du Sud, 1953.

Seyed, M., *Thus Spake the Prophet*. Madras, India: Sri Ramakrishna Math Publications, 1962.

Shah, Indris, *Tales of the Dervishes*, New York: E. P. Dutton, 1970.

Singh, Darshan, *The Alchemy of Love*, in *Satsandesh*. Bowling Green, VA: S. K. Publications, April 1979.

Singh, Darshan, *Break the Cup of Ego*, in *Satsandesh*. Bowling Green, VA: S. K. Publications, Nov. 1970.

Singh, Darshan, *Love Has Only a Beginning, The Auto-biography* of *Darshan Singh*. Bowling Green, VA: S. K. Publications, 1996.

Singh, Darshan, *The Secret of Secrets*. Bowling Green, VA: S. K. Publications, 1979.

Singh, Darshan, *Streams of Nectar*. Vijay Nagar. Delhi, India: S. K. Publications, 1993.

Singh, Darshan, *A Tear and A Star*. Bowling Green, VA: S. K. Publications, 1986.

Singh, Darshan, *The Wonders of Inner Space*. Bowling Green, VA: S. K. Publications, 1st Edition, 1988.

Singh, Rajinder, *Echoes of the Divine*. Naperville IL: S. K. Publications, 2004.

Singh, Rajinder, *Fragrance of the Divine*. Bowling Green, VA: S. K. Publications, 2003.

Singh, Rajinder, *The Role of a Living Master*. Pamphlet. Bowling Green, VA: S. K. Publications, 1986.

Singh, Rajinder, *Spiritual Pearls for Enlightened Living*. Naperville IL: Radiance Publications, 2006.

Singh, Kirpal, *Crown of Life*. Bowling Green, VA: S. K. Publications, 4th edition, 1980.

Singh, Kirpal, *Godman*. Bowling Green, VA: S. K. Publications, 1979.

Singh, Kirpal, *The Jap Ji: The Message of Guru Nanak*. Bowling Green, VA: S. K. Publications, 1981.

Singh, Kirpal, *Morning Talks*. Delhi, India: Ruhani Satsang, 1970.

Singh, Kirpal, *Naam or Word*. Sanborton, NH: Sant Bani Press, 4th printing, 1974.

Singh, Kirpal, *Portrait of Perfection*. Bowling Green, VA: S. K. Publications, 1981.

Singh, Kirpal, *Simran*. Delhi, India: Ruhani Satsang, 1973.

Singh, Kirpal, *Spiritual Elixir*, Part II. Delhi, India: Ruhani Satsang, 1967.

Singh, Kirpal, *The Teachings of Kirpal Singh*. Bowling Green, VA: S. K. Publications, Volume 3.

Singh, Sardar Sir Jogendra, trans. *The Persian Mystic, The Invocations of Sheikh Abdulah Ansari of Herat*. London: John Murray, 1939.

Sophic Hydrolith (*The Water Stone of the Wise*). Anonymous European author forming part of the Hermetic Museum, Vol. I, pp. 95–96.

Mother Teresa, *No Greater Love*. Novato, CA: New World Library, 1995.

Glossary

Abad: A Sufi expression that connotes the moment God created all souls. Hence, from a theological perspective it signifies the very beginning of our individualized existence and, simultaneously, the moment of our separation from God.

And: According to the Sant Theology, the first grand division of the universe; corresponding to the physical world.

Absence: A technical Sufi expression (*gha'ib*) that literally means "one who is not present." It has come to mean one who is spiritually asleep to the Perfect teacher, or *murshid i-kamil*, or more generally, to the reality of God in their lives.

Al-Baatin: One of the ninety-nine names of God in Sufism. This has come to mean one who hides or keeps hidden what should remain hidden. A true saint or Master will never reveal the negative aspects of any soul in public. He protects all those who come to him, operating under the law of *al-baatin*, which demonstrates God's quality of protection and compassion.

Alchemy: In medieval society, a process which is said to have been able to transmute iron into gold. In reality this was a spiritual metaphor for the transformation by which the material body is purified of all dross and turned into the spiritually charged entity.

Agape: A Greek word for non-physical universal or spiritual love. It can be compared to the non- personal, all-embracing love that sees beyond race, religion, ethnicity, or other temporal criteria.

Agna Chakra: One of the six charkas, or "wheels," located in the subtle body. Each chakra is responsible for the maintenance of a specific function within the physical body (i.e. beating of the heart, digestions, elimination, and so on). The sixth, or agna, chakra is the portal leading into the first spiritual plane, or *Pind* in Sant cosmology. It has also been referred to as the third eye or tenth door.

Al Hallaj: One of the most famous of Sufi martyrs, who was beheaded during the eleventh century for declaring publicly, "I am the Truth." His remarks ignited a firestorm of controversy over what was acceptable public revelation of inner experience according to Islamic canon. His utterances later came to be known as *Ecstatic Speech* and became part of a wider debate among Sufi Masters and scholars on the stages of mystical attainment.

Ansari of Herat: An early Sufi saint born in Herat (now Afghanistan), known for his exceptional devotional poetry. He, along with Hasan al Basri and Rabia Basra, helped return Islam to its fundamental principles of piety, inner purity, and mystical practice in the eighth and ninth centuries.

Anal al Haq: Sufi expression literally translated as "I am annihilated in the Truth"; a specific stage in the soul's inner journey in which is realizes it is no different than God in essence. This is attained in the fourth plane, or *Bhanwar Gupha,* according to the Sant teachings.

Apara Vidya: Knowledge of the physical world gained through the agency of the five senses. From a Western perspective this would be considered empirical data, but from the Sant, Sufi, and Hindu perspectives it is limited and passing and therefore not real knowledge.

Aphrodite: The Greek goddess of love.

Assembly: A poetic Sufi expression used to connote the gathering of Sufi lovers who are intoxicated or spiritually drunk on the love of the Spiritual Master or Pir.

Azal: A Sufi expression indicating the end of our individualized existence and, hence, return to the ocean of all consciousness.

This is the moment when each soul re-emerges into the divine presence and perfect unending reality of God.

Barbur: A Moghul Emperor during the sixteenth century, known for his brutality, inhumanity, and forced conversions of Hindus.

Bang i-Asmani: Literally the "great sound from the Beyond." A Sufi term referring to the divine inner music and inner light, also known in Sufism as *Nur Allah*, *Nur Mohammadiyya*, and *Suate Sarmadi*.

Bulleh Shah: As Sufi saint who was a disciple of Hazrat Inayat Khan. Well known throughout India for his devotional poetry.

Brahman: Absolute God in non-dual Advaita philosophy; also one of the Tripartite aspects of God (Brahma, Vishnu, and Shiva) in Hindu philosophy—Brahma in this case being responsible for creation. Also, the third grand division of the universe in Sant Mat cosmology.

Bhanwar Gupha: In Sant cosmology, the fourth plane and penultimate step before the final merger with God. The light of this region is equivalent to the light of 100,000 noonday suns. It is a region of almost pure spirit with little or no matter. It is here that the soul realizes its essence is no different than that of God.

Bhajan: In Sant Mat spiritual terminology, the spiritual practice of listening to the holy sound within, also known as the practice of *Anhat Shabda* or the primal sound current.

Balk Bokara: The town in present-day Afghanistan where Rumi was born and later migrated to present-day Konya. Also commonly associated with the Kingdom of Ibrahim Ibn Adhem, a well-known disciple of Kabir.

Bhai Kanehiya: A disciple of Guru Gobind Singh who was known for his selfless love of God. During the wars with Mogul kings, Bhai Kanehiya was found to be providing assistance to the enemy. When Guru Gobind Singh found out he singled him out as one who truly understood his teachings.

Bhai Lalo: Devoted disciple and traveling companion of Guru Nanak who accompanied Nanak on many of his tours in India, Asia, and the Middle East. Well known for his surrender, devotion, and extreme faith.

Baba Farid: Fourteenth-century Sufi Saint of the Chistiyya order in Delhi, India. Well known for his extreme piety and devotion to the poor.

Borhan al din: A renowned mystic and father of Jalalu'ddin Rumi. He left Balk Bokara to avoid the onslaught of the invading Mogul hordes and eventually migrated to Konya, where he and his son settled. He is credited for Rumi's early mystical training and spiritual development.

Boddhisattva Vow: A spiritual vow within Mahayana Buddhism which states that all *arhats,* or beings near perfection, refuse to cross over into enlightenment until all sentient beings are free from suffering.

Baptism: In early Christianity it was the esoteric rite of being initiated into the mysteries of the beyond by having a direct experience of inner light and inner divine music. Today it is commonly associated as the ritual that signifies one's becoming a Christian.

Caliph: Originally this term referred to the first four successors to Prophet Mohammed, later known as the four rightly guided Caliphs. Later on the term was applied to those individuals responsible for governing and applying Islamic law to the conduct of human affairs.

Caravanserai: A poetic term often employed in Sufi poetry which refers literally to the early caravans that crossed Arabia carrying large amounts of wealth. Metaphorically, in Sufi poetry, it refers to the transient nature of life, power, position, and wealth.

Chaitanya Mahaprabhu: A famous Hindu saint appearing at the same time as Kabir and Nanak and linked with the Bhakti and Sant revival of the Hindu religion in the fifteenth and sixteenth centuries. Often credited for his *sargun* worship (worship of God with form) and revival of the best elements of Hindu spirituality.

Clara Barton: Founder of the Red Cross and tireless worker for the weak and sick.

Conscious Co-worker: A term employed by Sant Kirpal Singh Ji to signify the highest state of consciousness, in which the individual soul works in total and complete harmony with the divine will. Such a soul is beyond the realm of death, causation, time, and space and outside the realm of mind, matter, and illusion. In short, a perfected being.

Crown of Creation: A Hindu term signifying the fact that the human being is the highest in all creation, for only in the human form can man evolve spiritually (whereas in all other forms spiritual evolution is not possible).

Cupbearer: A poetic Sufi name that refers to the Shaykh, Pir, or spiritual Master. The Master is referred to as the Cupbearer because he pours out the divine wine of God's love to all who come to him.

Darshan: Generally, to sit in the physical proximity of a Saint, Guru, or highly evolved being. Spiritually it is the act of sitting in their presence and receiving their spiritual power directly or indirectly. In common parlance it is the act of receiving the *glance of light* through the eyes of a living saint.

Dhikr: A Sufi term that literally means remembrance. It is the spiritual discipline of repeating or invoking one of the ninety-nine names of God, either internally or externally. Most commonly, in most Sufi orders, it is the repetition of the name of Allah with specific movements. It can be performed individually, in a small group, or communally. The practice leads to inner contemplation and spiritual absorption.

Dhyana: A Hindu term that refers to a state of one-pointed meditation. More specifically, it is the stage attained when the concentration becomes fixed and unwavering on the object of concentration. In more common usage, a general Hindu term for meditation.

Dzochen: A Tibetan Buddhist term referring to a more advanced form of meditation often practiced among the *geluk-pa*, or followers of the *virtuous way*, and other branches of Tibetan Buddhism. In this form the practitioner begins to connect with the Clear Light, or Light of Naked Awareness.

Dark Night of the Soul: A Christian term employed by St. John of the Cross to signify the purification of the soul on its ascent into spiritual beatitude. In this stage the soul often experiences great hardship and spiritual isolation as it divests itself of all that is worldly and material.

Dhammapada: Important scripture of the Buddhist canon and part of the *Sutta Pitaka*. Containing famous utterances ascribed to the Buddha.

Dehra Dun: A lush farm area at the foothills of the Himalayan Mountain range. The area is home to the Spiritual center called Manav Kendra, or Man center, developed by Sant Kirpal Singh.

Dharam Das: A wealthy Hindu Brahmin known for his scrupulous piety. Was later initiated by Kabir and eventually succeeded him.

Diksha: The Hindu rite of initiation or spiritual rebirth. Involves the investiture of sacred thread by Brahmins and spiritually signifies receiving a direct infusion of spiritual consciousness from a saint in the form of divine light and sound.

Dying While Living: The process of leaving the body and entering into higher realms of consciousness while in a state of conscious meditation. Often equated with the process of dying, in which the attention is gradually withdrawn form all lower chakras and centered in the agna (sixth) chakra, where it enters the first spiritual plane.

Ebrahim Ibn Adam: Early Sufi saint of the ninth and tenth centuries.

Eye of Kursi: This is a Sufi name used by certain orders to refer to the inner eye of spiritual perception opened by a genuine Master at the time of initiation.

Fana fil-Shaykh: A technical Sufi term that literally means annihilation of the soul in the being of the Shaykh. In common parlance it means the merger of the soul in the radiant or light form of one's spiritual master. This is a prelude to merging the soul in God.

Fana fil Allah: After the soul is merged in the soul of the Master, the Shaykh or spiritual Master merges the soul into that of God. In common parlance this is the final stage of the spiritual path, where the individual soul merges itself with the ocean of all consciousness.

Fiqh: An Islamic term that refers to the science of interpretation of the Qur'an. It later developed into four schools of jurisprudence, which were later accepted by Islamic Imans as authoritative.

Gabriel: An archangel who brought the message of God directly to Prophet Muhammad during his revelations.

Ganam Sakis: Earliest recorded stories of the Sikh gurus and their disciples. Most scholars do not consider it historically verifiable, but it is nevertheless accepted as spiritual canon within the Sikh tradition.

Gham: Persian word for sorrow.

Gha'ib: A technical Sufi expression that literally means *one who is not present*. It has come to mean one who is spiritually absent or asleep to the perfect teacher, or *murshid i-kamil*, or more generally to the reality of God in their lives.

Ganj i gham-ishiq: A technical Persian Sufi term literally meaning *treasure of sorrow*. It refers to the state of one who has accepted the burden of realizing the noble qualities of compassion and mercy (*sifat*) and returning to the source of His being in post-eternity.

Ghazal: A specific form of Persian poetry named after the gazelle for it large leaping jumps. The poetry was originally romantic in nature, but, beginning in the eighth century, came to be used by many Sufi poets to convey the mystical and spiritual relationship of the soul with God. It continued to be developed and refined by some of the greatest of Persian poets up to the present era.

Gospel of Thomas: An esoteric gospel of the early Christian church that was later expunged from Christian cannon at the Council of Nicea in 324. The Gospel of Thomas differs from traditional gospels in its portrayal of Jesus and his early mission.

Gnosis: A Christian term referring to the stage where the seeker attains direct mystical awareness and knowledge of God through inner meditative perception. This can be compared to the Sufi term *marifat,* or inner knowledge of God, which is attained through direct inner experience mediated through the *Nur Allah.*

Guru Gobind Singh: Tenth and last of the Sikh Gurus. Well known for his heroic fight against the senseless brutality of the Mogul emperors. He sacrificed his sons and family to protect the right of freedom of religion and battle against the oppression. Set up the institution later known as the *Khalsa,* or pure ones.

Guru Amar Das: The third Guru in the Sikh religion.

Guru Dev: The radiant or light form of the Spiritual Master, which appears after crossing the threshold of the first plane, or *Sahasar Kanwal.* In Sufism it has been called the Super Sensory Guide and Man of Light.

Guru Granth Shahib: The Sikh religion's Holy Scripture, which was first compiled by the fifth Guru, Guru Arjan. It contains the writings of many great spiritual masters from several different religious traditions. It is credited with being the first democratic experiment in religious history.

Guru's Word: Another name in Sikh terminology for the Naam or Word principle. This is the primal or first expression of God, which is given by the Sat Guru (guru of truth) and which expresses itself as the Light and Sound principle.

Havan: A sacred Hindi festival in which sadhus and saints are invited and feed so that the hosts may attain their blessings and favorable assistance in a given undertaking.

Hadith: These make up the sacred body of scripture that contains the words and recorded stories of Prophet Mohammad as he was inspired by God to speak. Sacred Hadith are second in importance only to the Qur'an itself.

Hal: A technical Sufi term indicating a temporary state of spiritual experience. Such states come and go on the spiritual path and are often juxtaposed with more permanent states called maqam, or stages. A hal state is best described as a sudden powerful moment of great insight, ecstasy, or inner absorption given as a matter of grace to those traveling the inner path.

Hanifi School of Law: One of the four most prominent and widely accepted schools of Islamic jurisprudence. During the early development of Islam, four schools emerged which represented four distinct modes of interpreting the meaning of the Qur'an.

Haqiqat: The fourth stage in Sufism mysticism, signifying the attainment of the highest truth through direct knowledge of God.

Hari Bol: Hari is another name for God and bol means to chant. Literally spoken it means to chant the Name of the lord.

Haram: An Islamic name for all actions, words, or deeds that are "forbidden" to practicing Muslims. May be compared to the niyamas of Hindus.

Hazrat Inayat Shah: A Sufi Shaykh of the late nineteenth century in India.

Hazrat Mian Mir: A great Sufi saint who lived during the time of the Mogul emperors and was a great friend of Guru Arjan, the fifth Sikh Guru.

Hazur Baba Sawan Singh: The spiritual successor to Baba Jaimal Singh in the Sant Mat lineage. Baba Sawan Singh was the first of the four great modern spiritual masters of the twentieth century to attract large numbers of followers in India, known for establishing a huge spiritual center on the river Beas.

Hitbutdedhut: A Jewish term used to connote intense inner concentration on God. In practical terms, another name of for meditation within the Jewish mystical tradition.

Hudar: A technical Sufi term that refers to the mystical state of being totally present or attuned inwardly to the Pir or Sufi Shaykh.

Ijtihad: A technical Islamic term that refers to the process developed by early Muslim jurists to interpret the meaning of the Qur'an according to "independent reasoning." The gates of *ijtihad* were later declared closed by certain schools of thought.

Jihad al-Akbar: A term found in the Qur'an and coined by Prophet Muhammad that refers to the inner struggle to overcome the *nafs*, or ego, and become a true believer who submits completely to Allah. Literally, it referred to the inner "greater struggle" to overcome one's selfish animal desires, as opposed to the lesser struggle to attain justice for the spiritual community, or *umma*.

Jap Ji: The prologue to the Sikh scripture or Guru Granth Sahib, written by the first Sikh Guru, Nanak. A highly condensed poetic summary of the Sikh teachings often sung or recited by devout Sikhs every morning.

Kabir Panth: A sect of the Hindu religion that follows the teachings of Kabir or, literally, the path of Kabir. Kabir is also associated with the revival of Indian spirituality at the turn of the fifteenth century. (See Chapter Three.)

Kashi: A holy city in traditional Hindu folklore known for being an auspicious place to die.

Karma: The law of action and reaction. This basic law states that every thought, word, or deed has an effect—whether positive or negative—for which we are responsible.

Kalma-i-Qadim: Literally, *kalma* means word and *qadim* ancient, therefore, according to Islamic theology, the original word or power responsible for manifesting all creation (see Nur Mohammadiyya). This Arabic term corresponds to the divine word of the Christians and Jews, and to *shabda* in the terminology of the Sant Mat Masters.

Kali Yuga: According to Hindu theology, the last of the four yugas or epochs, in which spiritual aspiration and interest is at its lowest ebb. Referred to by many spiritual masters and often associated with the darkest of times both morally and spiritually.

Kena Upanishad: One of the earliest Vedas and part of the Upanishads.

Kriyaman karma: One of three main kinds of karma an individual produces in classical Hindu and Sant Mat theology. Kriyaman karma refers to the thoughts, words, and deeds generated by an individual on a daily basis.

Kun-fia-Kun: An Arabic term derived from the Qur'an, usually translated as "Be and it Became," or "Be and it is." This refers to the primal or original impulse arising spontaneously from God, which brought all creation into existence.

Knothei septum: Greek term meaning to know oneself spiritually. This admonition appeared on the threshold of the Delphic Oracle, where the early Greeks went to receive the messages of the gods.

Insani-i-kamil: An Islamic term coined by the great Sufi Shaykh Ibn al Arabia referring to the *perfect man,* or one who has attained the highest state of spiritual consciousness and embodies all qualities of a full or complete human being.

La illah ilallah: This is traditionally part of the Muslim *shahada*, or profession of faith, which states "There is no god but God." Less literally translated it means, "there is no reality other than the reality of God," or in terms of Muslim praxis, to worship only God and not put anything on the same level of God in our daily lives. It is also used as a Sufi *zikr*, or invocation, during mystical meditation.

Leila: In early Arabic folklore, she was Majnun's lover. This early tale depicts the story of two lovers whose passionate romantic love reaches the zenith of total absorption. It was often employed as a teaching parable to mirror the disciple's relationship with the divine Beloved or spiritual Master.

Lisan al-ghayb: An honorific title given to Hafiz that literally means "tongue of the invisible." This accolade was bestowed upon him because of his acute insight into the nature of the higher reality and the intricacies of traveling the inner path.

Lord Vishnu: The third god in the Hindu triumvirate that includes Brahma, Shiva, and Vishnu. Vishnu is commonly associated with the power of maintaining and sustaining creation. It is also the primary deity and object of worship of the Vashnavites, a popular Hindu sect found throughout India, known for their worship of Lord Krishna.

Majnun: In classical Persian folklore, the mad lover of Leila who sacrifices everything for his beloved. Often employed by Sufis and other traditions as a metaphor to illustrate the pinnacle of selfless love of a disciple for his Spiritual master.

Mantra: A set of words or phrases used to invoke the presence of God. A mantra can be used with either the attributive or basic names of God. It can be recited out loud or repeated mentally. Its basic function is to help the aspirant still or quiet the mind in order to develop mental focus and one-pointed attention in meditation.

Manzil-i-wiraneh: Literally the Persian word for *ravaged heart.* This is the symbolic heart where each soul learns to accept the lessons of change in order to become a fully conscious human being. The ravaged heart is that which is torn asunder by the painful lessons of love on the spiritual path as it learns to become a fit receptacle for the gift of perfect love and compassion.

Master of the Magi: In classical Persian culture this term refers to the spiritual Master who dispenses the wine of God's love to the yearning lovers of God. The term Magi refers to the Zoroastrian priest who was not forbidden to drink wine and, therefore, became an apt poetic symbol for the spiritual Master who dispenses the wine of inner divine love.

Maqam: A technical Sufi term indicating a stage of spiritual attainment on the inner journey that is of a more permanent basis. Maqams are not usually subject to change once they have been attained. They represent significant milestones on the inner path. Some of the better-known ones are the stations of trust, asceticism, patience, detachment, and so on.

Marifat: The third mystical stage on the Sufi path to God realization, marked by inner or direct revelations of God or what Sufis called *ðwarq,* or tasting. This knowledge is obtained without the agency of the five senses and in the spiritual worlds of Lahut, Mahut, and Hahut.

Mother Teresa: The Great Catholic missionary known for her work with the poorest of the poor in Calcutta, India. Later established her own order called the Sisters of Charity, which emphasizes working with the neediest in every society, such as lepers, outcasts, the sick, and others.

Mushahada: A Sufi term for inner contemplative meditation.

Muraqaba: A technical Sufi term that connotes the state of inner reflection and meditation.

Mahabharata: One of the most important Hindu scriptures, which describes the epic battle between the forces of good and the forces of evil in the world. It contains the Bhagavad-Gita, the best known and most read of all Hindu scriptures.

Mecca: The holiest place for devout Muslims, associated with the first revelations of Prophet Muhammad. Today it is a place of holy pilgrimage, which all Muslims who have the means should make at least once in their life.

Medina: The city that Prophet Muhammad fled to after being forced to leave Mecca, and where he established the first community of Muslims.

Monet: Famous eighteenth-century French impressionist painter known for exquisite paintings of flowers.

Mohammad: Founder of the Islamic religion and considered the seal of the prophets by the Islamic tradition. He received the Qur'an, which is the Holy Scripture of Islam, through the agency of the angel Gabriel.

Murshid i-Kamil: A Persian Sufi term used to refer to the perfect spiritual Master who is capable of enlightening his disciples with the experience of the *Nur Allah*, or light of God.

Murid: A Persian Sufi term for a disciple or student who has taken initiation from a spiritual Master.

Nabhadas: The most widely respected biographer of Kabir.

Nafeh: A Persian term that refers to the musk bag of a gazelle. It is used in Sufi poetry to refer to the divine scent or attractive power of an authentic spiritual Master.

Nafs: An Arabic Sufi term that refers to the animal instincts in humans associated with self-preservation. More generally, most Sufi schools equate it with the Western idea of ego. Here ego refers to anything that reinforces or maintains the illusion of separation from others and God.

Nirgun: Hindu term that means formless. Often associated with devotion to God, which is formless or without physical attributes, hence non-dual or absolute.

Nur Allah: Literally the "light of God" in Arabic. This term refers to the inner divine light, which both created the world and maintains it.

Nur Muhammad: Literally the "light of Muhammad" in Arabic. This refers to the inner divine light or *Nur Allah* in Sufi mystical doctrines, which is at the heart of all prophetic revelations and both created and maintains the world.

Nuqta Sweda: A Sufi term referring to the inner eye of spiritual perception, which is opened by a competent spiritual Master at the time of initiation. It corresponds to the *single eye* in the New Testament, *Tisra Til* of the Sants, *Shiva Netra* of the Hindus, and *tenth door* of Theosophists.

Para Vidya: Hindu term that refers to the knowledge gained from direct experience of the soul without the aid of the five outer senses of sight, hearing, taste, touch, and smell. This knowledge is permanent and everlasting and considered by mystics to be the only real knowledge, as it comes as a direct unmediated experience of God's reality.

Paramhansa Ramakrishna: The great nineteenth-century Hindu saint who transformed the landscape of Indian spirituality, ushering in an era of authentic Hindu devotion and piety. Known for having approached God successfully through every religious path and found all paths as valid forms of realization.

Par Brahm: In Sant Mat theology, the fourth spiritual region above the casual plane. The five regions in ascending order are: *And*, or physical; *Pind*, or astral; *Brahman*, or casual; *Par Brahm*, or super casual; and *Sach Khand*, or realm of absolute truth.

Pind: The second division of the universe according to Sant theology.

Plotinus: Greek Neo-Platonic philosopher. In his *Enneads* Plotinus forged a diverse philosophical and religious doctrine into a systematic but vital whole. His account of the structure of reality can be viewed from both the metaphysical and individual perspectives. Plotinus's universe is comprised of three levels: the One or Good; the Transcendental Absolute and the Intellect—the universal mind, which eternally contemplates as a realm of pure immaterial essences; and Soul, a manifold reality that includes both World Soul and individual embodied human souls.

Pir-i-mughan: A classical Persian term that is poetically employed to refer to the master of the tavern of wine, the spiritual Master who dispenses the wine of spiritual love, also referred to as the Saki.

Pralabhd Karma: In classical Hindu and Sant theology, this refers to fate or destiny karma. These are karmas which must bear fruit or be experienced in this life. They generally include health or sickness, poverty or wealth, name and fame. They cannot be altered or diminished except by a competent Master of the highest order.

Rabia Basra: One of a group of early Muslim saints known for their extreme piety and devotion to the inner meaning and interpretation of the Qur'an. She became a model for the later development of Sufi methodology and praxis.

Saki: A poetic Sufi term that refers to the perfect master who dispenses the wine of love of God.

Sahansdal Kanwal: In Sant Mat theology, the first spiritual plane above the physical. This plane is associated with the appearance of the inner or radiant form of the spiritual guide, known in Sufism as the supersensory guide, or man of light, in meditation.

St. Teresa of Avila: Spanish catholic Carmelite nun and mystic, associated with John of the Cross. A monastic reformer, she addressed a book of spiritual direction, The *Way of Perfection,* to the nuns of her order. Her *Life of the Mother Teresa of Jesus* remains one of the most powerful Christian autobiographies.

St. John of the Cross: Spanish Carmelite monk and close associate of Teresa of Avila. Together with her, a major monastic reformer; one of greatest Catholic mystics and Spanish poets. John's description of the stages of mystic ascent has been deeply influential in Catholic spiritual literature.

St. Paul: A first-century Jew who was called to be an apostle of Jesus Christ to assure the gentiles (non-Jews) of their acceptance by God. Paul dominates the New Testament, and much of the traditional "life of Paul" derives from the Acts of the Apostles, a secondary source dating from the nineties.

Shams i-Tabriz: The wandering spiritual Master who transformed the professor Jalal al Din into Rumi, the mystic who poured out his love, longing, and visions in thousands of lyrical verses that he sang while in ecstatic trance. After Shams disappeared in 1248, Rumi realized the complete union between himself and his lost Beloved.

Sach Khand: According the Sant Mat lineage, the fifth and final region of pure or absolute Truth, where not a trace of mind, matter, or illusion remains. This is the final resting place of the soul and the consummation of the spiritual journey.

Simran: In the terminology of the saints, the name for the inner remembrance of God or repetition of the names of God inwardly with the tongue of thought. The equivalent to the practice of *zikr* in Sufism, *mantra* in Hinduism and Buddhism, and *rosary* in Christianity.

Sanchit karma: This refers to the vast storehouse of unfulfilled karmas or seed impressions, which lie dormant waiting to be realized or bear forth fruit in future lives.

Sheikh al Akbar Ibn al-Arabi: A great Sufi philosopher and mystic, also known as the seal of the saints, whose speculative mystical theories had a tremendous impact on later Muslim thought. Known preeminently for his articulation of the concept of the unity of being, or *wahat al wajud*.

Sat Naam: In Sant Mat theology, the term signifying the fifth and final spiritual region, which is the culmination of the souls' journey to God. This is a region devoid of the slightest traces of mind, matter, or illusion.

Satguru: A Hindu term used to refer to a perfect spiritual Master who has attained complete unity with absolute Godhead, or *Brahman*, and is commissioned to guide souls back to God. More literally, a teacher of universal Truth.

Sat-chit-ananda: "Being-consciousness-bliss"; a term used in Hindu Vedanta literature to indicate the positive attributes of non-dual *brahman*, the cosmic substratum. *Sat* is pure distinctionless being, *chit* the unconditioned self-luminous consciousness, and *ananda* is unqualified bliss beyond temporary human pleasures.

Satsang: A Hindu term that refers to sitting in the congregation of a true saint or realized being, or having the association with a perfect Master. It may also refer to listening to the discourse of an enlightened being.

Sahaja yoga: The yoga of light and sound, according to Kabir. Also known as *shahaja*, or the easy Union, because once connected to the divine current of light and sound the aspirant has little or nothing to do for himself or by himself.

Sangat: Hindu and Sant Mat term for the spiritual community. Literally, the community rooted in truth, or sat.

Sharia: Arabic term signifying the religious law of Islam. This law embraces the entire body of rules and moral directives that God has ordained. In essence, as the moral law by which humans being are to be judged in the hereafter, the *Sharia* may become part of the actual judicial apparatus of an Islamic state.

Suk Dev: Famous Indian renunciate and ascetic in the Hindu Bhakti tradition.

Sushmana: The threshold of the astral plane, in which the soul enters into the first plane of creation.

Sifat: A technical Persian Sufi term that refers to God's qualities or attributes as distinct from His essence, or *zaat*. These include preeminently the qualities of compassion and mercy.

Sultan-i-Azal: An Arabic term meaning the lord of pre-eternity. This refers to the absolute state of God's being before the moment of creation and, hence, before attributes or qualities and therefore nameless and formless.

Tarjuman al Asrar: A highly honorific title given to Hafiz meaning the one who is the *interpreter of mysteries*.

Qaws-i-nuzuli: The outpouring of God's being into creation, known as the "descent into creation" in Iranian mysticism. These twin movements—one originating from pre-eternity (*azal*) and the other starting from man and flowing back to God in post-eternity (*abad*)—is the cosmic topography from which Hafiz articulates his vision of self-surrender.

Qaws-i-uruji: The love of souls to return to their source, flowing back to God into post-eternity in a state of complete self-surrender.

Qazis: (Also *qadi.*) Islamic judges appointed by the ruler, responsible for the application of Islamic law in such matters as personal status, inheritance, and religious endowments.

Trikuti: The second spiritual plane in Sant theology, also known as the casual plane.

Tariqat: (Also *tariqa.*) A brotherhood of Sufi mystics following specific Sufi practices. Each *tariqa* developed its own characteristic methods of attaining stages and states of mystical union with god. It may also refer to the second grand pillar of Sufism, indicating the stage when an aspirant takes initiation into a Sufi order or *tariqa.*

Theosis: A Christian contemplative term indicating the state of divine union between the soul and God. It has also been employed in Christian esoteric traditions as referring to the process of divinizing man into God.

Tisra Til: The Hindu term for the eye of spiritual perception, also known as the third eye, single eye, or tenth door in various different sacred traditions.

Unstruck Melody: A mystical term referring to the light and sound principle, Shabda, holy word, or Nur Allah.

Yajna: Hindu religious festival or feast given to secure the blessings of saints for a particular occasion.

Zaat: Persian Sufi term referring to God's pure absolute essence, which is beyond form and formlessness, unknowable and inscrutable.

About Science of Spirituality

For Further Information on the Teachings of the Masters:

International Headquarters
Swan Kirpal Ruhani Mission
Kirpal Ashram
Sant Kirpal Singh Marg
Vijay Nagar, Delhi, 1100009 India
Telephone: 91-11-2722-333
E-mail: skrm@sos.org
www.sos.org

Western Headquarters
Science of Spirituality
48 Naperville Road
Naperville, Il 60563
Telephone: (630) 955-1200
Fax: (630) 955-1205
E-mail: info@sos.org
www.sos.org

Regional Centers
South East Regional Center, Science of Spirituality
5700 Markham Woods Rd.
Lake Mary, Florida 32746-4603
Telephone: (407) 549-3398.

Science of Spirituality Meditation Center
79 County Line Road
Amityville, NY 11701
Telephone: (631) 691-7100
Fax: (631) 691-7191
E-mail: NYinfo@sos.org
www.sos.org

Mid Altanitic Center, Science of Spirituality
Sawan Kirpal Meditation Center
19384 Smoots Rd.
Bowling Green, VA 22427
Telephone: (804) 633-5789.

Northwest Regional Center
11011 Shell Road
Richmond, BC V7A 3W7
Canada

About the Author
Andrew Vidich

Andrew Vidich, PhD, is an accomplished author, educator, and international speaker in the fields of meditation, mysticism, and leadership. He holds a doctorate in Religion with a specialization in the transformational methods within different religious traditions, and a specialization in Islamic Sufism. Dr. Vidich has taught courses in Meditation, Islam, Religion, and Death and Dying at Manhattan and Iona colleges. He has authored several books on modern mysticism and healing, among them *Love Is A Secret: The Mystic Quest for Divine Love;* he also co-authored *The Heart of the Healer* and *The Heart of Healing,* two anthologies of writings including chapters by Norman Cousins, Richard Moss, Bernie Siegel, Deepak Chopra, and Dr. Andrew Weill. He also co-authored with TAMIR *Rumi* the *Way of the Heart,* a CD featuring poetry and music performance of the best-selling poet-msytic Rumi. His consulting firm, The Leadership Institute, Inc., teaches contemplative practice, stress reduction, and conflict management in educational, corporate, and not-for-profit environments.

He has studied meditation and spirituality for over thirty-five years under the guidance of three spiritual luminaries, His Holiness Sant Kirpal Singh, Gracious Master Sant Darshan Singh, and the internationally honored H. H. Sant Rajinder Singh Ji Maharaj.

Contact Dr. Vidich:
E-mail: andrewtamir@optonline.net
www.Leadershipinstitute-inc.com

Index

A

Abad, 165, 166, 168, 315
abandonment, 190
absence, xiv, 27, 31, 76, 95, 184,
    129, 150, 315
acceptance, 69, 93, 129, 186
accusation, 77
Adam, Ehrahim Ibn, 321
agape, 214, 315
agna chakra, 253, 317
Al-Baatin, 134, 315
altruistic, 214
anal al haq, 30, 316
angel, 52, 166, 168, 258
anger, 27, 32, 34, 107, 122, 123,
    124–130, 236,
anger and resentment, 34
Ansari of Herat, 304, 314, 316
antrope gnothi seauton, 325
apara Vidya, 22, 23, 316
Aphrodite — the Goddess of love,
    283, 316
Arabi, Sheikh Akbar Ibn al, 201,
    332
art of alchemy, 236, 256
assembly, 119, 141, 184, 262, 316
austerity, 200, 206
authentic worship, 74, 87, 98, 114
azal, 165, 166, 168, 316, 333

B

Balk Bokara, 106, 302, 318
Bang i Asmani, 230, 237
baptism, 196, 250, 315
Barbur, 197, 209, 317
Barton, Clara, 129, 319
Basra, Rabia, 96, 97, 301, 330

Bhadra, Shil, 218
bhajan, 317
bhanwar gupha, 30, 316, 317
blood platelets, 125
Bodhisattva vow, 226
Borhan al din, 155, 318
brahman, 57, 317
brahmin, 77, 100, 103, 320

C

caliph, 173–179
caravanserai, 179, 180, 181, 318
circumcision, 194
communion, 82, 89, 166, 194, 262,
    289
compassion-in-action, 147
complaining, 68, 93, 114, 141
conscious co-worker, 97, 186, 319
contemplation, 14, 40, 89, 90, 253
contentment, 32, 120, 145, 152,
    194–196
continence, 196
Cortes, 249
Cosmic body of Christ, 227
courage, 58, 87, 175, 214, 229
criticize, 93, 128, 132, 136, 137,
    269, 268
crown of creation, 51, 52, 319
crucifixion, 150
cupbearer, 164, 169–171

D

dark night of the soul, 35, 240, 320
Das, Dharam, 99–105, 320
Das, Guru Amar, 264, 322
day of judgment, 150

death, 59, 60, 73, 74, 86, 106, 136,
   164, 169, 172, 240, 246, 247,
   280, 267, 288, 315, 337
deadly sins, 32, 33
Dehra Dun, 268, 320
depression and disappointment, 34
detachment, 115, 184, 185,
   237,249, 251
Dhammapada, 41, 311, 320
dhikr, 21, 255
dhyana, 21, 319
diksha, 320
Divine Light, vii, xviii, 40, 230,
   256, 290, 320, 329
doubt and uncertainty, 34
doubts, 65, 173–176, 178, 260, 286
dying, 58, 59, 131, 118, 240, 258,
   320, 337
dzochen, 21, 320

E
ecstasy, 30, 41, 101, 118, 157, 213,
   262, 323
ego, 23, 27,29, 32, 93, 96, 97,
   102–106, 108, 110, 120, 122,
   131, 139, 144, 146, 148, 153,
   156–158, 175, 179, 203, 210,
   264, 265–279
empty faith, 87
enlightenment, 37, 39, 49, 59, 62,
   104, 106, 200, 202, 250, 318
eternal light, xvii, 79, 119, 138,
   199
everlasting peace, 200
expectations, 26, 124, 204, 223
Eye of Kursi, 321
eye of wisdom, 96, 252

F
faith, v, 73, 87, 89, 90, 93–96, 98,
   104, 105, 113–115, 175, 178,
   186, 189, 194, 133–134, 185,
fana fil Allah, 120, 122, 240, 321
fear and worry, 34

fana fil-Shaykh, 122, 240, 321
Farid, Baba, 135, 169, 186, 318
fear of death, 58
fiqh, 163, 321
fellowship, 43–46, 150, 152, 195,
   209, 213, 224, 235
five thieves of the soul, 32, 33
forbearance, 128, 129
forgetting, 128, 129, 130
forgetfulness, 79, 123, 183, 265
free will, 64
four birds of prey, 31, 32, 33
fundamentalism, 78

G
Gabriel, 162, 321, 328
Galetea, 283
Gandhi, 129, 155, 235
generosity, 121, 135, 148–152,
   218, 219, 221, 222, 225, 226
ganj i gham ishiq, 164, 165, 186, 321
gha'ib, 184
gham, 163–165, 186, 321
ghazal, 164, 169, 179, 303, 322
Gnosis, 49, 79, 89, 90, 96, 121,
   204, 240, 322
Gospel of Thomas, 90, 322, 204,
   240, 322
grace, 90, 99, 123, 139, 197, 148,
   167, 169, 170, 172, 179, 194,
   199, 200, 216, 217, 222, 217,
   222, 257, 268, 269, 274, 276,
   304
gratitude, vi, 120, 125, 149, 177, 204
great essence, 106
Guru Granth Shahib, 199, 322
Guru's Word, 75

H
habits, 60, 61, 126, 136, 167, 243,
   245
hadith, 131, 140, 155, 163, 165,
   143, 272, 249, 303, 311, 323
hal, 171, 233, 323

Hallaj, Al, 171, 316
hanifi law, 155
haqiqat, 240, 323
haram, 172, 323
Hari Bol, 156, 157, 323
hatred, 79, 81, 128, 129, 195, 197, 209
havon, 100, 323
healing, 69, 93, 119, 126, 128, 129, 133, 232, 270, 278, 337
hitbutdedhut, 21, 324
hudar, 184, 324
holy awe, 206
humility, 36, 102, 120, 121, 141, 144, 145–146,147–149, 150, 178, 179, 240, 242, 272, 304
hypocrisy, 153, 157, 218

I
ijtihad, 163, 324
illusion, xi, 22, 25, 27, 40, 64, 82, 144, 169, 211, 242, 265, 319, 329, 331, 332
impermanence, 180, 181
initiation, 44, 76, 77, 90, 102, 107, 108, 239, 308, 320, 321, 328, 329
injustice, 129
inner remembrance, 39, 40, 89, 113, 201, 225, 331
inner resolve, 67, 248
inner vigilance, 126
insanil-i-kamil, 120, 326
invocation, 183, 201, 235, 155

J
Janak, Raja, 251, 250
Janam Sakis, 194
Jap Ji, 199, 200, 306, 307
jealousy, 129
jihad al akbar, 124, 324

K
Kabir Panth, 325

Kailash, 198
kali yuga, 325
Kalma-i-Qadim, 209, 325
Kanehiya, Bhai, 140, 141, 317
karma, 63, 64, 242, 325, 330, 332
Kashi, 73, 74, 325
kingdom of heaven, 41, 103
kriyaman karma, 64, 242, 325
Kena Upanishad, 300, 325
Khanid Empire, II, 172, 305
Kun fia Kun, 165, 325

L
la illah ilallah, 201, 326
lack of faith, 96, 150
Leila, 326
Lalo, Bhai, 94, 95, 96
law of sympathetic vibration, 130
letting go, 226
light of God, 38, 80, 86, 120, 138, 141, 143, 144, 199, 204, 230, 240, 328, 329
lisan-al-ghayb, 164
living faith, 111
Lord Vishnu, 76, 326
loving adoration, 106, 115

M
macrocosm, 127, 227
Madrassa, 195
magnanimity, 151
Mahabharata, 125, 328
Mahaprabhu, Chaitanya, 156
Mahatma Gandhi, 129, 155
Majesty, 55, 59, 60, 65, 97, 128, 148, 153, 206, 212, 215
Majnun, 326
mantra, 39, 77, 127, 183, 251, 255–256, 294, 327 332
manzil-i-wiraneh, 165, 327
maqam, 158
Mardana, 194
marifat, 327
Master of the Magi, 171, 327

maqam, 171, 323, 327
Mecca, 209, 217, 328
Medina, 217, 328
mercy, 30, 120, 130, 136, 139, 140, 167, 178, 180, 186, 187, 196, 235, 263, 264, 322, 333
Mir, Hazrat Mian, 98, 324
Mogul dynasty, 98, 140, 209, 317
monastery, 236
Mother Teresa, 139, 214, 302, 304, 308, 327, 331
Mohammad, 140, 150, 162, 171, 272, 323, 328
Monet, 208, 307, 328
murid, 164, 328
mushahada, 21, 328
muraqaba, 21, 328
Murshid i Kami, 120, 315, 321, 328
musk bag, 170, 328

N
Nabhadas, 76, 328
nafs, 120, 121, 164, 324, 329
nawab, 193–194
nafeh, 170, 328
Nalanda University, 218
negative thoughts, 129, 244
Nishapuni, Hasan Nizami, 197
Nobel Peace Prize, 104
non-violence, 120, 135, 136, 141, 242
nirgun, 77, 102, 329
non-retaliation, 125
nuqta sweda, 252, 329
nur Muhammad, 329
nur Allah, 70, 212

O
one-pointed attention, 327
outer and inner knowledge, 24

P
par Brahma, 30, 330
para Vidya, 22, 23, 329

Paramhansa Ramakrishna, 28, 329
patience, xv, 36, 58, 62, 54–67, 97, 200, 201, 249, 327
perfect man, the, 120, 326
perseverance, xv, 36, 62, 65, 67, 201, 249
Pind, 316, 330
piety, 115, 198, 316, 318, 330, 329, 330
Pilgrim's Progress, Paul Bunyan, 45, 304
pir-i-mughan, 330
Plato, 23, 83, 205, 243, 252, 301, 309
positive mysticism, v, 229, 237
Plotinus, 330
prayer, xii, xiv, 21, 35, 50, 133, 155, 158, 171–174, 177, 182, 185, 194, 198, 199, 153, 242
preciousness of life, 57
predicament of man, 165
presence, 25, 27, 34, 43, 44, 77, 91, 112, 120, 143, 153, 163, 184, 188, 206, 207, 215, 216, 219, 229, 231, 237, 257, 258, 260, 269, 272, 277, 279, 284, 284, 286, 288, 320, 317, 319, 327
profound longing, 164, 261
pseudo-righteousness, 98, 99
purity, 39, 55, 64, 99, 179, 200, 201, 241, 316

Q
qaws-i-nuzuli, 165, 333
qaws-i-uruji, 165, 333
Qazis, 196, 333
quality effort, xiv, 55, 68, 87, 207, 208, 220, 245

R
radiation, 88, 89, 157, 235, 258, 260, 288
ravaged heart, 164, 182, 327
Ravi River, 199

regularity, xiv, 50, 61, 196, 249
rejoice, 96, 109, 114
remembrance, 39, 40, 89, 90, 92,
    94, 111, 113, 127, 183, 84, 201,
    207, 213, 225, 268, 319, 331
renunciation, 155, 236, 249, 251
resentment, 34, 124, 127, 129, 130,
    247
resolve, 53, 67, 248, 249, 251
respect, vii, 66, 112, 132, 135, 179,
    219, 220, 223, 266, 270, 278, 279
restlessness and agitation, 34
rishi, 35, 36
root cause, 125, 244, 245, 265

S
sach khand, 330, 331
sahaja yoga, 74, 332
sahansdal kanwal, 330
saki, 169, 330
salvation, 155, 215, 226
sanchit karma, 63, 64, 332
sangat, 333
satguru, 241, 257, 323
sat Naam, 199, 206, 209, 225, 229,
    332
sat-chit-ananda, 82, 332
satsang, 51, 240, 257, 259, 260, 300
seeing is believing, 22, 85, 89
self-analysis, 240
self-giving love, 214
self-honesty, 237, 239, 244, 245
self-introspection, v, 17, 240
self-mastery, 237
self-purification, 248
self-centered, xv, 287
self-control, 176
self-discipline, 176
self-effulgent, 111
shabda yoga, 76, 102
Shah Abu Ishaq, 172, 173
Shah, Bulleh, 264, 317
Shah, Hazrat Inayat, 264, 324
shariat, 241

sifat, 163, 166, 167, 187, 322, 333
simran, 39, 115, 294, 255, 294, 300
sin, 100, 108, 136, 144, 183, 186,
    207, 219, 265
Singh, Guru Gobind, 35, 140,
    141, 317, 322
Singh, Hazur Baba Sawan, 139,
    142, 216, 229, 232, 233, 263,
    304, 324
Smiles, Samuel, 62
Smith, Elenor, 249
so hung, 30
Socrates, 210, 211
sovereignty, 109, 110, 115
spiritual love, 122, 264, 300, 302,
    315
spiritual millionaire, 109, 115
spiritual poverty, 146
spiritual revolution, 157, 234
spiritual teacher, viii, xiii, xvii, 42,
    44, 55, 76, 82, 84, 85, 112, 113,
    149, 155, 162, 164, 170, 174,
    180, 190
spiritual thirst, 153, 263
spiritually dead, 115
spontaneous illumination, 22, 26,
    90, 205, 232
St. John of the Cross, 230, 240,
    309, 313, 320, 331
St. Teresa of Avila, 21, 230, 331
St. Paul, 21, 122, 214, 331
sublimating anger, 126
sub-liminal, 245
submission, 120, 170, 171, 176,
    179, 182, 304, 312
Suk Dev, 251, 333
sultan-i-azal, 165, 333
surrender, v, 40, 93, 98, 161, 162,
    163, 164, 165, 169, 175, 176,
    179, 182, 186, 188, 189, 190,
    261, 204, 295, 318, 333
sushmana, 82, 84, 337
Sweet is Thy will, 94, 98

T
Tabriz, Shams i-, 118, 257, 331
taj ul Maasir, 197
tariqat, 239, 334
tarjuman al asrar, 197
Theosis, 240, 334
Timurlane, 197
tisra til, 253, 329, 334
transcendent, 73, 75, 79, 103, 196,
     204, 223, 226, 252, 275
trikuti, 29, 334

U
unity, xi, 61, 73, 79, 82, 119, 141,
     143, 144, 150, 197, 199, 201,
     213, 217, 240, 265, 272, 287,
     312, 332
universal man, 120
unstruck melody, 82, 84, 85, 86,
     334

V–Z
Vyas, Ved, 250
wine, 164, 169, 170, 171, 172–174,
     284, 319, 327, 330
yajna, 101, 103, 334
zaat, 163, 166, 187, 333, 334,